Russian Mass Media and Changing Values

This book provides a multi-faceted picture of the many complex processes taking place in the field of contemporary Russian media and popular culture. Russian social and cultural life today is strongly individualised and consumers are offered innumerable alternatives; but at the same time options are limited by the new technologies of control, which are a key feature of Russian capitalism. Based on extensive original research by scholars in both Russia itself and in Finland, the book discusses new developments in the media industry and assesses a wide range of social and cultural changes, many of which are related to, and to an extent generated by, the media.

The book argues that the Russian mass media industry, whilst facing the challenges of globalisation, serves several purposes including making a profit, reinforcing patriotic discourse and popularising liberalised lifestyles. Topics include changing social identities, new lifestyles, ideas of 'glamour' and 'professional values'. Overall, the book demonstrates that the media in Russia is far from homogenous, and that, as in the West, despite new technologies of control, media audiences are being offered a new kind of pluralism, which is profoundly influencing Russia's cultural, social and political landscape.

Arja Rosenholm is Professor in Russian Language and Culture at the University of Tampere, Finland. Her recent publications include, as co-editor, *Understanding Russian Nature: Representations, Values and Concepts* and *Recalling the Past–(Re)constructing the Past: Memorizing World War II in Russia and Germany.*

Kaarle Nordenstreng is Professor Emeritus in the Department of Journalism and Mass Communication, University of Tampere, Finland. His many publications include, as co-editor, *The Russian Media Challenge* and *The Information Society Reader* (the latter also published by Routledge).

Elena Trubina is Professor of Philosophy at Ural State University, Ekaterinburg, Russia. Her publications in Russian include, as co-editor, *Trauma: punkty* (Trauma: Points).

Routledge Contemporary Russia and Eastern Europe Series

1 Liberal Nationalism in Central Europe
Stefan Auer

2 Civil-Military Relations in Russia and Eastern Europe
David J. Betz

3 The Extreme Nationalist Threat in Russia
The Growing Influence of Western Rightist Ideas
Thomas Parland

4 Economic Development in Tatarstan
Global Markets and a Russian Region
Leo McCann

5 Adapting to Russia's New Labour Market
Gender and Employment Strategy
Edited by Sarah Ashwin

6 Building Democracy and Civil Society East of the Elbe
Essays in Honour of Edmund Mokrzycki
Edited by Sven Eliaeson

7 The Telengits of Southern Siberia
Landscape, Religion and Knowledge in Motion
Agnieszka Halemba

8 The Development of Capitalism in Russia
Simon Clarke

9 Russian Television Today
Primetime Drama and Comedy
David MacFadyen

10 The Rebuilding of Greater Russia
Putin's Foreign Policy towards the CIS Countries
Bertil Nygren

11 A Russian Factory Enters the Market Economy
Claudio Morrison

12 Democracy Building and Civil Society in Post-Soviet Armenia
Armine Ishkanian

13 NATO-Russia Relations in the Twenty-First Century
Aurel Braun

14 Russian Military Reform
A Failed Exercise in Defence Decision Making
Carolina Vendil Pallin

15 The Multilateral Dimension in Russian Foreign Policy
Edited by Elana Wilson Rowe and Stina Torjesen

16 Russian Nationalism and the National Reassertion of Russia
Edited by Marlène Laruelle

17 The Caucasus – An Introduction
Frederik Coene

18 Radical Islam in the Former Soviet Union
Edited by Galina M. Yemelianova

19 Russia's European Agenda and the Baltic States
Janina Šleivytė

20 Regional Development in Central and Eastern Europe
Development Processes and Policy Challenges
Edited by Grzegorz Gorzelak, John Bachtler and Maciej Smętkowski

21 Russia and Europe
Reaching Agreements, Digging Trenches
Kjell Engelbrekt and Bertil Nygren

22 Russia's Skinheads
Exploring and Rethinking Subcultural Lives
Hilary Pilkington, Elena Omel'chenko and Al'bina Garifzianova

23 The Colour Revolutions in the Former Soviet Republics
Successes and Failures
Edited by Donnacha Ó Beacháin and Abel Polese

24 Russian Mass Media and Changing Values
Edited by Arja Rosenholm, Kaarle Nordenstreng and Elena Trubina

Russian Mass Media and Changing Values

Edited by Arja Rosenholm, Kaarle Nordenstreng and Elena Trubina

LONDON AND NEW YORK

First published 2010
by Routledge
2 Park Square, Milton Park, Abingdon, Oxon, OX14 4RN

Simultaneously published in the USA and Canada
by Routledge
270 Madison Avenue, New York, NY 10016

Routledge is an imprint of the Taylor & Francis Group, an informa business

Typeset in Times New Roman by Exeter Premedia Services
Printed and bound in Great Britain by
CPI Rowe, Chippenham, Wiltshire

British Library Cataloguing in Publication Data
A catalogue record for this book is available from the British Library

Library of Congress Cataloging in Publication Data
Russian mass media and changing values / edited by Arja Rosenholm, Kaarle Nordenstreng and Elena Trubina.
p. cm. – (BASEES/Routledge series on Russian and East European studies ; 67)
Includes bibliographical references and index.
1. Mass media–Social aspects–Russia (Federation) 2. Mass media–Political aspects–Russia (Federation) 3. Mass media and culture–Russia (Federation) I. Rosenholm, Arja.
II. Nordenstreng, Kaarle. III. Trubina, Elena.
P92.R9R87 2010
302.230947–dc22

2010003865

ISBN 10: 0-415-57746-2 (hbk)
ISBN 10: 0-203-84664-8 (ebk)

ISBN 13: 978-0-415-57746-5 (hbk)
ISBN 13: 978-0-203-84664-3 (ebk)

Contents

List of illustrations

Tables

Figures

List of contributors

Bondarik, Marina, studied at Moscow State Technological University and has been involved in a number of research projects on social policy, health education and healthcare in the Russian Federation. Her fields of research include health and media studies, sociology of medicine and public health.

Fomicheva, Irina, is professor of sociology of Journalism at the Faculty of Journalism, Moscow State University. Her research interests include typology of social communication and empirical research methods of media. Her publications include *Industriia reitingov. Vvedenie v mediametriiu* (The Industry of Ratings, Introduction to Mediametrics) (2004) and *Sotsiologiia SMI* (Sociology of Mass Media) (2007).

Litovskaia, Maria, is professor of philology at Ural State University, Ekaterinburg. Together with Arja Rosenholm, Irina Savkina and Elena Trubina, she co-edited *Obraz dostoinoi zhizni v sovremennikh rossiiskikh SMI* (The Ideas of Good Life in Contemporary Russian Mass Media) (2008). Her publications are on Soviet and post-Soviet culture and include *Massovaia literatura segodnia* (Mass Literature Today) (2009).

Mikhailova, Natalia, is a PhD student at the School of Modern Languages and Translation Studies at the University of Tampere. Her research focuses on contemporary Russian mass culture and media, particularly entertainment TV.

Nordenstreng, Kaarle is professor emeritus of journalism and mass communication at the University of Tampere. His main research interests are theory of communication, international communication and media ethics. He has been a member of Unesco's panel of consultants on communication research (1971–6) and European Science Foundation's research programme 'Changing Media – Changing Europe' (2000–4). His research on Russia is based on Academy of Finland projects 'Globalisation and localisation as societal processes in former Soviet Union' (1998–2000) and 'Media in a changing Russia' (2006–8). His books include *Russian Media Challenge* (edited with Vartanova and Zassoursky, Prologue by Mikhail Gorbachev, 2001) and *Normative Theories of the Media: Journalism in Democratic Societies* (with Christians *et al.* 2009).

Pasti, Svetlana, received her PhD from University of Tampere, Department of Journalism and Mass Communication, where she is currently a researcher. Her research areas are development of journalism as a profession and generational differences among Russian journalists. She has published two monographs and several book chapters as well as articles in international journals.

Pietilä, Ilkka, received his PhD from University of Tampere and is currently a researcher at Tampere School of Public Health and the University of Tampere Centre for Advanced Study. He has specialised in sociology of health and illness and gender studies. He has published on Russian public health, lay interpretations of health, as well as men's health and masculinity.

Pietiläinen, Jukka, received his PhD from University of Tampere, Department of Journalism and Mass Communication and is currently affiliated with Aleksanteri-Institute, University of Helsinki. Fields of scholarly interests include Russian media and journalism, quantitative audience studies and foreign news. He has published a number of articles on the post-Soviet media.

Ratilainen, Saara, is a PhD student at the University of Tampere, Department of Russian Language and Culture. She is writing her dissertation on the contemporary popular print media focusing on the development of female target audience in the late Soviet and post-Soviet Russia. Her scholarly interests include literary and culture studies, and gender and media studies.

Resnianskaia, Liudmila, is a docent of periodical press at the Faculty of Journalism, Moscow State University. Her research interests include typology of media, political journalism, media in political processes and media texts in electoral campaigns. Her publications include *Desiat' intervi'iu o politicheskoi zhurnalistike* (Ten interviews about political journalism) (Moscow, 2001) and *Obshchestvennyj dialog i politicheskaya kul'tura obshchestva* (Public dialogue and political culture of the society) (Moscow, 2003).

Rosenholm, Arja, is professor in Russian literature and culture and director of the Russian studies Program in the School of Modern Languages and Translation Studies at the University of Tampere. Her expertise encompasses various aspects of Russian and Soviet literature and culture, especially women's writing, popular culture and media, and ecocriticism. Her publications include *Gendering Awakening. Femininity and the Russian Woman Question of the 1860s* (1999). She is the co-editor of *Models of Self: Russian Women's Autobiographical Texts* (with Marianne Liljeström and Irina Savkina) (2000); *Understanding Russian Nature: Representations, Values and Concepts* (with Sari Autio-Sarasmo) (2005); *Recalling the Past – (Re)constructing the Past. Collective and Individual Memory of World War II in Russia and Germany* (with Withold Bonner) (2008).

Salmenniemi, Suvi, received her PhD from the University of Helsinki and is currently a post-doctoral fellow at the Collegium for Advanced Studies at the University of Helsinki, Finland. She specialises in cultural and political sociology and gender studies. She is the author of *Democratization and Gender in Contemporary Russia* (Routledge 2008).

Savkina, Irina, PhD, is lecturer in Russian literature at the Department of Russian Language and Culture, University of Tampere. Her fields of interest include Russian literary history, gender studies and popular culture. She is the author of *Razgovor s zerkalom i zazerkal'em: Avtodokumental'nye zhenskie teksty v russkoi literature pervoi poloviny XIX veka* (Autodocumentary Women's Texts in the Russian Literature of 1800–1850) (2007).

Shaburova, Olga, is docent in social philosophy at Ural State University, Ekaterinburg. Her academic interests span masculinities and gender representations in Russia, as well as political theory. She is the author of numerous articles devoted to political theory, gender representations, collective memory and masculinity.

Smirnov, Sergei, is a lecturer in media theory and economics at the Faculty of Journalism, Moscow State University. He specialises in the models of media business in Russia, economics of TV-industry and media concentration. He is one of the authors of *Perspectives to the Media in Russia: 'Western' Interests and Russian development* (Aleksanteri Institute 2009). His current project investigates the economic crisis in the Russian media industry.

Trubina, Elena, is professor of philosophy at Ural State University, Ekaterinburg. Her research deals broadly with social theory, urban and cultural studies, and the interactions between urban space, politics, memory and subjectivity. She is co-organiser of the interdisciplinary international project, sponsored by the Kennan Institute, which resulted in a book *Dilemmas of Diversity after the Cold War: Analyses of Cultural Differences by United States – and Russia-Based Scholars* (2010, in print), co-edited with Michele Rivkin-Fish. Her publications in Russian include two books devoted to post-Soviet identities and *Trauma: punkty* (Trauma: Points) (2009), co-edited with Serguei Oushakine. She is currently working on a project devoted to mobility and cosmopolitanism.

Vartanova, Elena, is professor, chair of media theory and media economics department and dean of the Faculty of Journalism, Moscow State University. Her research interests include media systems in Nordic countries, information society, post-Soviet transformation of Russian media and media economics. Vartanova is an author and an editor of numerous books (in Russian) on Nordic media systems, information society and media economics.

Introduction

Arja Rosenholm, Kaarle Nordenstreng
and Elena Trubina

This volume includes analyses that emerged during co-operation between two Finnish-Russian scholarly teams, located at the University of Tampere and their Russian counterpart projects at the State University of Moscow and the University of Ural in Ekaterinburg. Each team had a record of earlier projects with joint publications (Nordenstreng *et al.* 2002; Litovskaia *et al.* 2008). The research reported in the present volume was funded both by the Academy of Finland and its special programme 'Russia in Flux' during the period 2005–8, and by the Russian Fund for Humanitarian Sciences.

This volume gives a multifaceted picture of the complex process taking place in the contemporary Russian media and popular culture, inseparable from the changes in society. The authors, from a variety of fields of study, analyse latest developments in the Russian mass media, adopting different perspectives and methodological approaches that help to reveal the complex processes at work. The multiplicity of perspectives and approaches includes surveys, interviews and cultural studies-oriented readings, as well as various sources of material such as major Russian newspapers and lifestyle magazines cultivating a special Russian flavour of 'glamour' for the new consumer culture.

Overall, the volume focuses on the structural and cultural changes taking place in the Russian media industry and the political and economic spheres of the Russian media landscape. Some chapters, especially those in Parts Two and Three, using a more cultural studies viewpoint, suggest that within the media and popular culture and inseparable from social and cultural processes, changes have a decisive impact on how the identities associated with these social changes are re-formulated. Thus, the study of 'glamour' and lifestyle magazines is relevant, inviting us to consider various cultural products of entertainment and how they construct new identities and 'imagined communities', lifestyles, etc. This link – we contend – should not be underestimated or seen as isolated from the political, but rather inextricably linked with politics as 'one of the constitutive parts of culture and [...] itself a subject to culturological analysis and justification', as Epstein (1995: 284–5) argues.

While following the changes taking place in the Russian media and society in the last few years, the chapters raise questions and topics exemplifying the ambiguity of the historical situation, namely, how the post-socialist transformations and the global media market offer readers a new kind of pluralism combined with a fragmentation of knowledge, norms and values. This requires of the individual reader new skills and media literacy in order to navigate the plethora of fragmented messages, new genres and media formats. Beyond the audience, journalists, too, are concerned over the new situation, some articles showing the professional ethos and responsibility of journalism as a field of challenge. In the markedly individualised situation that characterises Russian social and cultural life today, the reader is offered innumerable options and alternatives, but simultaneously, this freedom also involves a conflict originating in the new technologies of control and normalisation inseparable from the new market.

What the chapters also bring out is that the Russian media are far from being homogeneous, and that the mass media are – not unlike the 'Western' media – a powerful, albeit not primary, social agent appealing to readers of different social strata in developing different social, political and cultural interests and classifications of the habitual capital. The chapters illustrate how the issue of widening social inequalities in society goes hand in hand with new forms of classification and division throughout the cultural and media field. In this differentiating function the media re-produce new audiences according to class, gender and lifestyle.

As a field of study the mass media can provide us with a profound knowledge of Russian society and culture, especially if we aim – as is the ambition of this volume – to draw a picture of reality that challenges binary paradigms by listening to people's collective voices and popular attitudes ranging from grass-roots level to beyond the political authorities (Borenstein 2008: 3).

The book is structured in three parts that highlight the contemporary Russian media from different angles.

Part one: Mapping the media landscape

This section provides a structural contextualisation to the rest of the volume by presenting a map of the media industries and their consumption in contemporary Russia, with a separate look at the changing profession of the journalist.

Elena Vartanova and **Sergei Smirnov** focus on the economic structures of the media industry. They demonstrate, first of all, the impressive size and diversity of the current industry in terms of numbers and their growth rate, especially for advertising, which, during the first decade of the new millennium, has reached the level of the Western industrial countries (typically 1 per cent of the gross domestic product). Actually Russia has become the 10th-largest media market in the world (Pankin 2010). Ownership of this industry is divided between governmentally controlled state capital and privately controlled commercial capital, the latter comprising both domestic and foreign ownership. The trend in the 2000s has been a decrease in commercial capital and a relative increase of state capital as the basis for media enterprises, notably through mixed forms of ownership. This trend has been accompanied by a concentration of the media industry, with three main players in the arena: a state enterprise (VGTRK) operating in TV, radio and the Internet; a mixed conglomerate (Gazprom-Media) running TV, radio, press, cinema and advertising agencies; and a purely commercial structure (Prof-Media) in TV, radio, press, cinema and the internet. The Russian media system is also characterised by a trend towards regional agencies in co-ordination with the central players. Regionalisation and convergence of different media, including the Internet, are key aspects of the dynamically developing system.

This chapter is based on the situation until 2008. However, in 2009, it became obvious that the media market in Russia had significantly suffered from the economic crisis – the global crisis, which was particularly felt in countries of 'transition economy' such as Russia. The Russian media as a whole lost about one third of their income, mostly because of reduction in advertising revenues. Media and radio suffered most, while television found itself in a more advantageous position while the on-line sector had turned out to be the safest. However, the structure of the media market remained more or less unchanged: the key players did not leave the market and, in spite of the uneasy economic situation, chose not to give up their prospective media projects. Accordingly, this chapter duly represents the contemporary structure of the Russian media industry.

Jukka Pietiläinen, **Irina Fomicheva** and **Ludmila Resnianskaia** offer basic data on the use and consumption of different media in light of recent research. They show with national survey data (over 2,000 interviews throughout Russia in 2007) how television continues to be the most important medium among the Russian people at large. Practically every Russian is a regular TV viewer, whereas two-thirds of the population read newspapers and about half listen to the radio. Newspaper readership is in decline, whereas the electronic media and magazines are gaining in following. High exposure figures do not guarantee great appreciation: trust in them is on the decline. As the authors summarise, the Russian media today are typically 'tolerated rather than liked'. No doubt this is related to the fact that the stereotype media have changed over the past two decades from advocates for democratic change to soft instruments in the power struggle among the political and business elites, not far removed from their role during the Soviet era.

Svetlana Pasti summarises case studies on how journalists, particularly those of the younger generation, view their profession amid changing media structures and political conditions. She begins with a paradox in journalism in contemporary Russia: the profession is particularly popular as measured by the large numbers of young people applying for places in journalism schools, but journalism is one of the least trusted professions in the eyes of the general public. Commercialism, with entertainment and public relations, has occupied more and more ground as opposed to quality journalism, replacing its critical function in society by what is understood to be a 'polit.PR contract' between media and government. Based on in-depth interviews with 30 journalists in St. Petersburg in 2005, Pasti demonstrates how the younger generation of journalists is no longer inspired by the public interest but rather by self-interest. Nonetheless, there are differences, such as types of professionals whom the author calls 'mercenaries' (in government-oriented media), 'artists' (in commercial-popular media) and 'experts' (in quality media). Two-thirds of those interviewed said that they did not produce corrupt materials or hidden advertising, although most of them admitted that these practices do indeed exist among journalists. Moreover, practically all associated corruption with professionalism, thus legitimising such doubtful practices. As one respondent put it: 'A journalist is not from another planet, he takes bribes just like a doctor and a pedagogue'. Under these circumstances the old Soviet journalists are viewed by the young with greater respect than ten years ago, when the younger generation distanced themselves sharply from the recent past. Such discoveries give rise to paradoxes and reflections, but show nevertheless how the profession is domesticated by the industry and the market with all its political implications. Yet, despite generally gloomy prospects for the future, Pasti offers a brighter perspective in counting on those outsiders who are not integrated into the present system and who one day could unite and fight for the profession.

These three chapters remind us of the drastic change that the Russian media system has undergone during the past two decades. As summarised by Elena Vartanova:

> today the market-driven media, increasingly dependent on new information technologies, take into account interests of advertisers and audiences more than ever. The structure of national and regional/local media markets is being increasingly shaped by wants and needs of these players in the media market, and this process seems to minimize the traditional impact of politics on Russian media performance and activities.
>
> (Vartanova 2009: 283)

However, the change is complex and fraught with contradictions, as is Russian society at large. Accordingly, the contemporary media landscape also reveals 'a replacement of information with opinions, self-censorship and the large role of the state in the public space' (ibid.: 297).

The changing Russian media landscape is dominated by the 'old' media – print (newspapers and magazines) and electronic (radio and television), as well as the 'cultural' media of books, records and films. However, like other countries, Russia is experiencing an expansion of 'new' media based on video, cable and Internet technologies. Today Russians – especially young Russians – are playing the same kind of video games, listening to music with the same MP3 portable devices and interacting with the same kind of 'social media' as their Western counterparts. Most of these new media applications are not merely imported copies but genuinely adapted to Russia by the use of Russian language. For example, Russian blogging already has its own institutional history (Dragileva 2009).

This notwithstanding, the new media do not yet dominate the media field except in relatively small metropolitan elite circles. For the majority of the population it is the traditional media that continue to constitute the media environment. This is also the case in general in most Western industrialised countries, and especially in Russia, where most of the population resides outside the metropolitan centres of Moscow, St. Petersburg, Ekaterinburg, etc. Internet access has undoubtedly burgeoned, attracting ever more advertising even during the recession years of 2008–9, and this while the rest of the media has experienced a decrease in volume as well as in advertising revenue. Nevertheless, the Internet in late 2009 regularly reached some 40 million Russians out of a population of 143 million – about a quarter.

Russian media professionals continue discussing the digital revolution, which is taking place in journalism. One of the difficulties involved is that many business models, which used to work well in journalism for decades now, collapsed everywhere. However, given the current rapid growth in the number of the social network users and, in general, increasing popularity of opportunities that the Web 2.0 offers in Russia, most journalists understand that it is better to embrace the change brought along by the convergence of off-line and on-line media than to try to avoid it.

Part two: Biopolitics of the media

The four chapters in this section address the physical and psychological health of Russian citizens, their well-being and personal growth. Of special interest is the question of how the consumers of the Russian media, of newspapers, special magazines and popular literature are expected to construct their understanding of welfare policies, of crises such as the 'health crisis' and the 'demographic crisis', raised and widely discussed due to the National Projects (2006–7) announced by the Russian government in 2005 and 2006, advocating positive programmes to overcome the problems of transition.

The point of departure for the chapter by **Arja Rosenholm** and **Irina Savkina** is the speech delivered by the former president, Vladimir Putin, in his annual address to the Federal Assembly of the Russian Federation in 2006. This topic was the 'crisis' in the demographic situation in the country, the main focus being childcare policies, which were to stimulate population growth, and in particular to encourage having a second child. The speech, especially the exhortation to 'have children', was vividly and broadly commented on in the Russian mass media, both the newspapers and the Internet. That the speech was so much quoted motivates the main question of *how* it was quoted and the way in which the media negotiated themselves into competing political positions. The authors are interested in the rhetorical practices of the media discourse. Accordingly, they explore how the Russian mass media reacted to the speech, and what kind of a speech was re-constructed by the media discourse. Of special interest is how the implications of gender and nation are involved in other current discourses, and what kinds of positions are offered to the reader in the public discourse, who will be addressed and with what kind of rhetoric?

Marina Bondarik's chapter focuses on the Priority National Project 'Health', which was by far the largest of the four projects announced by the government in 2005 and 2006. Bondarik examines how the federal health policy was being addressed in the most widely circulated newspapers. She inquires as to what were the dominant cultural and political manifestations, as well as what differences prevailed among interests related to the development of the Russian healthcare system as expressed by the newspapers reporting on the National Project? Bondarik's analysis of the mass media as the main source from which people learn about health issues is significant in that there are very few studies available on how the post-Soviet media have presented health matters. Consequently, the study contributes to new knowledge regarding health communication.

The chapter by **Ilkka Pietilä** is devoted to the question of how the Russian edition of *Men's Health* magazine, while combining topics of lifestyle, gender and health issues, constructs its male readership by re-formulating ideal masculine characteristics in the context of a 'health crisis', and especially of what is called 'stressful life'. Pietilä is interested in the assumptions made concerning the new Russian middle-class and upper-class male readers, the main focus being on how the discourse on stress, as the only permanent health-related topic in the magazine, is conceptualised in the reader's social and cultural environment, his particular context of the masculine self. Pietilä finds that stress is a 'prism through which several and different kinds of issues are projected onto the public screen'. Accordingly, stress is more an element of the young, urban professional's *habitus*, making the model reader, than an element to be considered in social relations. Social references, writes Pietilä, particularly those addressing the topic of stress, are strikingly vague and trivial, but, as he puts it, do not contradict the genre of a lifestyle magazine, being less oriented towards social problems than focusing on the individual.

Gender and lifestyle are also the keywords for **Suvi Salmenniemi**, who looks at the contemporary 'self-help literature' as part of the mass media. The main focus is on two famous authors, N. Pravdina and V. Malakhov, whose advice books belong to this popular self-help genre assumed to wield important cultural power in re-defining the gendered ideals, values and lifestyles prevailing in society. Self-help literature is particularly popular in Russia today, but is still, according to Salmenniemi, an unexplored terrain in academic research. For this reason, Salmenniemi's chapter will give us important information concerning 'technologies of the self', i.e. how do individuals in contemporary Russian everyday life work on their bodies, souls and conduct, and how are representations of gender (re-)produced and offered as individual ideals? The chapter deals with the questions of why this genre is so popular today, what kind of advice is given to strengthen personal growth, how gender and sexuality are signified in this literature and in what contexts, and how they operate within the discourse on individual happiness and harmony as important elements by which the ideal subject – happy and healthy – will be depicted?

The common methodological approach to the media adopted in these different chapters shows how the modern media are seen as part of the operating principle of what Michel Foucault has called bio-power and bio-politics (Foucault 1998: 102). The media's rationality is shaped not only through the media's role as a mediator of information and meanings repeating cultural rituals, or as an arena of public debate, but also, and perhaps even more strongly, different media are seen to emerge as technologies of power that generate, adapt, cultivate and control life. They actually reveal life by bringing it into the area of transparency and of knowledge. Instead of being secret and 'private', life has been made visible and audible; accordingly, an object for public observation, control and normalisation.

The chapters quite clearly show how the media, as one of the central technologies of bio-power, are present in people's everyday lives, in multiple ways capturing the social body that is newly re-produced along the lines of the ideals, values and patterns of the new post-socialist consumer culture. Scholars do not pinpoint bodies and sexuality by chance in the focus of their articles: social reality is made visible in the bodies, in gestures and appearance, with how symbolical meanings are articulated by bodies being the very intersectional point and object of bio-power. It is the aim of the demographic discourse, health reforms and various lifestyle discourses to guide and manipulate individuals through their bodies. This takes place not only overtly, but also discretely, imbuing the individual with a desire for a healthy and happy lifestyle. It is to be represented by 'normal' bodies, which follow the hetero-normative ideology of dual gender patterns, by that of a new self-made (business)man with a healthy, self-reliant, independent and virile body, which learns to master 'stressful' moments as symbolic signs of the new efficient lifestyle, and by that of a female individual whose body is the very battleground between medicalised, religious and nationally idealised imagery. If the male body and lifestyle, as the chapters claim, still seems to be defined along the lines of the public and without any of the caring obligations or rights in the private domain quite explicit in demographic discourse, women, as the audience, are addressed with a view to being persuaded into the roles of mothers, forming the core of the Russian family. Whereas men totally fail to play the role of father in the future family unity, the Russian female body is challenged by various and contradictory needs; both in the roles of maternal caregiver and as a career woman independent, although not inseparable, from the family, as Salmenniemi takes the advice books to imply.

The object of control is a new individual who – surprisingly not very different from *Homo Sovieticus* – is to be taken over by society to be normalised, now, however, through a process of differentiation into classes and gender, by national categories, age and professional status. Individuals themselves are expected to enjoy the mastering of various technologies of self; they are offered discourses on how to master one's life, being healthy and harmonious, being simultaneously themselves re-produced as the objects of the very discourses that the media run for them bottom-up. In view of this mode of working, of bio-power, it is important to study the contemporary Russian media as the central technologies that reproduce the object of their discourses. The mass media, in close connection with popular culture, have assumed a core role in providing readers with tools to work on their bodies, souls, conduct and ways of being. For there is no longer any single or dominant discourse giving the Russian reader clear-cut answers, nor one single elite culture to pass judgement on what is 'right' or 'wrong', it is the media and popular culture that assume the status of mentor (Barker 1999: 30). They offer the individual various, often ambiguous, eclectic and quite contradictory patterns of life, yet, or perhaps because of this, they are so well-liked; one can pick out any advice that seems to suit one's own lifestyle.

The advice the cultural entrepreneurs give the public may often sound authoritative and dictatorial. For instance, 'They will follow whatever we say' is the slogan of the popular *Afisha* magazine (Moscow's equivalent of *TimeOut*). Rhetorically, authoritativeness expresses itself in the ease with which the word 'right' figures in the reviews, as in the 'right length of a blouse', or the 'right place for a girl to be seen at'. Their position as experts in the community of 'right shoppers' is thus sustained by phenomena already described in the 1950s by the American anthropologist W. Lloyd Warner, who emphasised that striving for the 'right car' or the 'right area to live in' comprises important expression of one's status in the community (Warner *et al.* 1949: 23). However, by virtue of being involved in innovative activities, the trend-setters are free from any association with authoritarian pressure. In this sense, our argument comes closer to the insights of the American philosopher Barbara Hernstein Smith regarding that certain inevitability with which the conflict takes place between, on the one hand, conservative 'practices of the relevant community' and, on the other, 'destabilizing practices' of those 'who stand to gain from a reclassification, circulation, and redistribution of commodities and cultural goods and, thereby, of social power – including the profit and power to be had just from *mediating* their circulation' (Smith 1988: 131). These 'new cultural intermediaries', as Pierre Bourdieu calls them, help consumers to traverse the confusing realm of goods and services, strive to improve their taste and, surely, translate the producers' need into the consumer market. The significance, and even prestige, that their activities achieve have to do with lifestyle as the major constituent in a new understanding of culture.

It is enough to take even a brief, passing look at the crowd in central Moscow to be struck by the variety of appearances, from 'respectable' to bohemian, from low-key to flamboyantly ostentatious, from unassertive to overtly kitschy. The social and cultural differences in the patterns of consumption are there but, rather than being related directly to one's class or status, they express innovative forms of personal and group identity, new kinds of social experiences. Describing the Americans' stylistic preoccupations, James Twitchell has pointed out that 'Your lifestyle is not related to what you do for a living but to what you buy [...]. No one wants to be middle class, for instance. You want to be cool, hip, with it, with the "in" crowd, instead' (Twitchell 2000: 288–9). With the only reservation being that, apparently, for many Russians, to define themselves as belonging to the middle-class comprises an important component of 'coolness' or 'chic', this observation explains the growing popularity of the expertise the above-mentioned cultural entrepreneurs offer – through consulting, specialised editions and general interest magazines. One is increasingly valued not on the basis of one's consumption per se, but on how cleverly and adeptly one does it.

Consumer appetites, those which began to build up under socialism and remained ever-unfulfilled, have led to rather intimate consumer attitudes towards things that are perceived as not just goods capable of satisfying basic needs but as everything one can have dreamt of aesthetically. Middle-class consumption styles have been absorbed and imitated through fashion magazines, advertising and the very practice of leisurely browsing amidst brand names. The consumption of goods, both purchased and dreamed of, enables people not only to identify with the most popular strata, 'those who have money', but also to enact the ongoing narratives of their lives, which take their form from, and secure their enjoyment through, the investments of the imagination in acts of purchase and the subsequent combination of things. Meanwhile, the leaders of the Russian top-quality publications have moved from being oriented toward 'New Russians' to 'Global Russians'. This is how Vladimir Iakovlev, editor of a new magazine entitled *The Snob*, puts it: 'Global Russians are the group that is in search of self-identification and are in the process of development and, most importantly, in the process of the development of a new system of values' (Morev 2008). It seems unlikely that downshifting and frugality will be at the top of this prospective hierarchy even in times of financial austerity, as the cost of a single issue is about 20 dollars.

Part three: Media as the arbiters of style

The chapters in this section are devoted to the symbolic production of popular values and meanings by the various media. Three chapters look at lifestyle journals, including one originating in Soviet times (*Krest'ianka*), and the fourth concerns a local version of the reality TV show *Survivor*. The media, as the authors of this section convincingly demonstrate, have played an integral part in the legitimisation and promotion of popular culture. The transformations of the consumer market involved a change not only in the amount and variety of goods actually consumed, but also in the meaning attached to everyday life, one's living conditions, one's understanding of civility and civilised life. This change in meaning mirrored a metamorphosis of the configurations of cultural relations and the circulation of culture among socially active Russian citizens. The new understanding of culture that has recently come to the fore differs radically from that according to which culture is always 'high' and classic, and thus needs to be promoted by specific cultural institutions. The new agents of cultural industry that emerged in the 1990s and 2000s, those working in the private and state-sponsored mass media, advertising agencies, publishing houses, fashion and design agencies, architectural offices, show business and marketing departments, have been promoting a different idea of culture, one closely related, first, to a notion of profit, second, to one of lifestyle.

Regardless of whether one tries to promote a new novel, a TV show, an advertising idea, or a profession, understood as goods, they are placed hierarchically, depending on their utility. Thus the boundaries between cultural institutions and the market-place become porous, the proponents of high culture begin to take into consideration the issue of profit, while the new cultural practitioners become increasingly involved in (and handsomely paid for) 'selling expertise regarding the technical, social, or aesthetic appropriateness of commodities'(Appadurai 1986: 54). As a part of this process, home interior specialists give technical and aesthetic advice. The glamour expensive commodities convey comes to the fore, as Litovskaia and Shaburova show. The very notion of a cultural commodity becomes very broad, including, for instance, expansion of a 'celebrity value' towards ordinary people as it takes place in reality shows (Collins 2008). The new cultural workers seem to be eager to educate the public, to transmit their collectively held values to groups and individuals.

Saara Ratilainen poses related questions in her article on *Krest'ianka*. This magazine is a fascinating example of connecting the traditions of the Soviet ideological edition and new ways of promoting consumerist standards. The irony is that the publication entitled, literally, *The Peasant Woman*, which used to tell collective farmers both about the infinite wisdom of the Communist Party and new and practical fashions, came to be adorned with faces of movie stars and other celebrities and to advertise the same series of perfumes, brands of clothing and cars that may be found in any lifestyle publication. On the other hand, there are attempts to capitalise on the Soviet nostalgia, visible in a drastic change of cover design. After a decade of employing a standard commercialised aesthetic, the magazine now resorts to simplified, poster-like covers reminiscent of those of the Soviet era depicting devoted professionals, happy families, etc. How about family traditions, asks Ratilainen? How is a new woman who reads *Krest'ianka* supposed to reconcile professional demands, impulses to creativity and her role as wife and mother? It turns out that the heroes of the new life propagated by the magazine convey those same patriarchal stereotypes that governed the Soviet way of living behind the facade of gender equality. The figure of a man as breadwinner, supporter, significant other, and caring husband is so powerfully propagated that Ratilainen draws a witty analogy with the ancient myth of Pygmalion. It is only the male creator who counts, whereas the only way for a woman to prove that she is creative is to give birth to Pygmalion's child.

Natalia Mikhailova demonstrates how the producers of a Russian version of *Survivor* (entitled *The Last Hero*) gradually stripped down most of the ethical connotations the notion of hero might have held for the Russian audience, by choosing each successive year a more handsome actor resembling those seen on the covers of glossy magazines. Having compared the early and the latest versions of the show, Mikhailova observes a similar tendency in the producers' choice of winners: whereas the early winners embodied the traditional patriarchal Soviet ideas of masculinity, including the values of loyalty and courage, the present heroes are simply good-looking. In Mikhailova's opinion, this represents the tendency to glocalise the Western TV formats and explains the show's popularity: the audience does not want to be challenged, it wants to be entertained, and the closer the 'ordinary celebrities' are to those with whom people are already accustomed the better.

Maria Litovskaia and Olga Shaburova trace the genealogy of the adoption and interpretation of the 'glamorous' lifestyle by the Russian media, showing how the unprecedented popularity of the word 'glamour' itself and the luxurious and expensive mode of living it came to designate generated rather ambivalent attitudes towards the publications and shows that endlessly depict the lives of the rich and famous. As a rule, Russian academics' texts on the 'glossies' condemn their superficial rendering of reality and the promotion of extremely one-sided views. The reason that 'glamour' became a target of criticism lies in the conflicting understandings of culture and human worth mentioned above. The problem of cultural legitimacy of the commercial media expresses itself in intellectuals distancing themselves from 'glamour', either by saying that an educated person is not supposed to even notice such 'glossy stuff' or cynically sharing the opinion of the heroine of a recent film *Glianets (Gloss*) that 'Smart people don't read the glossies. They make them.' Trying to capture these controversies, Litovskaia and Shaburova look at the magazines' discussions of the phenomenon of 'glamour' itself. What are the links between creativity and 'glamour'? Does real talent need to be processed by show business? Can the glamourising of one's wealth as opposed to one's other achievements set a good example for youth? Although most people realise that what is at stake is the profit of those who make the 'glossies', these questions abound.

Elena Trubina looks at the magazines specialising in home design, first, from the point of view of normative concepts, second, with an eye to the complex intersections of economic and cultural interests. The juxtaposition she creates of 'good house' and 'good city' is meant to emphasise the increasing privatisation and individualisation of the post-Soviet way of life, as well as a trend towards a privatised urban space that has differential outcomes in terms of the allocation of urban resources. Her chapter is one of the few in the volume to analyse readers' opinions. One reader quite perceptively formulates the paradox related to the profit orientation of the magazines offering practical advice: 'We want to use their expertise but they are more successful in using us'. Together with the readers she interviewed, Trubina seeks to make sense of their mistrust of the magazines' policies. The readers' access to professional expertise, which these magazines make possible, comes together with an intense promotion of goods and services, so that one is never sure of the impartiality of the advice tendered. The other possible reason for this mistrust is that the interiors the magazines praise are too perfect, too polished, and too remote from real life, where one always has to negotiate between one's aesthetic aspirations and financial or temporal constraints. Close reading of the concrete configurations of the readership, context, content and meaning of certain media products presupposes, we believe, challenging some embedded orthodoxies. For instance, when it comes to the interrelations of the Western and Russian formats and journalist practices that are of interest to many of the authors in this volume, does it make sense to account for this process solely in terms of 'borrowing' or 'imitating' successful shows or publications? Similarly, to what extent is it productive to think of this, as conventional wisdom often has it, as only one-way traffic of goods and ideas?

There does indeed exist a conventional narrative of globalisation, which tends to emphasise, first, the triumph of consumerism and, second, the death of distance, i.e. a growing difficulty of distinguishing between what is internal and external, national and international within a particular society. It is also commonplace to say that the media not only constantly promote the globalization discourse, but also comprise an integral component in globalisation. The economic dimensions of globalisation (international trade, capital flows and global markets) have profoundly influenced the cultural industries (Louw 2001; Fursich and Roushanzamir

2001). The expansion of global culture, and global media as its major part, has turned the national media systems into a competitive field. As a result, the greater profit expectations of media companies often involve conservative ('non-risk') programming and, in general, compromise of credibility in favour of commodification. The number of TV channels, journals and online sources has soared in Russia during the last 20 years, and in many cases it is Western media products that comprise their main source of profit.

That the media have played an important role in the rapid recovery of millions of Russians from the years of their country's self-imposed international isolation hardly needs to be argued. The impact of globalisation upon personal experiences is remarkable. The frames of meaning, slogans, celebrity figures and lifestyle emblems carried by the Western media are enthusiastically shared by many. Whether it is *House M.D.* or *Heroes*, *Cosmopolitan* or *Forbes*, *Discovery Channel* or *Euronews*, many people derive a special pleasure from their awareness that they are watching and reading popular media products together with the rest of the world. Indeed, the simultaneous consumption of media products brings a real sense of empowerment to people, many of whom too well remember the times of aggressive state propaganda.

Global trends and national media

There are, however, three points that need to be emphasised with regard to the dynamics between global trends and national media. These are, first, the thorny problem of the interconnection between the media and democracy; second, the role of the nation-state; and, finally, the specifics of the intertwining of post-socialist and global change.

When it comes to the interconnection of the media with democracy, what we believe needs to be more actively accounted for is that the globalisation of the media is a controversial process. It involves the promotion of democracy and universalistic cosmopolitan culture while putting significant pressure upon local economies and politics. It has also become apparent that the prevailing normative models according to which the freedom of the press has been conventionally judged, are often used without paying sufficient attention to the complex ways in which journalism, market interests, electoral processes and public relations are linked even in the most democratic nations (cf. Christians *et al.* 2009; Kunczik 1999). The American media sociologist Michael Schudson argues that traditional normative notions, i.e. 'objectivity' and deviations from it, need to be reconsidered in the light of the broader social tendencies and cultural peculiarities, which have an impact on contemporary journalistic practices (Schudson 2003). Although 'critics of political bias ordinarily presume that the journalist should be a professional who tells the truth and that it is possible to do this without prejudice' (ibid.: 47), it is also possible that the traditional normative assessments remain too detached from organisational routines, managerial pressures and financial constraints to which journalists are subjected, not to mention their habits of gathering and producing news resulting from the complex interplay of societal, political and cultural forces. In a similar vein, objecting to the widespread equating of journalism with democracy, the Australian media scholar Beate Josephi notes that 'using terms such as Chinese, Qatari or Singaporean journalism would be incorrect as these countries do not provide the democratic basis seen necessary for journalism' (Josephi 2005: 575).

The reason we think these analytic discussions are highly relevant in the Russian context is that the debates within Russian society on the current state of its media go along similar lines. Excessive moralising and normative preaching long characterised the culture of the educated strata of Russian society. Today, it seems, the journalists and the media in general are the favourite target of those disappointed with the state of democracy, high culture or 'truthfulness'. The accusations of journalists as being corrupt, too willing to 'sell themselves out' or being guilty of betraying justice and democracy are numerous and often apocalyptic: 'All mass media today belong to somebody and the ease with which the journalists sell themselves is truly catastrophic' (Poptsov 2008). Many commentators blame the media and the 'liberals' for contributing to the fragmentation of Russian society and 'betraying the interests' of the Russians (Kara-Murza 2007). The tone of other media experts and practitioners is more reserved. Many note that it is the market that decides everything because the main source of profit for all public (free for all) channels is advertising. Under these conditions, the major criterion for the success of a show or a channel is its rating. Given that the system of rating measurement in Russia is not able to account for the diversity of the TV audience and its preferences, TV and other media producers only orient themselves toward the market of advertising (Golubeva 2005).

If in some countries (France for example) there are debates about a complete removal of advertising from the state-funded TV channels, the Russian government generally refrains from any legal regulation of advertising, confining itself to minor matters such as the prohibition of showing beer commercials in the daytime. However, in many other respects the nation-state remains a major player in the national media system. This brings us to our second point, namely, the disagreement among media scholars with regard to the role of the nation-state under globalisation. Although some tend to put great hopes in the 'global public sphere' (Castells 2008; Volkmer 2003) and enthuse about the expansion of the media markets and the internationalisation of cultures that can make the state obsolete, others are more cautious regarding the liberating opportunities of the Internet, cultural globalisation and the putative withdrawal of the state (Morris and Waisbord 2001). In particular, it is important to acknowledge that in many countries nation-states continue to run media systems and that the fields in which most communication occurs often remain nationally defined. Not only do states determine who controls the media, they 'have a range of informal ways of influencing the media, from information management to the provision of loans', as suggested by James Curran and Myung-Jin Park in trying to 'de-Westernize media studies' (Curran and Park 2000: 12).

To revert to Russian matters, the deregulation of the media that marked the early 1990s was replaced by an increase in governmental regulation and ownership of media outlets. However, there still exist commercial stations alongside the public service systems, foreign ownership and cross-ownership of television and other media outlets. The collusion of political and commercial interests often takes place when the state channels, on the one hand, produce shows that picture the liberal ideology as 'alien' and 'imposed' on the Russians by the politicians who, in the early 1990s, developed liaisons with Westerners, conducted shock therapy to the detriment of the Russian people, worked hard to spread the ideology of 'political correctness' and contributed to the 'chaos of El'tsin's era', and on the other hand, promote entertainment-oriented, profit-driven, utterly simplified ventures that do not question the social order and governmental decisions.

According to the editor of the analytical magazine *Pro et Contra*:

> the government broadcasts to the population the "right" set of events with the coverage of concrete events carefully calibrated: some of them are totally excluded, some are mentioned in passing while some are persistently emphasized [...]. Discussions are minimal, and the skillful hosts of the talk shows put in a favorable light those who express "right opinions"[...]. The managers of all three federal channels duly share the "right" position with those from the Kremlin administration who see making flattering image of Russia as their task.
>
> (Lipman 2006)

Looking at the way the numerous images of war are employed in order to symbolically unify an increasingly individualised Russian (*Rossiiskaia*) nation, the Russian cultural studies scholar, Galina Zvereva, emphasises their functioning as the basis of building a 'positive, national-patriotic, mobilizing identity', which prevents the development of patterns of behaviour independent of the state (Zvereva 2005).

Reaching our third point, namely, reflection on the complex intertwining of specifically post-socialist and global change, we argue that what makes the Russian case sadly interesting is that at the moment the concept of public interest is identified entirely with the goals of government. How did this come about? Drawing on a vast number of sociological polls, one of the most prominent Russian media sociologists, Boris Dubin, argues that a widening gap is emerging between the various systems of social relationships and types of communicative communities (Dubin 2006: 3, 38). In a sense, a general public still needs to be brought into being, at least when it comes to the expression of public as opposed to official interests. This process of social fragmentation could have been neutralised by building a system of regulation of social relations, which would include civic values, symbols and articulated legal and ethical norms. Instead, using TV as a single virtual unifying umbrella, the government places special emphasis on the unity of the state and the nation, on the imperial 'we' whose glorious past is praised ad nauseam and who are currently exemplified by the figure of the prime minister.

In the history of North America and Europe, mechanisms were found through which genuine public interests could be expressed by the media, namely, public broadcasting (at least relatively) free from both political and commercial pressures. Whether it is the wide choice of programmes or the media presence of the independent voices expressing public concerns, all this is possible through fund-raising, non-commercial foundations and other means to gain independence. As TV expert Anna Golubeva rightly notes, 'it doesn't make sense to talk about public donations in a country where some people are not able (and not willing!) to pay for their utilities' (Golubeva 2005). She goes on to say that there are no public foundations powerful enough to finance a national TV channel. This is the reason why only the state-controlled channels implement 'public' broadcasting. There is one national channel in Russia that is completely free from advertising, namely, *Kul'tura*. However, the irony is that this broad gesture toward the educated Russian audience was possible because the state is the major stakeholder in the media market, receiving about 70 per cent of its revenues from advertising.

With this complicated juncture of contemporary trends and historical legacies in mind, let us take a brief look at the attempts to summarise the development of the Russian media in recent decades, which, again, Russian practitioners themselves have made. In one attempt, a truly troubling case is recalled when the day after the Moscow Mayor Iurii Luzhkov suggested while taking part in the 'Posner' talk show that the governors should be elected once again and not appointed by the state as this is the only way to give them legitimate rule, President Dimitrii Medvedev aggressively announced that those who do not like the current system of governors' appointment should seriously consider retirement (Baskov 2009). Even more significantly, at the moment when completing this introduction (winter 2009), all analytical talkshows ceased to exist: independent opinions seem to be completely out of fashion on Russian TV. In the press reviews, a more encouraging case is brought up (Mostovshchikov 2009). The commercial channel *2X2*, which broadcasts adult animation movies, was accused of incitement to violence by several senators and religious organizations. In particular, the provocative series *South Park* has made many conservative viewers unhappy. The channel received quite extensive public support and continues broadcasting. Although we would be reluctant to make a bold statement about a Russian spectators who seem to care more for their favourite animation movies than analytical programmes, the question of the controversial consequences of the growing individualisation of society remains.

The differentiation and dispersion of the media taking place in the contemporary world no doubt problematises traditional theories of mass media as vehicles of monopolistic concentration of power and manipulators of the tastes and mores of the populace. Indeed, the unprecedented degree of connectivity and interactivity that the new media make available makes it impossible to rely on once-effective methods of socialist time propaganda. At the same time, as this volume demonstrates, the Russian mass media becomes both the testing ground for the new approaches and the last resort of those who believe that it is only from top to bottom that information should be distributed.

References

Appadurai, A. (1986) 'Introduction: Commodities and the Politics of Value', in A. Appadurai (ed.) *The Social Life of Things: Commodities in Cultural Perspective*, Cambridge: Cambridge University Press, 3–63.

Barker, A. (1999) 'The Culture Factory: Theorizing the Popular in the Old and New Russia', in A.M. Barker (ed.) *Consuming Russia*, Durham, NC: Duke University Press, 12–45.

Baskov, M. (2009) 'Etot god my uzhe otpisali', *Lenta.ru*, 4 January 2009. Online. Available www.lenta.ru/articles/2009/01/04/finalmedia/ (accessed 11 December 2009).

Borenstein, E. (2008) *Overkill. Sex and Violence in Contemporary Russian Popular Culture*, Ithaca, NY and London: Cornell University Press.

Castells, M. (2008) The New Public Sphere: Global Civil Society, Communication Networks, and Global Governance, *The Annals of the American Academy of Social Science*, 616(1): 78–93.

Christians, C., Glasser, T., McQuail, D., Nordenstreng, K. and White, R. (2009) *Normative Theories of the Media: Journalism in Democratic Societies*, Chicago and Urbana, IL: University of Illinois Press.

Collins, S. (2008) 'Making the Most out of 15 Minutes: Reality TV's Dispensable Celebrity', *Television & New Media*, 9: 86–109.

Curran, J. and Park, M.-J. (2000) 'Beyond Globalization Theory', in J. Curran and M.-J. Park (eds) *De-Westernizing Media Studies*, London: Routledge, 3–18.

Dragileva, O. (2009) 'The Story of Livejournal: How Russians Started Blogging', unpublished master's thesis, University of Tampere.

Dubin, B. (2006) 'Mass-media i kommunikativnyi mir zhitelei Rossii: plasticheskaia khirurgiia sotsial'noi real'nosti', *Vestnik obschestvennogo mneniia*, 3: 36–48.

Epstein, M. (1995) *After the Future. The Paradoxes of Postmodernism and Contemporary Russian Culture*, Amherst, MA: The University of Massachusetts Press.

Foucault, M. (1998) *The History of Sexuality*, vol. 1: The Will to Knowledge, London: Penguin.

Fursich, E. and Roushanzamir, E.L. (2001) 'Corporate Expansion, Textual Expansion: Commodification Model of Communication', *Journal of Communication Inquiry*, 25: 375–95.

Golubeva, A. (2005) '"Iashchik". Intellektual'naia igra. Pravila', *Kriticheskaia Massa*, 3–4. Online. Available http://magazines.russ.ru/km/2005/3/gol17.html (accessed 11 December 2009).

Josephi, B. (2005) 'Journalism in the Global Age: Between Normative and Empirical', *Gazette: The International Journal for Communication Studies*, 67: 575–90.

Kara-Murza, S. (2007) *Sovetskaia tsivilizatsiia*. Moscow: Izd-vo Klub Semeinogo Dosuga.

Kunczik, M. (1999) 'Freedom of the Press: Where to Draw the Line?', in M. Kunczik (ed.) *Ethics in Journalism: A Reader on Their Perceptions in the Third World*, Bonn: Friedrich Ebert Stiftung, 5–30.

Lipman, M. (2006) Editorial, *Pro et Contra*, July–August.

Litovskaia, M., Rosenholm, A., Savkina, I. and Trubina, E. (eds) (2008) *Obraz dostoinoi zhizni v sovremennykh rossiiskikh SMI*, Ekaterinburg: Izdatel'stvo Ural'skogo universiteta.

Louw, P.E. (2001) *The Media and Cultural Production*, London: Sage.

Morev, G. (2008) '"Snob" eto ne shliagernaia zhurnalistika. Interv'u s Vladimirom Iakovlevym', *Openspace.ru*. Online. Available www.openspace.ru/media/paper/details/3763/ (accessed 11 December 2009).

Morris, N. and Waisbord, S. (ed.) (2001) *Media and Globalization: Why the State Matters*, Lanham, MD: Rowman & Littlefield.

Mostovshchikov, E. (2009) 'My nichego pro tainyi hod ne znaem', *Openspace.ru*. Online. Available www.openspace.ru/media/air/details/8769/page3/ (accessed 11 December 2009).

Nordenstreng, K, Vartanova, E. and Zassoursky, Y. (eds) (2002) *Russian Media Challenge*, 2nd edn, Helsinki: Aleksanteri Institute.

Pankin, A. (2010) 'Democracy is Dangerous for the Media', *The Moscow Times*, 25 May.

Poptsov, O. (2008) 'Vlast' i TV udarili po rukam', *Zhurnalist*, April: 47–8.

Schudson, M. (2003) *The Sociology of News*, New York: Norton.

Smith, B.H. (1988) *Contingencies of Value. Alternative Perspectives for Critical Theory*, Cambridge, MA: Harvard University Press.

Twitchell, James (2000) 'Two Cheers for Materialism', in J.B. Shor and D.B. Holt (eds) *The Consumer Society Reader*, New York: The New Press.

Vartanova, E. (2009) 'Russian Media: Market and Technology as Driving Forces of Change', in E. Vartanova, H. Nieminen and M-M. Salminen (eds) *Perspectives to the Media in Russia: "Western" Interests and Russian Developments*, Helsinki: Aleksanteri Institute, 283–300.

Volkmer, I. (2003) 'The Global Network Society and the Global Public Sphere', *Development* 46(1): 9–16.

Warner, W.L., Meeker, M. and Fells, K. (1949) *Social Class in America: the Evaluation of Status*, New York: Harper Torchbooks.

Zvereva, G. (2005) 'Vechnaia voina', *Kriticheskaia Massa*, 2005: 2. Online. Available http://magazines.russ.ru/km/2005/2/zv7.html (accessed 11 December 2009).

Part 1

Mapping the media landscape

1 Contemporary structure of the Russian media industry

Elena Vartanova and Sergei Smirnov

In one word, the basis of the contemporary media system in Russia is the *market*. In spite of all the difficulties accompanying the media market, the market brings tangible changes into the structures and typology of the media, the practices of professional journalists, the audience demands and the patterns of media consumption. In this chapter, we will map out the main trends of the present media industry as shaped by the market.

It is not an easy job to attribute a general character to the structure of Russian media. First of all, Russia has the largest territory of all the countries in the world. This has many consequences for the mass media. The number of distinct regional and local media markets considerably exceeds even the number of subjects of the Federation (local governments) of the country, which is 83 in 2009.

The quantitative diversity of the Russian media market is indisputable. As of 1 December 2008, the number of media outlets registered in Russia was 101,000 (Roskomnadzor). Among the officially registered Russian media, some do not really exist. This is why the national media register includes only 66,032 print and electronic mass media (Reestr SMI). They are as follows: Television programmes 5,254, Radio programmes 3,769, Newspapers 28,449, Magazines 21,572, Digests 1,378, Other media 5,610.

Another reason why it is very difficult to characterise the Russian media is the lack of transparency in the market in general, and in the media market in particular. The most obvious problems are the overstated circulation of newspapers and magazines and the falsified ratings of the broadcasting channels, aimed at comforting advertisers. In addition, a debate around the concept of 'oligarchs' has become popular recently, as a result of which we now know some 'names' but do not have a full understanding of how they correlate with ownership of particular media companies. In fact, no government agency today possesses exhaustive statistical data on the condition and dynamics of the national media market as a whole.

Key segments of the media market

All data show that whereas in the USSR the key role in the media system was played by print media, in post-Soviet Russia this role is played by television. Today there are three main types of terrestrial broadcasters: centralised national channels, networked national channels and regional channels. In 200 cities and towns of Russia, 10–12 publicly accessible TV channels are available. In addition, cable and satellite TV are rapidly developing. Market experts believe that the total number of channels broadcast in Russia is about 1,500. Today, TV is the most important source of information and entertainment for most citizens of Russia. About 40 per cent of Russians watch the central TV channels from Moscow daily. Public opinion polls also show that for another 40 per cent of the population it is local TV that is the main provider of information and entertainment. The changing attitude of Russians to different media is not the only explanation of the growing role of TV in the national media system. For many families, an important factor in the choice of this or that medium is money: they do not have to pay for TV (leaving aside the cost of electricity as insignificant).

The newspaper sector of the Russian media market can be divided into three almost equal parts: national newspapers account for 35 per cent of the total circulation, regional papers for 33 per cent and local papers for 32 per cent. In 2007, the total circulation figure for regular newspapers was about 7.8 billion copies. Market experts hold that of the 28,449 registered newspaper outlets (daily and weekly), only about 15,000 are actually being published. The total audience for national newspapers does not exceed 20 per cent of the population, but local print media, and in particular rural papers, are as much again. The main tendency in the newspaper market, however, is a reduction in circulation. This is accounted for by the demographic situation (the number of traditional newspaper readers is decreasing), as well as by a general decrease in interest among Russian citizens, especially young people, in newspapers as a source of current information, which results from the rapid development of online media. Publishers have to spend additional resources on confronting this threatening tendency. Free newspapers have become a good way to solve the problem.

The magazine sector of the Russian media market is developing more rapidly. In the past three years its annual growth has exceeded 13 per cent (only in India and China it is developing faster). The total circulation of Russian magazines in 2007 was 1.9 billion copies. These include 900 million glossy magazines, 600 million of which were printed abroad. Magazine periodicals in Moscow far outperform those in the regions, in a ratio of 60:40. However, as was the case with newspapers, out of the total number of registered magazines titles in the country (21,572), only 12,000 are really being published. One of the major problems with this sector is the imperfect system of distribution, especially when it comes to subscription. The main consumers of magazines are citizens of metropolitan areas.

A positive dynamic is also observed in the development of the radio market. It comprises national networks and local radio stations. The market started to grow in the mid-1990s with the emergence of local FM stations. Wired broadcasting has become less popular since then, both because of the strong competition in large cities, and because of the wearing out of equipment in distant regions. The key players in the radio market are a few core central stations. The development of radio broadcasting in the regions occurs through local broadcasters joining existing networks – altogether 31.

The fastest-growing sector of the media system in Russia is the Internet. In the Russian-language area of the Internet (RUnet), almost 2.5 million domain names were registered in November 2009 (Stat.reg.ru 2009). Notably, some RUnet sites position themselves as a mass medium, and their number amounted to 2,018 outlets in 2008. The total Russian audience of the Net is estimated to be 30–40 million in 2009. Many of these users search for the news, which suggests that the Internet is really making its way next to traditional news media. On the other hand, Rambler's rumetrics service, for example, measures only about 10 per cent of news-oriented hosts (visits to webpages) in the RUnet. Although news is the most popular search topic, about 90 per cent of activities online happen around other subjects such as games, social networking and shopping. In terms of the size of the Internet audience, the clear leader is Moscow, where more than 5 million people a month use the Net. In Russia as a whole, 6 per cent of the population has not heard of the Internet and 73 per cent do not have any opportunity to use it regularly.

Advertising in the Russian mass media

With the introduction of market relations, the Russian economy found itself in need of a new type of information: advertising. So, against the background of the economic growth of the mid-2000s, the development of the advertising market was especially important for the media industry, as it became the primary vehicle for advertising. Research shows that there are obvious connections between the national economy, the development of the advertising market and the media industry as a whole. Between 1997 and 2008 the total growth of the advertising market was 650 per cent, with its annual growth around 30 per cent. By 2008 the share of the advertising industry in the gross domestic product (GDP), calculated as the percentage of advertising market volume within GDP, was 0.9 per cent. The contribution of the Russian advertising industry to the GDP is comparable to that of Austria, where it is about 1 per cent. As a result of the intensive growth of its advertising market in recent years, in terms of its volume Russia was number 13 in the world in 2008 and sixth among the European countries. According to estimates by the Association of Communication Agencies of Russia, this figure amounted to 8.9 billion dollars in 2008 (including outdoor, indoor and the below the line (BTL) sector).

It is clear that the 2008 crisis could not but be reflected in the general situation in the Russian advertising market. However, in comparison with the problems facing the economically developed countries of Europe and the USA, the dynamics are better in Russia. As a well-known advertising analysis agency pointed out in December 2008,

> we have to reduce our prognosis for the advertising market growth in 2009 for the countries of the Asian-Pacific region from 5.2 per cent to 3.2 per cent and for the countries of Central and Eastern Europe from 12.7 per cent to 1.5 per cent. For the rest of the world our prognosis remains the same… In the

> most rapidly developing markets of Brazil, Russia, India and China we predict further growth in 2009: 5 per cent in Russia, 9 per cent in China, 13 per cent in India, and 30 per cent in Brazil.
>
> (ZenithOptimedia 2008)

Since these predictions, fresh data show that the first nine months of 2009 have in fact experienced 30 per cent decline of the Russian advertising market size compared to the previous year. Internet was the only segment that demonstrated some growth (3 per cent), whereas the rest of the segments showed minus ranging between –55 per cent for advertising publications and –21 per cent for TV advertising.

In the long run, however, the Russian advertising market will continue growing, pushed also by globalisation. The Russian consumer market remains insufficiently developed and less attractive to global advertisers. The removal of barriers against foreign companies gaining access to Russian consumers has resulted in intensive foreign capital investment into the media business. The same process has caused an acceleration in the development of the Russian advertising market. Since 2000, many foreign media corporations have bought Russian media companies or established subsidiaries in Russia. Compared with the first wave of foreign media capital in the early 1990s, the second is more substantial. Its first tangible result is the growth of the Russian advertising market. The second result is that global media companies are making preparations in case Russia joins the World Trade Organization, which might be quite profitable for them.

The Russian advertising market is based on all kinds of agencies: full-service agencies, specialised agencies and mega-agencies. A natural tendency towards concentration can be clearly seen here: more than 75 per cent of advertising on TV is controlled by Video International. Among other specific features are the leadership of TV, slower development of print advertising and an increased interest in the Internet. But the most pervasive tendency for the advertising market is its growth hand in hand with the Russian economy, which introduces new challenges to the media, such as a better understanding of the audience and a more precise measurement of its size, structure, demands and interests.

Ownership structures

The central feature of the modern media market in Russia is the heterogeneous character of its economy. This is caused not only by the uneven development of Moscow and the regions but also by the differences in the ownership structures in the media market. Considering the formation of the Russian media market in the 1990s to 2000s in terms of ownership structure, one can observe two basic components: state capital (or, to be more precise, budget capital) and commercial capital. Of the latter there are two varieties, that of Russian financial and industrial groups (also known as 'oligarch' capital) and foreign capital (historically always concerned with the media).

In our experience, state capitalisation and commercial capitalisation have proved to be effective in the Russian media not only separately but also in combination.

There are three main types of media companies in Russia: state, commercial and mixed companies ('hybrids'). It is no exaggeration to say that the media industry in Russia has, almost without exception, developed through total diversification, which manifests itself in the entry of Russian financial, industrial and financial and industrial groups' capital into the media market. It was the latter type, commonly known as the *FPG* C° business, that was the basis for the foundation of the Russian media enterprises.

Forms of ownership

The main tendency in the evolution of large media ownership in this country in the 2000s has been a decrease in commercial capital and the proportionate increase in state capital and mixed capital. The media are concentrated (directly or indirectly) in the hands of governmental or government-controlled structures. The following three companies of national importance lead the media market today: VGTRK, a state enterprise, Gazprom-Media, an enterprise with a mixed form of ownership, and Prof-Media, a purely commercial structure.

- The Russian Federation Broadcasting Company (VGTRK) controls the national TV companies Rossiia, Kul'tura, Sport, Vesti, RTR-Planeta, Sport-Planeta, Bibigon, regional TV and radio companies (GTRK), the radio companies Radio Rossiia, Maiak, Kul'tura, Vesti-FM, and the Rossiia Internet channel.
- Gazprom-Media controls the TV companies NTV, TNT, NTV-Mir, NTV-Plus, the publishing house Sem' dnei, the newspapers Tribuna, Chas pik, the radio companies Ekho Moskvy, Siti-FM, Popsa, Nekst, Relaks-FM, Detskoe Radio, NTV-Kino movie company, NTV-Media advertising agency, and the movie theatres Oktiabr' and Kristall-palas.
- Prof-Media controls the publishing houses Afisha, B2B-Media, the radio companies Avtoradio, Avtoradio Sankt-Peterburg, Iumor-FM, NRJ, Alla, the TV companies TV-3, 2X2, MTV-Rossiia, VH1-Rossiia, the Central Partnership movie company, the Cinema Park movie theatre chain, and the Rambler Internet portal.

The 'second echelon' players include nearly 30 media companies beginning with: Aksel Shpringer Rossiia (magazines), and ending with RBK-Informatsionnye Sistemy (newspapers, magazines, TV, the Internet). Based in the capital, all these structures are also active in the regions, so they may be said to have the status of federal media companies. Most of them are purely commercial, but some are state-run and others have mixed capitalisation.

In the regions, there are few large media enterprises comparable in size with the metropolitan players. The most successful are: Abak-Press (the Altai territory), Baltiskaia Mediagruppa (St. Petersburg), Bonnier Grupp Rossiia (St. Petersburg), Korporatsiia Fedorov (the Samara region), Provintsiia (40 regions), Tomskaia Mediagruppa (the Tomsk region), Chetvertyi Kanal (the Sverdlovsk region), and Iuzhnii Region (the Rostov region).

As in other countries, media companies in Russia have several sources of income: payments by audience, direct or indirect governmental subsidies, sponsorship, overt or covert advertising. There are also new sources of profit, such as product placement in the audio-visual media and books, and selling of client databases by the new media. Advertising remains the main source of income for media enterprises regardless of the type of ownership. In this respect, the Russian media faithfully follow the laws of the market. For state-run media enterprises it is vitally important today not only to act in the advertising market but also to consider commercial advantages of doing so. This certainly helps many companies to survive and to be relatively free from political bias, but at the same time journalistic activities are highly dependent on market requirements.

The new media economy being formed in Russia shapes the modern media system. The Russian media have to function within a market that is still partly dependent on state ownership and state monopoly. The areas of printing, distribution, and signal re-translation are still closed to private initiative and therefore require government investment. The paradox of the Russian media market is that competition, an inherent value of the Anglo-Saxon ideal of independent journalism, does not guarantee economic freedom to the Russian media. Far from it: the decentralisation of economic resources in the regional markets and the strong competition between newspapers and TV companies turn out to be beneficial not to the media and their audiences but to the authorities, enabling them to control the media more efficiently. In fact, competition in economically weak markets should be regarded as a shortcoming of the modern media system in Russia.

Growth strategies for the media enterprises

Undoubtedly one of the key processes determining the development of the media industry in modern Russia is business concentration. It has been proven statistically that business concentration contributes to the general expansion of the Russian media industry and stimulates the development of all its sectors. First, new large media corporations are formed in order to accumulate and optimise the distribution of the financial flows necessary for the implementation of projects requiring substantial investment. Second, a wider range of the projected audience increases the attractiveness of the media to advertisers. In addition, bringing together the production and distribution of the information and advertising product results in a synergetic effect.

In 2008, 874 million dollars were spent on merger and acquisitions deals in the media, and market experts believe that in the medium term the tendency will continue. At present there are over ten large diversified media companies in this country with the real total capitalisation amounting to 500 million dollars or more. All in all, the number of players in the market is about 50. According to estimates by experts in the Federal Agency for Print Media and Mass Communications (FAPMC), several companies with capitalisation running into billions are likely to appear in the near future. The number of new media outlets acquired or founded by

Table 1.1 The top 10 Russian publishing houses in terms of the audience of any one issue of all newspapers in 2007 (in cities with a population over 100,000)

Publishing house	*Audience of any one issue*	*Percentage of urban population aged over 16*
1. Ashet Filipachi Shkulev i Intermedia Grup	10,121.7	17.8
2. Komsomol'skaia Pravda	8,435.0	14.8
3. Argumenty i fakty	7,042.3	12.4
4. Bauer-Rossiia	4,615.1	8.1
5. Pronto-Moskva	2,855.1	5.0
6. Moskovskii Komsomolets	2,733.2	4.8
7. S-info	2,245.1	3.9
8. N'ius media-Rus	2,219.1	3.9
9. Media mir	1,950.9	3.4
10. Kommersant	237.5	0.4

Source: TNS Gallup Media (2008: 32).

the leading companies has been increasing annually. Thus, there is every reason to claim that today the level of concentration in the Russian media is in fact growing (Table 1.1).

The Russian model of media concentration as a whole is characterised by an apparent centripetal tendency. There is clear predominance of metropolitan and federal media companies, which locate their assets and management units in Moscow. Given its special status and strong potential, economically Moscow leads the field among the constituent members of the Russian Federation. It is not surprising, therefore, that Russian media tycoons tended from the very start to develop their businesses in the capital, where conditions were most favourable. The expansion of media companies into regional information markets is secondary. The growing interest of the largest media companies, especially network broadcasters, in the regional media can be accounted for by their closeness to the audience, local content oriented towards the local consumer and a new tendency towards spot advertising. In regional companies themselves, however, concentration of the media system is still poorly developed.

Chronologically, the stages of concentration in the Russian media completely coincide with the stages of media commercialisation, because concentration was a logical consequence of the capital flow into the national media system. The stages are as follows: Stage one covers the years from 1991 to 1996. This was the time of initial commercialisation and initial concentration of media assets in post-Soviet Russia. Stage two lasted from 1996 to 2000, and it was during those years that the process of media concentration in Russia reached its climax. Stage three, from 2000 to the present day, is characterised by the redistribution of media assets and changes in the rules for operating media businesses. Thus the process of media concentration is far from being simply cumulative; rather it consists of two clearly distinct vectors, one of which replaced the other at the turn of the century.

However, certain peculiarities of the Russian model of media concentration have not changed considerably over time. The main one seems to be the predominance of a 'diagonal' growth strategy (also known as a 'cross' strategy). The fact that the diagonal type of concentration prevailed in Russia can be accounted for by the specific rules of the game that took shape in the information market in the early 1990s. New businessmen used the opportunity to start acquiring any property that was available. Mass expansion began in all the sectors of the national media industry, first in newspapers, magazines, TV and radio, and later in the film industry, video and audio recording and the Internet. Notably, some large media owners tended to gain control over already existing outlets, whereas others preferred to found their own. Second echelon media companies are more likely to practice horizontal concentration.

The integration of the Russian media market into an overall media system required new approaches to the media business, and gradually these came to be more transparent. In the 2000s, annual reports published on corporate websites contained data on the income of the large media structures. From such documents it is known that in 2007 the annual earnings of Gazprom-Media, for example, totalled 1,275 million dollars, those of Prof-Media 480 million dollars, and those of VGTRK 900 million dollars. It must be noted, however, that few media enterprises have chosen the route of transformation into an open public company with prospects of listing on international markets.

The first company to place its shares on the international market was Rambler-Media. It has been listed on the London Stock Market since 2005. In 2006, the STS Media company's shares were entered on the New York Stock Market. As a result both companies gained a lot of 'cheap money'. Through its IPO Rambler-Media added 50 million dollars and STS-Media 346 million dollars. RBK-Informatsionnye Sistemy is listed internationally, on the Moscow Interbank Currency Exchange (MMVB) and on the RTS Stock Market. According to estimates by financial analysts, the most likely candidates for successful flotation are Gazprom-Media and Prof-Media. Allegedly, the government intends to reincorporate VGTRK as a joint-stock company. However, all these mega-projects have not been realised so far.

As a result of these changes, 'pure' media capital has begun to emerge in the Russian information market. The large diversified companies of the older type (such as Gazprom-Media) are already giving way to large companies of the new type (such as STS-Media), which are based on current assets acquired in the media market as such. New development strategies, various combinations of different concentration types, and mutual penetration of the state approach and the commercial approach to the information business have all contributed to a kind of recovery, a reversal of diversification of media capital holdings in Russia. Gradually, stable civilised patterns of interaction among media companies are being established, and a pool of efficient media managers is being formed.

It is not surprising that portfolio investors have put their faith in the large and medium Russian media businesses. Three companies today are most attractive to investors: STS-Media, Rambler Media (owned by Prof-Media), and

RBK-Informatsionnye Sistemy. Over the past year, the capitalisation of STS-Media has grown by 72 per cent, and that of RBK-Informatsionnye Sistemy by 66 per cent. The saturation of traditional sectors with investment resources inevitably leads to a search for new outlets for capital investment. Obviously, under such conditions, the media market will remain especially attractive to Russian investors, including those for whom the media business is not a primary concern.

The influx of foreign capital

Some prosperous media enterprises were established through the influx of foreign capital into the national media system, although in the 1990s, especially during the period of initial capitalisation, this influx was not widespread. The wide-scale expansion of foreign media enterprises into the Russian media market began in the 2000s, in response to increased stability in the country's general economic development.

Over recent years the following big players in the world media market have been successful in Russia: the German companies Axel Springer Verlag (Aksel Shpringer Rossiia), Bauer Verlagsgruppe (Bauer-Rossiia), Bertelsmann-Konzern AG (REN-TV Media Holding), and Hubert Burda Media (Burda-Rossiia); the Swedish companies Bonnier AB (Bonnier Grup Rossiia) and Modern Times Group (STS Media); the French Hachette Filipacchi Medias (Ashet Filipachi Shkulev and Intermedia Grup) and Lagardere Group (Evropeiskaia Mediagruppa); the American Conde Nast, the Swiss EDIPRESSE Group (Edipres-Konliga), the Finnish Sanoma WSOY (Independent Media), the Dutch Trader Classified Media NV (Pronto-Moskva) and others (Table 1.2). Interest in Russian media is shown by other owners of famous international brands, in particular American media giants.

Table 1.2 The top 10 Russian publishing houses in terms of the magazine audience in 2007 (in cities with a population over 100,000)

Publishing house	*Cumulative audience in Russia, October 2007*	*Percentage of urban population aged over 16*
1. Burda	10,607.7	18.6
2. Sem' Dnei	5,920.9	10.4
3. Independent Media Sanoma Magazines	5,841.2	10.2
4. Bauer Rossiia	4,225.1	7.4
5. Za Rul'em	2,881.7	5.1
6. Conde Nast	2,176.1	3.8
7. Ashet Filipachi Shkulev i Intermedia Grup	2,015.0	3.5
8. Media park	1,653.0	2.9
9. OVA-Press	1,296.1	2.3
10. *Health* magazine	1,046.8	1.8

Source: TNS Gallup Media (2008: 50).

The key strategy for foreign media enterprises in Russia is adaptation of famous foreign media brands. This approach is fully represented in the fast-growing magazine market. Today, almost all the world's largest magazine brands can be found here. In compiling Russian-language versions the following techniques are used: business franchising, co-operation, and co-branding. Notably, few foreign media organisations have decided to open their own offices in Russia; most of them have confined themselves to buying large share-holdings of publishing houses or forming joint enterprises with Russian partners.

Recent tendencies

The key peculiarity of the modern media system in Russia is related to the changes in the market structure and the new correlation between the national and regional/local markets. The vertical hierarchical structure of the newspaper and magazine market that used to be predominant in the USSR has given way to horizontal configurations in the regional markets.

Regionalisation of the market and media systems

Nowadays, readers are increasingly interested in their local newspaper published near their homes, as it refers to their everyday concerns; so are advertisers. The news broadcast by local TV is of greatest interest to viewers, and this leads to relatively high ratings. According to the annual report by FAPMC, 'two thirds of the circulation of socio-political newspapers is created by regional and local editions' (Russian Periodical Press Market 2008: 30).

In view of the evident interest of the audience in local information and the new economic foundations of the media business, it is possible to distinguish the main reasons behind the regionalisation of journalism and the modern media system in Russia.

First of all, print media markets are strongly dependent on their distribution systems. The Russian Post, virtually the only national enterprise able to deliver newspapers and magazines throughout the country, has never been able to create a cheap and efficient distribution system. In the late 1990s to early 2000s, subscription circulation dropped and retail sale became the main method of distribution. Also print media became an element of urban life only because the transport and trade communications of cities and towns made the press distribution possible. Television, in fact, remained the sole truly national mass medium and possessed the only comprehensive infrastructure in Russian information space.

Apart from reductions in distribution, the deterioration of print media has had other negative effects on journalism. Serious political and intellectual public discussion has suffered above all. The national agenda has 'lost' a number of issues important to a sense of national identity. Today, only weekly business magazines are trying to resume the traditions of the quality press, though discussions of non-economic issues are minimal. The attempts to create a universal (in terms of the audience), national (in terms of distribution and agenda) magazine have yielded insignificant results. And although the success of *Russkii Reporter* (a project by the Ekspert publishing house) in the regions calls for some optimism, its sales in Moscow and other large cities are far from satisfactory.

Second, TV, as a medium that has a particular effect on the centrifugal forces in Russian politics, has come to play the key role in the media system. However, this resulted in the subsequent division of labour: the central (federal) channels took upon themselves the functions of covering national politics and of mass entertainment (as a consequence of their co-operation with global and national advertisers), whereas the regional media (both audio-visual and print media) focused on regional/local audiences and advertisers (Rantanen 2002; Vartanova 2009). It is obvious that the potential of the federal channels in forming the national agenda has not been fully realised. In an attempt to satisfy advertisers' needs as well as political interests, Russian TV has shifted the emphasis to entertainment, with elements of 'infotainment', tabloid style and journalism 'on demand'. This in turn leads to audience preference for the regional media, which outperform the national media in providing information that bears close relation to audience interest.

Third, the current state of Russia's economic development has strengthened the role of regional advertising markets, which results in higher incomes for the regional media. As pointed out in the annual report by FAPMC:

> while in the mid and late 1990s the most attractive advertising vehicles were the national media, primarily TV, over recent years the interest of advertisers in regional media has considerably increased. The growth rates of the advertising component in regional media, including the network media, have exceeded those of most federal editions. As a result, the local press is becoming increasingly attractive to investors and among the subjects of the Russian Federation regional and inter-regional media holdings are rapidly emerging.
>
> (Russian Periodical Press Market 2008: 30)

By the mid-2000s, the volume of regional advertising accounted for 28 per cent of the total volume of advertising in Russia, that is, a growth of over 30 per cent. Alongside this, it should be noted that the Russian advertising market has not yet been fully developed. Russia is lagging behind many countries of the world both in terms of the proportion of the total volume of the advertising market in the GDP and in terms of advertising expenses per capita (about 50 dollars).

Another important consequence for the typology of the Russian media system resulting from the growth of the advertising industry was the passing of the Act 'On Advertising' in 2006. By imposing stricter limitations on the length of blocks of advertising time, the Act did not only encourage the flow of some advertising from the federal to the regional channels, but also revived the regional broadcasters' hope for improvements. Advertisers themselves admit their readiness to invest in regional TV, provided the quality of coverage and transmission is not inferior to that in Moscow.

The formation of the content production market

As the number of media outlets in Russia is growing as well as the number of channels concerned with content delivery, the need for content in the media industry has increased. Television channels, the number of which has grown over recent years both on federal and regional levels, were the first to face this problem. In response to their demands, a sector that was new for the Russian media business, content production, began to emerge.

In this context, let us consider the dynamics of movie production, TV programme production, and the purchasing of foreign TV content. The consequences of this process are obvious: the more investments are made in TV production, the higher the quality of the Russian TV product becomes. Good examples are programming dynamics, changes in the most frequent formats and dynamics in programme-producing countries. Serials, being, in terms of popularity, format number three on six main channels, are most indicative. Over recent years, the proportion of serials in viewing time has remained about the same, 15–17 per cent. But at the same time there are significant changes within this format: in 1997 the number of Russian serials was 103, in 2002 it was 292, and by 2005 it had grown to 538. The number of American serials on Russian TV showed slower growth: in 1997 there were 87; in 2002, 130; in 2005, 153. The number of European serials remained relatively stable: in 1997, 111; in 2002, 115; 2005, 101. A negative dynamic is apparent only in the showing of serials produced in other regions, mostly in Latin America: in 1997 there were 38; in 2002, as many as 56; but in 2005, the number dropped to seven.

The reasons for the increase of the number of Russian serials on TV are first and foremost economic. It is known that the increase in financial investment in TV production made it possible to establish production capacities for cheap Russian serials and then progress from criminal serials (the genre that dominated the screen in 1997–2002) to more expensive serials, such as production of screen versions of Russian classical literature, e.g. *The Idiot* and *Master and Margarita*, each part of which cost as much as 650,000 dollars.

Influenced as it was by the transformations of the market, the Russian media industry was unable to escape the pressure coming from the global media industry, particularly the tendency to form an individual segment of content production for TV. Broadcasters' need for quality programmes is determined by the demands of advertisers and the interests of politicians, as well as the desires and tastes of ordinary people. Notably, in recent years of intensive economic growth, the Russian producers of TV content have been able to deliver a sufficient number of programmes, serials and entertainment shows. This enabled the heads of the producing companies to claim, in the autumn of 2008, that Russian TV was in a position to survive the crisis in 2009. The capacity for production of TV content has been built up in the country, and this is why TV will overcome the present hard times more smoothly than in 1998.

Segmentation in the media market and changes in the media typology

Since 1991 Russian society has changed considerably. This is not merely a matter of political, economic and institutional change, but a matter of changes in the social structure, which resulted in considerable shifts in the values and media demands of the Russian people.

In spite of the predominant opinion among researchers that the modern structure of Russian society is very different from that of Soviet society, there is no scientific evidence of this. However, the 2006 research by the Institute of Social Projection, entitled 'The Real Russia. Social Stratification of Modern Russian Society' (Real Russia 2006), can be regarded as a step in this direction. According to this research, which posited a model of the structure of the Russian society on the basis of its own surveys, 25 per cent of the population belong to the middle-class, whose level of income was 72,000 rubles or more per month (about 3,000 dollars) and who had entered the 'zone of social and economic safety' (Table 1.3).

The factors that helped to build up the hierarchy were: the declared level of personal incomes, the material quality of life, the level of adaptation to the labour market, and the psychological adjustment to the market. It is important that here

Table 1.3 The social hierarchy in Russia (as of 2005)

Declared level of incomes, rub.	*Social stratum and its characteristics*	*Proportion of population as %*
25,000	'White collars 1': top-managers, owners of small enterprises, highly skilled specialists	1.8
10,300	'White collars 2': medium-level managers	5.4
	'Blue collars 1': highly skilled workers	2.7
7,200	'Light-blue collars 1': intelligentsia/non-manual workers (mostly women), teachers, doctors	10
	'Blue collars 2' (men, private sector)	5.5
5,600	Students	3.3
	'Blue collars 3' (those working in state sector, women, small towns)	10.8
3,000	'Light-blue collars 2': servants, kindergarten teachers, nurses (women)	5.0
	'Grey collars-1': unskilled workers (state sector, men)	10
1,030	'Grey collars-2': health service, agriculture (mostly women in rural areas)	4.8
	Non-workers (mostly women)	9.7
2,300	Pensioners	31

Source: Real Russia (2006: 66–7).

not only quantitative but also qualitative measures of social strata come into play, and, in the first place, self-positioning within the conditions of the market economy.

The conclusion is obvious: over recent years the structure of Russian society has changed considerably due to the changes in people's material status. Russians differ both in their levels of income and in their forms of consumption, and therefore in their media interests. The growing demand for oil in the mid-2000s resulted in a certain stability in the Russian economy, which, in turn, led to an increase in people's purchasing power. In spite of the existing social inequality, media consumption, as well as the consumption of goods and services advertised, has tangibly increased. There are other social changes too: in the lifestyle of many social groups variety of consumption has become dominant, leisure activities have diversified and the role of education in career-making has strengthened.

All these tendencies have had effects on the development of the media typology, specifically, the expansion of entertainment and of clearly specialised media. They also account for the increased interest of the audience in quality political editions of a general character and in analytical programmes on TV. According to a ten-year specialist forecast, the popularity of this sector will steadily grow.

The decrease in political content in the media results from the fact that owners and managers of Russian media enterprises have developed a new economic logic. They are faced with the task of increasing the profits of media company assets. An important symptom of this process is the change in content of many mass media: there is an increase in the proportion of entertainment content and of material dealing with specific interests, such as leisure, sport, health, fashion, music and the consumer market in general. Content commodification has become the main criterion when launching new formats and genres, as well as in formulating the strategies of media companies.

A good example of such transformations on the level of large national media companies is the step-by-step reformation of Prof-Media. Within Russia's information market, this private company is oriented exclusively towards the entertainment sector. Today it does not have any social or political TV channels at the federal level. In recent years, the company has also got rid of its leading political publications, the newspaper *Izvestiia* and the magazine *Ekspert*. It is developing economically through special interest concerns: the *B2B* magazines, musical radio stations, specialised TV channels and movie companies.

A number of second echelon media companies, which originated in the 1990s, have chosen to take the same direction. Such companies as Moskovskii komsomolets, Komsomol'skaia Pravda, Promsviaz' Kapital and Ekstra M Video are developing through establishing new print editions dealing with leisure, education, advertising and business, which suits the demands of the Russian audience. Naturally, the companies that were initially oriented towards the entertainment sector are going the same way. Independent Media, Burda Russia, Conde Nast, Ashet Filipachi Shkulev and Intermedia Grup are launching new glossy magazines, whereas STS Media, Russkaia Mediagruppa, Evropeiskaia Mediagruppa and Arnol'd Praiz Grup focus on music radio stations and specialised TV channels.

It is important to mention that in the Russian media market subsidiaries of foreign media companies or companies backed with foreign capital play an active role in developing the range of topics and the format of content. It is the activity of these trans-national structures that encourages the transformations in the typology and content of the media. The same tendencies have equally affected the state-run and mixed media companies. A striking example of the emergence of new major trends is the foundation of the Sport TV channel within the context of VGTRK (this will be closed in January 2010 and its place will be taken by a new channel for youth Rossiya 2), as well as expansion in the category of music stations (Pervoe Populiarnoe Radio, Radio Nekst) of the Gazprom-Media company. The increased proportion of non-political content can also be observed in the programme strategies of the largest national TV companies, Pervyi Kanal, Rossiia and NTV. They supply many programmes about cuisine, cars, housekeeping, design, fashions and so on.

Another indicative example of how the changes in social structure influence the typology of print media is the segmentation and development of the magazine market. According to the annual report by FAPMC (2007), in 2005 magazine earnings from advertising totalled 580 million dollars, which exceeded the level of 2004 by 110 millions. As regards the quantity of advertising in any one issue, many Russian magazines are very close to the best foreign counterparts. The estimates by the RPRG company indicate that the money earned this year by advertising, in a single issue of the Russian version of *Elle* magazine is about 2 million dollars. The situation with *Cosmopolitan* is about the same. *VOGUE* and *Za rul'em* lag slightly behind. Among the weeklies, the winners are, among others, *7 dnei*, *Liza*, *Kommersant-Den'gi*, *Ekspert* and *Afisha*.

Advertising is financially more rewarding for magazines than for newspapers. According to estimates by the Association of Russian Communication Agencies, the growth of advertising income in 2004–5 was 23 per cent for magazines and 16 per cent for newspapers. The proportion of magazines in the advertising market at that time was 12 per cent, whereas that of newspapers was only 7 per cent. It is not surprising, therefore, that the FAPMC report pointed out the cause of stability among magazines being that 'the magazine business is more profitable and less labor-consuming than the newspaper business'. This is just one more proof that the structure and the typology of the Russian media clearly depend on the advertising market. There are some objective reasons for this. Magazine distribution is cheaper and more reliable, and it does not depend on daily delivery. One may think that readers trust magazines more than they trust newspapers, the prestige of which has severely dropped since the beginning of *perestroika*. The analytical level of weekly social and political magazines is higher than that of daily newspapers, one of the reasons being that the business-cycle of magazines is much longer. Lastly, magazines are certainly superior to newspapers in terms of graphic arts. Therefore, magazines are more attractive both to the audience and to advertisers, and they have better prospects for the future than the daily print media.

From what has been said above, one can conclude that social transformation in Russia, in terms of economic and demographic characteristics, lifestyle and values, is becoming more and more evident. As a result, the mass audience that used to be relatively homogeneous is developing into a heterogeneous one. And the changes in the structure and typology of the media are determined not only by the process of social transformation, but also by digital information and communication technologies.

Convergence

The advance of information and communication technology (ICT) generates changes, which, in turn, lead to a fragmentation in the mass audience, a fact that seems to be having a negative impact on the traditional relationships between advertisers and the media. The new media, the Internet and mobile phones significantly contribute to the process of reduction: the information consumer is becoming not only a consumer but also a mediator and a producer. Under these circumstances, the Russian media market, affected by social and political reforms, has been changed by the technological progress. At least four main tendencies in the transformation of the market can be distinguished.

First, the Internet and mobile telephones have expanded the access of Russian people to information. According to data obtained in 2008, the number of regular RUnet users is about 28 million, in addition to which are 11 million habitual users. This is nearly 25 per cent of the population (Table 1.4). In the 2000s, the inequality of the regions in terms of digital access has been going down, and the social, age and gender balance among Russian mobile and Internet users has been improving. Today, the proportion of women among RUnet users is about 40 per cent, although a typical user is an educated male city dweller having a high level of income, aged between 25 and 35, an official, a politician, a businessman, a journalist or a student. Another trend in the development of the Internet is the predominance of individual users over corporate ones. However, the ratio between Internet connections from homes and from offices is still 35:65.

Second, it is obvious that for modern Russians the Internet is an essential part of the media system. The increase in their purchasing power undoubtedly contributed to the development of the new media: pay digital TV (cable and satellite),

Table 1.4 The number of Internet users in the Russian regions

Region	*Penetration, %*
Central (including Moscow)	24.9
North-West	27.8
The Southern region	24.5
The Volga region	23.7
The Ural region	23.6
Siberia	22.7
The Far East region	29.8

Source: Yandex (2008).

the Internet and the mobile telephones as vehicles for distributing news, weather forecasts and advertising. According to the FAMPC data, in recent years the proportion of Russians who have no contact with the media has gone down, and the proportion of the audience using the Internet as a mass medium has gone up. In 2007, the number of Russians who use only the audiovisual media (TV and radio) dropped: it was no more than 55 per cent. At the same time, the proportion of the audience in contact with the other major older sectors (TV, radio and the print media) dropped too: in 2007, it was about 10 per cent of Russians, which was 10 per cent lower than in 2006. Meanwhile, a growth in the media audience in general could be observed: from 2006 to 2007 it totalled 32 per cent, so more than 35 per cent of Russians use the print media, TV, radio and the Internet every day. (Russian Periodical Press Market 2008). FAMPC data from 2009 show that 48 per cent of RUnet users connect to the Internet every day.

Third, the Internet is becoming increasingly popular as an advertising vehicle, which strengthens its position in the Russian media system. Over recent years, the Russian Internet advertising market has developed dynamically and progressively. According to the Association of Russian Communication Agencies, this segment of the advertising market displays the highest growth dynamic, twice as high as the traditional media. The total volume of advertising on the Internet was 7.5 billion roubles in 2008, or just about 2.3 per cent of the advertising market as a whole, but this share is growing fast: from 2006 to 2007 it was an unprecedented 92 per cent and from 2007 to 2008 the rise was still 30 per cent. After 2008 its growth was only 3 per cent – against the general media market decrease of about 30 per cent.

Lastly, the process of technological convergence is proving beneficial first and foremost to large companies, which succeed by establishing multimedia newsrooms and by repeatedly using their own resources for content. The instances are relatively few but the tendency can be observed in the establishment of print media by *RBK* for recycling their online content and in the purchasing by the Prof-Media company, which specialises in the traditional media, of the leading enterprise of Rambler's Internet sector. Online media projects are gradually becoming fully fledged media market participants, and this dynamically growing sector of the information and communication industry attracts the attention of all players in varying degrees. The pioneering companies in this field were RBK-Informatsionnye Sistemy, Yandeks and Rambler-Media. In time, new departments specialising in the global computer net emerged within other media empires too. As media and communication channels are closely interwoven today, large media companies tend to occupy other new market niches. The Gazprom-Media, Sistema Mass-Media and Renova-Media companies are developing cable and satellite TV in order to realise interactive and multimedia projects. In other words, the global process of 'new media' market expansion has become a reality for Russian media companies too.

Russia's switch-over to digital broadcasting will certainly have a special role to play in strengthening the new media. The technical aspects of the change-over have been defined by the regulation of the Russian Federation Government 'On the Adoption of the European System of Digital Television Broadcasting in the Russian Federation'. In accordance with the federal plan, the process will be completed by 2015. The project will cost 10 billion dollars. The chosen broadcasting standard is the European DVB-T with MPEG-4 coding. Experimental digital DVB-T broadcasting was launched in Russia in 2000 in the city of Nizhnii Novgorod. Today it is used in the Khanti-Mansi autonomous area, the republic of Mordoviia, the Sverdlovsk region and the Kurgan region. The population of these parts of the Federation enjoys between ten and 12 digital channels. The body responsible for the adoption of digital TV throughout the country is a state-run enterprise, the Russian Television and Broadcasting Net (RTRS). The key problem is that in Russia there is no federal target-oriented development programme for broadcasting, no frequency-territorial plan for digitalisation and the package of free channels has not been defined. This package is likely to include the channels today covering more than 60 per cent of Russia's territory, plus one local channel in each member of the Federation. Also, the national legislation on communication licensing is too old to take into account the new technical achievements. The question of the so-called last mile, that is re-equipping households with digital devices, DVB-T antennas and set-top-boxes, is still open. Today, only 10–15 per cent of the population have TV sets designed for digital input. Unless a re-equipping is carried out, it is likely that in 2015, immediately after analogue broadcasting has been discontinued, the most underprivileged sections of the population, especially in far-away areas, will find themselves without TV.

The new digital technologies are actively being developed by non-terrestrial pay-TV operators. Each region in the country has its own cable TV companies; the Association of Russia's cable TV alone includes 100 regional companies. All in all, according to the data supplied by the Association, there are 22 million cable net subscribers. The regions most highly developed in this respect are Moscow and St. Petersburg. At the same time, not more than 10 per cent of Russia's population has access to digital cable supplying 'Triple Play': Internet, TV and telephone. The leading players in the national cable and IP-TV system are Nafta-Moskva, which has about 5 million subscribers, Sistema Mass-Media with 1.5 million and Renova-Media with 730,000.

Direct satellite broadcasting (Direct TV) is carried out by two powerful companies, NTV-Plius and Natsional'naia sputnikovaia Kompaniia (Trikolor TV). NTV-Plius has broadcast via the Bonum-1 satellite since 1998 and the number of its subscribers is 550,000. In 2006, the company extended broadcasting into Siberia. It was the first company to try experimental high-definition broadcasting (HDTV). Natsional'naia sputnikovaia Kompaniia emerged on the Russian market in December 2005. The Trikolor TV package is distributed in the European part of Russia via the Eutelsat W4 satellite. It has 3 million subscribers.

The development of the modern media system is closely related to the development of the Russian mass media into an individual industry steadily increasing its attractiveness to both Russian advertisers and foreign investors. Today, the most evident process encouraged by the introduction of the market philosophy and economy into the media system is the transformation of their economic and typological foundations. In the modern Russian media industry, there exist some drastically new business models, which were impossible under a state-controlled economy. The Soviet mass media and journalism played the role of an ideological, pedagogic and educational institution, but they did not care much about audience demands. In fact this was not necessary, as all the money they received was allocated from the state budget. Audience demand, especially when analytically monitored, is a vitally important mechanism for adjusting media activity to the market.

The fundamental change that triggered the transformation of the media system in post-Soviet Russia was the intensive growth of the advertising industry. As a result, the basic law of the media economy came into play, the law of constructing an audience for advertisers. In accordance, the media form their content with the aim of attracting precisely the audience whose custom is most advantageous to the advertisers, who are the main source of financing media enterprises (Picard 1989). It has to be admitted that under the market conditions the performance of any social functions by the media often becomes a secondary concern, commercial interests being regarded as more important.

For most media researchers, it is clear that the modern mass media, their economic foundations, their structures and institutions, have all been shaped by market influence. In many studies, it is emphasised that the mission of the media and journalism in democratic countries to provide unbiased information and a broad and fair reflection of existing views and ideas goes hand in hand with the commercial need to make a profit. (McQuail 2005; Croteau and Hoynes 2001: 6–7). This situation results in inevitable internal contradictions in the media systems of market economies. In other studies, these contradictions are labelled as contradictions between the commercial media and social interests, between culture and commerce, or between a prosperous business and a weak democracy (Croteau and Hoynes 2001; De Bens 2007; McChesney 1999). Whatever the definition, in each case the idea is that there are inseparable ties between the market as an economic structure of society and the media system existing within its context. Many researchers stress that because of these close ties the market influences the character of the media, in effect imposing its own values and thus leading to commercialisation, which, in turn, results in such characteristics as sensationalism, the tabloidisation, emphasis on entertainment (Sparks 1992; Esser 1999; De Bens 2001: 92).

In spite of all its peculiarities, the media system in post-Soviet Russia has changed profoundly over the recent decades and its restructuring has been quite similar to developments in other countries: quantitative growth, increased diversity in media channels and media content, regionalisation of the media markets, and the introduction of ICT into the media infrastructure and into the media system itself.

References

AKAR, Association of Russian Communication Agencies. Online. Available www.akarussia.ru (accessed 5 June 2009).

Croteau, D. and Hoynes, W. (2001) *The Business of Media. Corporate Media and the Public Interest*, Thousand Oaks, CA: Pine Forge Press.

De Bens, E. (ed.) (2007) *Media Between Culture and Commerce*, Bristol: Intellect.

Esser, F. (1999) 'Tabloidization of news: a comparative analysis of Anglo-American and German press journalism', *European Journal of Communication*, 14: 3.

FAPMC, Federal Print Media and Mass Communications Agency. Online. Available www.fapmc.ru (accessed 7 June 2009).

Gazprom-Media. Online. Available www.gazprom-media.ru (accessed 10 June 2009).

Internet in Russia. Survey. Online. Available http://bd.fom.ru/report/map/int0801 (accessed 5 June 2009).

McChesney, R. (1999) *Rich Media, Poor Democracy: Communication Politics in Dubious Times*, Urbana, IL: University of Illinois Press.

McQuail, D. (2005) *McQuail's Mass Communication Theory*, 5th edn, London: Sage.

MediaAtlas. Online. Available www.mediaatlas.ru (accessed 13 June 2009).

Merger&Acquisitions. Online. Available http://www.ma-journal.ru (accessed 3 June 2009).

Picard, R.G. (1989) *Media Economics: Concepts and Issues*, Newbury Park – London – New Delhi: Sage.

Prof-Media. Online. Available www.prof-media.ru (accessed 1 June 2009).

Promkatalog. Online. Available www.promkatalog.ru (accessed 5 June 2009).

Rantanen, T. (2002) *The Global and the National: Media and Communications in Post-Communist Russia*, Lanham, MD: Rowman & Littlefield.

Real Russia. (2006) *Social stratification of modern Russian society*. Moscow: Expert.

Reestr SMI. Online. Available www.reestrsmi.info (accessed 15 May 2009).

Roskomnadzor. The Federal Service supervising the Observance of the Legislation on Mass Communications and Connection. Online. Available www.rsoc.ru (accessed 14 June 2009).

Rumetrica. Online. Available www.rambler.ru/db/rumetrica (accessed 2 June 2009).

Russian Periodical Press Market. *Situation, Trends and Prospects*. Annual Report (2008), Moscow: FAPMC.

Russian Media-Industry: The General Situation and Development Perspectives. Report (2007), Moscow: BDO UNICON.

Russian Television: Structure, Production & Audience. Report (2005), Moscow: Internews.

Sparks, C. (1992) 'Popular journalism: theories and practice', in P. Dahlgren and C. Sparks (eds) *Journalism and Popular Culture*, London: Sage.

TNS Gallup Media (2008). *The Russian market for periodicals. Condition, Tendencies, and Prospects for Development. A report.* Moscow: FAPMK.

Vartanova, E. (ed.) (2009) *Osnovy Mediabiznesa*, Moscow: Aspect Press.

Yandex, VCIOM 2008. Online. Available http://advertising.yandex.ru/fomspring08.xml (accessed 13 June 2009).

ZenithOptimedia. Online. Available www.zenithoptimedia.com (accessed 20 May 2009).

2 Changing media use in Russia

Jukka Pietiläinen, Irina Fomicheva and Liudmila Resnianskaia

In the international development of the media market Russia presents a unique case in many ways. Russian development has followed many of the international trends, but many of these trends have assumed more radical forms. Whereas in other countries the process of change has been more gradual, in Russia the collapse of the former system has meant re-building much of the media structure from the ground up. Yet the Russian development differs from situations in Eastern and Central Europe, because the change in the media system has not been as complete as it was in many of those countries. In Russia, the media market has greatly changed the former socialist media system, and the increasing number of media outlets is restructuring the audiences.

This chapter identifies the trends in media usage, stressing outlets rather than content. It presents a concise description of the audience–media relationship in Russia, including the press, radio, television and the Internet. It does not address media ownership or structure, but examines the changes from the point of view of media audiences and media use with the main emphasis being on the ten years from 1998 to 2008.

The data for this chapter come mainly from a survey conducted by the Institute of Sociology of the Russian Academy of Sciences under the supervision of Mikhail Chernysh in February 2007. The survey (referred to below as 'our survey') was carried out at 52 locations. The sample included 2,014 respondents from towns of all types as well as from the countryside. The data are compared in part with an earlier, similar survey for which data were collected in 1998, involving 2,600 respondents; most of the locations and questions were the same (Nikula 2002: xv–xvi).

Television continues to be the most important medium in Russia. As reported by earlier research (Vartanova 2002; Belin 2002), TV became the dominant medium in the 1990s. Owing to lack of money for subscriptions or buying newspapers, people stayed by their TV sets. According to our survey in 2007, the situation remains the same: over 98 per cent of Russians watch TV regularly, 66 per cent read newspapers, 53 per cent listen to the radio and 38 per cent read magazines. Compared to other media, magazines are the only type of media to have significantly widened their audience (see Figure 2.1).

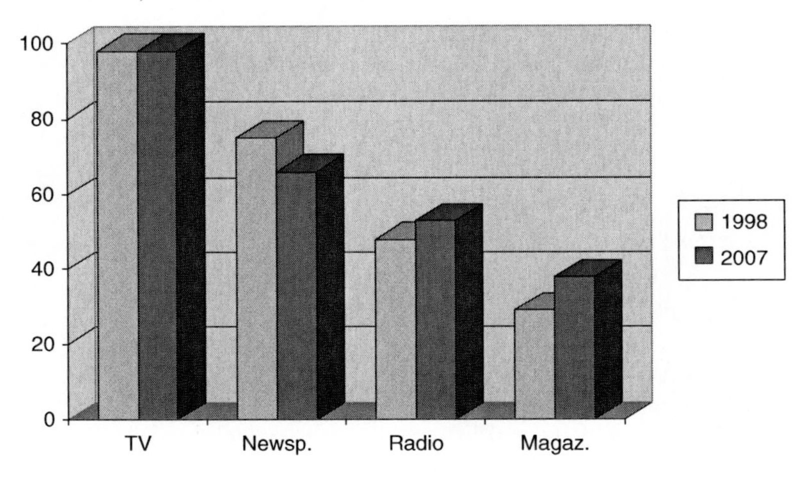

Figure 2.1 Audience of different media in 1998 and 2007, per cent of Russians regularly using.

Newspaper reading in modern Russia

Of all media, newspapers[1] suffered the most from the transition to a market economy, which started in 1991. The ensuing growth in the number of outlets failed to meet the expected response from potential readers (Benn 1996: 473–4). The main reason was a dramatic fall in the standards of living, which persists to this day: in 2007 over 27 per cent of non-readers thought newspapers were too expensive. The galloping inflation of the 1990s devastated the subscription system, while retailers were unable to arrange distribution. *Soiuzpechat*, the Soviet monopoly, was too unwieldy, and alternative services were not yet available. As a result, the readership suffered both in quantity and in quality. Readership dwindled, and reading became less regular (Resnianskaia and Fomicheva 1999: ch. 1). In 1993, as many as 93 per cent of Russians read newspapers, a figure that fell to 78 per cent in 1997 (ibid.: 87–8). In 2004 and 2005, around a quarter of Russians did not read newspapers (Zorkaia 2003: 61). According to our survey in 1998, 75 per cent read some newspapers regularly, whereas in 2007 only 66 per cent had read a newspaper during the previous week.

The mid-1990s witnessed a drastic change in the volume of publications appearing at various intervals. Some publications began to turn out special sizeable weekend supplements, later turned into separate editions, and were sold through subscription and retail. These were primarily the Friday edition of *Komsomol'skaia pravda* and *Trud-7*. The preference given to weeklies proved stable. Today's top five dailies have an audience share ranging from 1 to 3.4 per cent, whereas weeklies are far more popular, with audience shares from 3.9 to 17.8 per cent (TNS Gallup: 2007). Later arrivals among the weeklies have also gained readers (Pietiläinen 2002: 124).

Another trend in reader preferences apparent towards the end of the 1990s was a preference for local papers. National newspapers had to reposition themselves, some seeking to retain their status as quality papers (*Izvestiia*, *Trud*) and others drifting towards becoming tabloids (*Argumenty i fakty*, *Komsomol'skaia pravda*). *Komsomol'skaia pravda*, the national paper initially targeted at the young, and *Moskovskii komsomolets*, the metropolitan paper, gradually changed from being youth papers into general-interest papers and survived thanks to non-specific marketing. In the austerity of the 1990s, readers could not afford several publications, preferring one in which all members of the family could find something of interest. Likewise in 2007, most Russians read only one or, less often, two newspapers and only 5 per cent read four or more. Towards the late 1990s, both *Moskovskii komsomolets* and *Komsomol'skaia pravda* began to form networks with their regional partners, setting up regional editions with a national news section complemented by a local one.

Two new publications, *Nezavisimaia gazeta* and *Kommersant*, which appeared by the end of *perestroika*, tried out the new concepts. The former featured content of a universal character, exerting influence on intellectuals. The latter relied on analysis, pioneering in the emerging group of national business publications. The declared intention of the *Kommersant* editors – not only to work for the emergence of the middle-class, but also actively to promote the middle-class – was in itself a challenge. The paper's subjects range from politics to restaurant criticism, in an effort to shape business behaviour and lifestyle, offer comment on the economic and political situation, and monitor the financial and other markets.

The 1990s also saw some attempts to launch new national quality newspapers such as *Vesty*, *Russkii telegraf* and *Segodnia*, but they all failed, and two quality papers, *Obshchaia gazeta* and *Moskovskie novosti*, folded.

Nowadays the differentiation of newspapers continues, with some papers serving 'the information needs of an educated elite, while other newspapers are catering for the mass taste' (Voltmer 2000: 494). Such groups as the quality and business press, popular papers and tabloids have evolved among Russia's national newspapers, which is novel, for in Soviet times there was no explicit division into quality and popular press, not to mention tabloids.

In our survey 2,014 respondents mentioned having read 1,980 newspapers in total, on average one newspaper per person. The total number of different newspaper titles was 399 or, on average, five readers per title. Only a few newspapers had a significant national readership, and, as shown in Table 2.1, newspaper audiences have continued to shrink. *Komsomol'skaia pravda* tops the list. It is popular in cities and towns, among the middle-aged, the poor and low-level professionals. *Argumenty i fakty* is read equally across all age groups except those under 30. It is more popular in Moscow, St. Petersburg and in the villages than elsewhere.

The third most popular newspaper is *Antenna-Telesem'*, a television guide, and the fourth, *Zhizn'* (Life), is a tabloid, which came out in 1991 as part of an expanding network of regional newspapers and was integrated into a national newspaper in 2001. *Zhizn'* is especially popular in mid-sized cities. *Moskovskii komsomolets* is Moscow's most popular newspaper with regional editions in other cities.

Table 2.1 The most popular national newspapers in Russia

	Read regularly in 1998 (%)	*Read during previous week in 2007 (%)*
Komsomol'skaia pravda	10.1	10.7
Argumenty i fakty	15.1	10.6
Antenna-Telesem'	0.1	8.0
Zhizn'	–	5.4
Moskovskii komsomolets	5.1	2.9
SPID-Info	10.1	2.1
Trud	4.4	1.6
Rossiiskaia gazeta	1.6	0.9
Sport	0.1	0.8
Sport ekspress	0.3	0.6
Sovetskii sport	0.5	0.4
Izvestiia	0.6	0.4

SPID-INFO (AIDS-INFO), the first erotic publication, was read by 2.1 per cent of respondents in our survey, though from the mid-1990s until recently it was at the top. The monthly appearance of this newspaper may explain part of the lower reading share according to the 2007 survey, when only one week's reading was observed. *Rossiiskaia gazeta*, the government paper, was read by 0.9 per cent of respondents, and *Trud* (Labour), the former trade union paper, by 1.6 per cent.

TNS Gallup (2007) has provided higher readership figures. This may be explained by the use of different methods. As the National Readership Survey by TNS Gallup shows, TV guides are the clear winners in the competition, *Antenna-Telesem'* coming first, followed by sports papers.

A trend that proved common in the press at the provincial, regional, city and district levels in the late 1990s was that, against the background of low incomes, undeveloped distribution, and waning interest in politics, weeklies turned out to be best suited to meet demand. Compared with 1998, the reading of newspapers fell, especially among those under 30 (−17 per cent), the highly educated (−15 per cent), men (−15 per cent), the well-off (−15 per cent), managers (−24 per cent) and middle-managers (−16 per cent). Newspaper reading decreased in the groups that could have taken an interest in newspapers economically and culturally. Yet the highest proportion of non-readers can still be found among the poor, the unemployed and those with little education, as well as among the young and big-city residents. These figures differ somewhat from the earlier data, according to which the lowest readership levels were to be found in villages and among those over 55 (Zorkaia 2003: 61). In 2007, there were more readers in the rural areas and small towns, 73 per cent, owing to availability of city and district newspapers, compared to 57 per cent in the capital and in major cities. This may be due to the spread of the Internet and to the high prices charged for regional and national newspapers.

In some regions and communities the local newspapers are doing especially well. For example, in Podporozh'e, a town in the Leningrad region, the local newspaper *Svirskie ogni* (Lights of the Svir River) was read by 60 per cent of respondents; in a Buriat village in the Tunka district the local paper *Saiany* (The Saian Mountains) was read by 49 per cent of respondents. Other studies confirm this relative success of local newspapers (Eismont 2007: 2008).

The decline of readership in cities is so great that it cannot be entirely explained by a different formulation of the questions used in the two surveys (1998 – 'reading regularly'; 2007 – 'read during the previous week'). In Moscow, even the most popular newspaper, *Moskovskii komsomolets*, has seen a fall in its readership from 41 per cent to 13 per cent, and the share of people not reading any newspaper has increased from 24 per cent to 52 per cent. In St. Petersburg, the most popular newspaper is *Metro*, a free paper (part of an international corporation), which was read by 18 per cent. Compared to 1998, the size of the *Sankt-Peterburgskie vedomosti*'s audience has fallen from 15 to 4 per cent, and the number of people not reading any newspaper has risen from 32 to 48 per cent. Other big cities show the same trend: in Nizhnii Novgorod the readership of *Avtozavodets* (Car Factory Worker) has fallen from 36 to 9 per cent, and in Cheliabinsk, reading of *Cheliabinskii rabochii* (The Worker of Cheliabinsk) has diminished from 20 to 5 per cent. It is clear that a sharp growth in the number of publications, local and free included, characteristic of big cities, as well as greater access to the Internet has fragmented audiences.

Figures from TNS Gallup available since 2002 do not indicate as clear a drop in newspaper readership, even if some decline can be found. Between 2005 and 2006 eight national newspapers lost on average 14 per cent of their readers, and none increased their readership. *Kommersant* suffered the most (–34 per cent), whereas *Komsomol'skaia pravda* lost a mere 1 per cent (Russian Periodical Press Market 2007: 15). The trend continued in 2007 with 'waning interest in print media among the population as a whole, and especially among young people, due to the rapid development of online media' (Russian Periodical Press Market 2008: 21). In 2008 this trend has turned, and in conditions of crisis in the fourth quarter of 2008, the circulation of daily and weekly newspapers increased by 5–7 per cent, mainly because of growth in business and quality newspapers (Rossiiskii rynok periodicheskoi pechati 2009: 19–21). In spite of the economic crisis, regional and local newspapers have also been able to expand.

The factors contributing to the fall in newspaper readership since the 1980s are the cessation of weekend delivery at the end of the Soviet era (even though distribution was mostly subscription-based), the fall in living standards, galloping inflation, high delivery costs, undeveloped retail distribution, the absence of free papers in small settlements, and delays in payments of old-age pensions and salaries to the so-called budget-sector intelligentsia, which constitutes the major share of readership. Price as a reason for not reading newspapers was mentioned mainly by elderly people. Younger people more often mentioned lack of time and uninteresting content. The number of people who felt that newspapers had become more interesting dropped rapidly from 58 to 34 per cent in 2001 (Zorkaia 2003: 65).

On the other hand, factors contributing to retaining the audience are a switchover to weeklies, the emergence of new delivery services, increasing diversity in the forms of subscription and delivery, various discounts for some population groups, habitual reading of certain publications, person-to-person transfer of copies, subsequent increase of earnings, and continuing interest in politics and economics among some sectors in the population.

New prospects for magazines

Although most of today's popular newspapers existed in the Soviet era, the current most popular magazines were almost all founded after the Soviet time. Two approaches were taken to address the transformation in the magazine market. The first was to retain the existing publications, primarily, the group of literary and opinion magazines popular during *perestroika* as forums for public discussion. The second was to cater to the new public needs that had evolved by the late 1990s.

The first approach failed because books became more readily available, readers no longer needed to look for works printed in magazines, and the declining political awareness of a large share of the population dampened public interest in political journalism.

The launching of new magazines proved more successful. Business magazines appeared to cater to the needs of the emerging Russian business world. Unlike the Soviet system of trade publications, the new business magazines, including *Den'gi*, *RBK*, *Finansy*, *Sekret Firmy*, *Businessweek*, *Forbes*, *Delovye Liudi* and *SmartMoney* (closed in the spring of 2009) target much wider professional audiences. Newly produced business-to-business magazines are aimed at both individual and corporate readers. On the other hand, some magazines tend towards in-depth specialisation as indicated by the existence of *Bukhgalter* (Accountant) and *Glavnyi bukhgalter* (Chief Accountant). There are also news-and-opinion weeklies that cover a wide range of subjects, offering analysis and discussion. These include *Vlast'*, *Russkii Newsweek* and *Itogi*; their content is close to that of quality newspapers.

Magazines advocating consumerism are the most popular. Of the total annual circulation of 1.85 billion copies, 'glossies' make up 900 million, two-thirds of which are printed abroad (Russian Periodical Press Market 2007: 23). These brightly coloured magazines have taught Russian women to follow fashion and take up the newest housekeeping gadgets, as well as initiating them into the latest in make-up and how to be alluring.

Some old-timers known to have had a huge circulation began to search for a new identity as their audiences dwindled. For example, *Ogonek* went up from 1.5 million copies in 1987 to 4.6 million in 1990, but fell to 0.2 million copies in 1993 (*The Post-Soviet Media Law and Policy Newsletter* 1993: 7). *Ogonek* also had to change its style completely in the post-Soviet era (Lovell 1996). Having copied the Europe-based *Focus* format in the mid-1990s, it lost its former audience and failed to find a new one.

The old Soviet publications *Rabotnitsa* and *Krest'ianka* were for many decades the only substitutes for a fully fledged women's magazine, and they were the last to change. In the old days, going through their copy on daily work and Party policy, one could come across the occasional recipe, advice on skin care or a dress pattern. Nowadays, both are glossies, but, glamorous as they are, they do not rank at the top in the ratings, which are dominated by the Russian versions of Western glossies (Stephenson 2007: 618–9).

In our survey, the 2,014 respondents mentioned 833 magazines that they had read, i.e. 0.41 magazines per person. The total number of titles mentioned was 353. The most popular Russian magazines are intended for women and target the upper strata of society (Table 2.2). One of the few exceptions is *Liza*, which has a wide readership both demographically and geographically. *Za rulem* (Behind the Wheel) came second, its readers being men under 40 from all types of settlements. The car magazine family is fairly large, catering to readers of different income groups.

On the whole, there is a trend towards differentiation of the press to meet diverse consumer needs. This accounts for the leading positions of women's magazines in the ratings, *Vogue* and *Cosmopolitan* being the fare for the rich and successful, and *Liza* for the less affluent. The majority of *Cosmopolitan* readers are women under 30, mainly big-city residents. Magazines for girls (*Girl*, *Cool Girl*) appeared less popular in the survey than *Cosmopolitan*. This is probably because these magazines target those under 17, who were not included in the sample.

Table 2.2 Magazine readership in Russia in 2007

Name of magazine	*Started in Russia*	*Number of copies printed*	*Published*	*Readership (survey 2007)*
Liza	1995	750,000	Weekly	6.4 %
Za rulem	1928	570,000	Monthly	3.6 %
Cosmopolitan	1994	980,000	Monthly	2.7 %
Sem dnei	1995	1,000,000	Weekly	1.8 %
Zdorov'e	1955	170,000	Monthly	1.6 %
Glamour	2004	600,000	Monthly	1.4 %
Karavan istorii	1998	300,000	Monthly	1.3 %
Domashnii ochag	1995	280,000	Monthly	1.0 %
Otdokhni!	1997	300,000	Weekly	0.9 %
Krest'ianka	1922	89,000	Monthly	0.8 %
Burda	1987	460,000	Monthly	0.6 %
RBK	2006	90,000	Monthly	0.5 %
Rabotnitsa	1914	100,000	Monthly	0.3 %
Ekspert	1995	78,000	Weekly	0.3 %
Itogi	1996	85,000	Weekly	0.3 %
Ogonek	1899	72,000	Weekly	0.2 %
Vogue	2000	150,000	Monthly	0.2 %
Kommersant Den'gi	1994	59,000	Weekly	0.2 %
*Gloria**	2006	375,000	Weekly	0.2 %
ELLE	1996	220,000	Monthly	0.1 %

* Closed temporarily in February 2009.

Readership shares do not directly correlate with the number of copies printed. One explanation may be that, in a long-standing Russian tradition, different publications are shared by relatives, friends and acquaintances in different ways. These readership shares are lower than those in the TNS Gallup (2007) ratings, because the latter focuses on cities with over 100,000 inhabitants.

As Table 2.2 indicates, the majority of the ten most popular magazines were founded after 1991. Only three of these, *Krest'ianka*, *Za rulem* and *Zdorov'e*, existed in the Soviet period. News-and-opinion weekly magazines, such as *Ekspert*, *Den'gi*, *Itogi* and *Finansy* are not very popular (see also Kozlova 2000: 3–13). Compared to 1998, readership of some other old magazines like *Ogonek* (from 0.9 to 0.2 per cent) and *Rabotnitsa* also decreased (from 1.7 to 0.3 per cent).

According to TNS Gallup (Russian Periodical Press Market 2007: 26), the most popular magazine categories are women's magazines (19 per cent market share), collections of crossword puzzles and other word games (18 per cent), and TV guides (16 per cent).

Magazine reading went up from 29 per cent in 1998 to 38 per cent in 2007, mostly among those under 30, those having a higher or secondary education, those who were well-off and women. These new magazines are mostly oriented towards the new middle-class and elites, thus increasing their popularity as newspapers decline.

Television: A wide audience for major channels

The two main TV channels, First Channel and Rossiia, are the only media to reach over half the Russian population weekly, but there is also strong competition in the TV market. Television networks such as REN TV, STS, TNT, TV-Tsentr, Rambler-Teleset and RBK are growing rapidly. The number of specialised channels is also growing, including MTV, Muz-TV, TV-3, 7-TV, and Sport. A channel for children appeared on the national service Rossiia and Kul'tura in 2007, allocated special frequencies for viewing. Among other channels are Domashnii for family viewing, Spas for believers and Zvezda for the military and paramilitary.

NTV, which focuses on crime prevention, and the new entertainment channels such as STS and TNT as well as several others are watched several times a week by sizeable audiences. The most popular channels are the same as in the mid-1990s, but STS and TNT have become more popular, especially in cities (Starobakhin 2007: 27–31). Other channels include various specialised and regional programmes watched by a large audience overall, even if the share for each channel is rather small.

Off-the-air TV, i.e. cable and satellite TV, is also expanding, involving pay packages, thematic programmes and niche channels. Thus, the Animal Planet audience went up by 13 per cent in 2007 alone. Yet access inequality is great, the share of high-income viewers of the terrestrial channels being on average 13–15 per cent and reaching 40–52 per cent for the niche channels (Achkasova 2008).

Table 2.3 Share and characteristics of regular audience for major television channels in Russia

Channel	*Share of weekly audience (%)*	*Highest audience*	*Lowest audience*
First channel	75	Rural areas; age over 60	Moscow; age under 30
Rossiia	69	Small towns	Moscow
NTV	45	Moscow	Rural areas
STS	28	Big cities; age under 30	Rural areas; age over 60
TNT	18	Big cities; age under 30	Rural areas; age over 60
Ren-TV	12	Middle-sized and small towns	Rural areas; age over 60
Kul'tura	8	Moscow; age between 50 and 60	Small towns; age under 30
Sport	7	Moscow	Small towns
Domashnii	4	Moscow	Middle-sized towns
Muz-TV	3	Middle-sized towns	Rural areas
MTV	3	Big cities	Rural areas
TVC	3	Moscow	Big cities
Some other channel	20	Big cities	Middle-sized towns

The terrestrial First Channel and Rossiia, which are the oldest and general purpose by subject scope and audience, are still in the lead (Table 2.3). Apart from the national service channels Rossiia, Kul'tura and the associated regional broadcasters, other channels are independent, which is not to say that they are free of governmental influence.

The main change is in the increasing popularity of the entertainment channels TNT and STS, especially among the youth, in big cities, and in higher income groups. On the whole, the entertainment programmes are the clear leaders (Dubin 2005: 24). People with higher incomes watch several channels more often, but the average difference by income is a mere 2.7 to 3.5 channels.

Television is a trend-setter in fashion, behaviour and retention or change of social values. Anchors are rated as stars, TV guides are very popular, and the heading 'what's to be shown on TV' is not confined only to the popular papers. Yet vis-à-vis the dwindling readership of the national press and smaller radio audiences, TV in Russia today has to provide national communication, a function it is ill-equipped to perform, because it is increasingly becoming the predominant vehicle for doing business.

Radio: Dominance of networks and new opportunities

The proportion of Russians listening to the radio in 2007 compared to that in 1998 remained the same or increased slightly, being 53 per cent and 48 per cent respectively. Most people listen to one or, at most, two stations. Even the most popular stations do not regularly reach more than 10–12 per cent of the Russian population (see also TNS Gallup, 2007).

Radio's fastest growth is in the FM band. This caused even the biggest state networks Maiak and Radio Rossii to use FM, while retaining operation on their other wavebands. Compared with earlier research (Vartanova 2002: 55; Bolotova 2005: 330–1), the FM stations Avtoradio and Retro, in particular, have improved their ratings, whereas those of the more traditional Radio Rossii are declining. The use of a stricter definition of listening (at least three times a week) in the 2007 survey also reduced the share of audience for each channel. Radio is clearly dominated by networks.

Listening to the radio is more common in cities (except Moscow) than in small towns or rural areas, among the higher strata of society and among youth. For example, 71 per cent of managers listen to the radio, whereas only 56 per cent of ordinary workers do so; 64 per cent of students are listeners as opposed to 38 per cent of pensioners and 41 per cent of housewives. One reason for this break-up is the changing lifestyles of some groups in the population; in particular, this involves listening to the radio in the car, whereas in Soviet times most city dwellers used public transportation and read newspapers there.

Young Russians listen to Evropa Plus, Russkoe radio, Avtoradio, Shanson and Hit-FM; the middle-aged prefer Russkoe radio, Avtoradio, Maiak, Retro and Shanson, whereas those over 60 listen most often to Radio Rossii, Retro and Maiak, the oldest Soviet networks that were completely re-formatted in 2007.

Driving time became a new niche market, with the number of drivers growing very fast. The share of respondents who listened while driving went up from 4.3 to 56.7 per cent between 1994 and 2002, whereas the number of those who listened at work went down from 80.9 to 12.5 per cent (*Issledovaniia auditorii: Televidenie, radio, Internet* 2005).

Geographical differences are fairly small and become significant mainly in the case of local stations such as Ekho Moskvy, its listeners being chiefly residents of large cities with a population of over one million.

New stations are very 'lively' and interactive in style, leaving no room for conventional formality. Stations targeting older audiences are dominated by hosts offering their listeners heart-to-heart talks, whereas hosts at stations geared towards younger audiences are glib, if not shallow. This style implies the direct involvement of listeners who are invited to participate in talks, ask and answer questions, and share opinions using mobile phones, pagers or the Internet. Phone-in subjects are diverse, with listeners calling from home or the office or while stuck in a traffic jam to chat about what to give on Valentine's Day or the best place to sunbathe on holiday.

Most FM stations discuss such subjects as meeting and dating, leisure or music. So-called talk radio, Ekho Moskvy, which is also an FM station, is the only exception, discussing civic subjects and asking phone-in listeners to vote on socially significant issues. The station's audience amounted to 2.2 per cent in 2007.

Internet: Agent of great change

It is rather hard to assess the online media–media audience relationship because relevant research on the whole is in its infancy. The new media environment increasingly manifests itself through changes in audience behaviour. So far, these changes have not been so profound as to be revolutionary. It is true that only 6 per cent of respondents over 16 knew nothing about the Internet in 2006 as opposed to 20 per cent in 2000, and yet 73 per cent of those over 16 had no access to the Internet in 2007. The Internet can be accessed from home by 10 per cent, from the office by 7 per cent, and from both home and office by 4 per cent (*Obshchestvennoe mnenie. Ezhegodnik* 2007: 191). According to our survey, 33.1 per cent had computers at home in 2007, but access to the Internet was available to only 12.2 per cent of those over 18.

According to the Public Opinion Foundation (2009a), in the summer of 2009, 37 million, i.e. over one-quarter of Russians over the age of 18 years, had used the Internet at least once in the previous month. In the summer of 2008 this figure was 30 million.

As in other countries, Russia too has a digital divide created by age, income, education and type of residence. Differences by type of residence are enormous. The gap is particularly great between the capital and the rest of Russia. According to the Public Opinion Foundation, the Internet was used at least once a month, nationwide, by 62 per cent in the 18–24 age bracket, the corresponding figure for Moscow being 91 per cent. In Moscow, the Internet is used at least once a month by 16 per cent of those over 55, the corresponding figure for the whole of Russia being 5 per cent (Public Opinion Foundation 2009b). In our survey, access was available to 8.4 per cent of respondents with secondary education and to 25.4 per cent of those with higher education.

Russians are gradually coming to use the Internet mostly at home rather than at the office, which is conducive to free personal development. In 2006, the Internet was accessed at home by 64 per cent of users outside Moscow and 75 per cent of Moscow residents, office access being 42 per cent and 41 per cent respectively (TNS Web Index 2006). In 2009, the Internet was accessed at home by 79 per cent of all users, whereas use in Internet cafes or at friends' homes is decreasing. In Moscow 90 per cent accessed the Internet at home (Public Opinion Foundation 2009b).

The Internet is mostly used as a source of information, benefiting the converging media. In February 2008, 34 per cent of over eight million hosts searched for news through Yandex.ru; 20 per cent were interested in e-trade, and 20 per cent consulted dictionaries (Yandex 2007).

The Internet increases the audience of the traditional media. This may mean a gain for quality newspapers, their readership being better equipped. The popular *Argumenty i fakty*, for instance, rated at 11–13 per cent, increased its readership in Moscow by 3 per cent of the population in 2006, whereas the gain for *Kommersant*, with its smaller audience, was 4.9 per cent (ibid.).

Non-readers of newspapers use the Internet at home more often than readers, especially if they are middle-aged, highly educated and middle-level managers. It appears that some people who used to read newspapers now turn to electronic versions, and the TNS Web Index data are likely to confirm this. The Internet version of *Komsomol'skaia pravda*, for example, had over 1.1 million readers, or

16 per cent of Muscovites aged 12–54, in March 2007. Half of the audience was 25–44 years of age. The share of managers and specialists among these was 55 per cent, Moscow's total being 36 per cent (Russian Periodical Press Market 2007: 61). On the other hand, those who have access to the Internet at home are more active magazine readers: two-thirds of them read magazines.

The traditional media are going online at a very fast pace. Even information agencies are now available to individual users. This is the case with the former Soviet monopoly ITAR-TASS, RIA Novosti, Interfaks, RIA Vesti, and the specialised supplier of economic and financial information RBK (Rosbizneskonsalting), which, having begun with the Internet, now continues to develop offline, producing a newspaper, a magazine and a TV channel.

Russia's blogosphere is developing faster than that in the rest of the world, with over 2 million Internet diaries and 11 per cent of the world's postings falling to Russians (in April 2007; see Yandex 2007). Russian journalists can use the great need for public communication to consolidate relations with their audiences. Practically all Internet media resources have forums to exchange views journalist-to-user or user-to-user. This is extremely important for the development of civic culture and the fostering of debating skills.

A cooling relationship

Regular opinion polls conducted since the late 1980s have registered a gradual loss of public confidence in various social institutions, the media included, over the past eight years – the President being the only exception (Table 2.4).

Our survey sought to determine what topics people thought were lacking in the media. The most often mentioned were human rights issues (41 per cent), viewpoints of the common people (35 per cent) and criticism aimed at local officials (25 per cent). The answers suggest mutual alienation. The media prefer to skate over dangerous issues rather than encourage people to speak up. In response, people lose confidence in the media and feel estranged. Characteristically, the responses were shared both by those who read newspapers and those who do not. This means that people read newspapers, not because they like them, but rather because they are accustomed to reading them and need information. This situation, however, cannot last for long, even if habitual newspaper reading has helped such

Table 2.4 Answers to the question 'To what extent are today's press, radio and television trustworthy?' (per cent of those surveyed)

Responses	*1989*	*1999*	*2007*
Quite trustworthy	38	25	25
Not quite trustworthy	40	44	39
Not at all trustworthy	6	19	22
Undecided	16	12	14

Source: *Obshchestvennoe mnenie. Ezhegodnik* 2007: 160.

old papers as *Komsomol'skaia pravda*, *Trud*, *Izvestiia*, *Moskovskii komsomolets* and *Argumenty i fakty* to survive in the transition to a market economy. As for the new papers, their ratings have never exceeded a few decimal points (Resnianskaia and Fomicheva 1999: chs 2 and 3).

The alienation from the mass media does not mean that Russians would like the media to be suppressed. The number of those who believe that greater governmental control would benefit Russia went down from 38 per cent in 2000 to 26 per cent in 2007. Yet the share of those who are indifferent, who believe that this would be neither to their benefit nor to their detriment, increased from 25 to 38 per cent. The public is also unsure as to whether the media have any sway with the powers that be. Those undecided about whether criticism of the authorities in the media improves or exacerbates the situation in the country made up 30 per cent as opposed to 18 per cent in 2000. Accordingly, the share of those interested in the political subjects covered in the media went down from 42 per cent in 2006 to 33 per cent in 2007 (*Obshchestvennoe mnenie, Ezhegodnik* 2007: 53). It does not follow, however, that this interest is non-existent. For several reasons, it is not only a question of depoliticisation. First, in surveys people give a negative response to the very concept of politics. Upon more detailed questioning, the same people show interest in subjects clearly associated with politics such as human rights issues, local government performance and so on. Second, TV ratings are constantly in the limelight, affecting journalists' judgements of audience preferences and leading journalists to believe that the audience is interested in nothing but entertainment, disasters, crime and sex. According to our survey in 2007, quality paper readers watch the same channels, with First Channel and Rossiia coming first, whereas the audience of the new off-the-air channels varies within a 1–3 per cent range. Thus, it would be rash to judge what people really want from all the media on the basis of TV ratings alone.

In 2002, a survey of Moscow residents showed that 26 per cent took an interest in economic reform issues, 25 per cent in the democratisation of society and 22 per cent in political reform (*City of Moscow sociological survey* 2002). The same survey indicated that 25 per cent showed an interest in the democratisation of society, but only 10 per cent took an interest in publications relating to government by the people. Respondents, it appears, show a negative attitude to trite words like 'politics' or 'power', which call for a finer approach to pinpointing genuine preferences.

Some media traits cause growing dissatisfaction. In 2007, when asked in our survey if the coverage of certain subjects should be banned, restricted or unrestricted, the respondents most often wanted a ban on scenes of violence (78 per cent in all age groups), the emphasis on bad news (67 per cent, the percentage growing with age), erotic scenes and the display of naked bodies (55 per cent, especially the elderly). As can be seen, the dissatisfaction is connected to the violation of cultural norms, the overblown coverage of persons of little importance and the media's obsession with emergencies.

It is worth noting that nearly 90 per cent of those surveyed in 2007 would like media advertising to be banned or restricted. This is not without justification, for unscrupulous advertising of the financial pyramids in the 1990s led many people who were completely inexperienced in such matters to lose their savings. The advertising spots were very appealing, humorous, had plot continuity with characters easy to identify with and, therefore, were trustworthy. Not many people at the time could distinguish between what was advertising and what was not, given that the Soviet media carried practically no advertising at all. Some people are currently extremely displeased with TV advertising breaks in general.

Most media are tolerated rather than liked. This is particularly true of television: 60 per cent of respondents said they did not like television very much, but watched all there was, or just chose some programmes (*Obshchestvennoe mnenie, Ezhegodnik* 2007: 163). Meanwhile, journalists and media managers take ratings of the audience size as a sign of a positive attitude. Low-income Russians do not have much choice as regards leisure, their information and cultural consumption being limited to several terrestrial channels. Thus, 11 per cent stated that they did not watch television at all. Nowadays, there is a gradual return to the traditional forms of leisure such as going to the cinema or visiting clubs.

Trends of change

A nation of readers becoming a nation of TV viewers is the most important development of the past two decades. This means that the Russian nation is joining the world trend of information consumption going visual.

The space for reading is becoming more limited because most readers turn to fewer publications and read less. At the end of the 1980s most Russian families read four or five publications fairly regularly. It follows that, obviously, more than one publication was read per person. In our survey there were 1,980 mentions of titles read, i.e. slightly less than one title per person, with regularity reduced. If we counted only those who read newspapers, then the result would be 1.5 titles per reader. Over two-thirds read only one newspaper.

Another important change consists of media channel differentiation and audience fragmentation. This may indicate a decline in newspapers that fail to meet the needs of the population. This might also be a result of the rising standards of living and the spread of middle-class attitudes. The same goes for radio and TV.

Magazines, radio and entertainment TV are the most Westernised sectors of the media and the best adapted to the new economic and political conditions. Radio, especially music radio, has been one of the success stories, mainly because of its lower production costs and attractiveness to advertisers due to high targetability, decreasing politicisation and improved professionalism (Vartanova 2002: 57).

Newspapers are lagging behind. Some newspapers have successfully adopted a popular style, gained readers and acquired a certain financial independence. Serious quality papers (e.g. papers oriented to middle-class and elite audiences) are seldom independent. Therefore, it may well be that newspapers are losing readers who are dissatisfied with the popular style, whereas quality papers are regarded as too partisan and uninteresting. The readers of business newspapers seem to be accustomed to a mixture of news and opinion and are not pressing for too rapid a shift towards fact-centred news writing (Koikkalainen 2007).

People whose position in the social structure gives 'them the most control over their own lives' (Schudson 1978: 119–20) apparently need other kinds of newspapers. This is most apparent in big cities and in the upper levels of the social structure, where people are most keen on adopting new middle-class identities.

The public's attitude towards the media is ambivalent. One can hardly do without the media, but their credibility suffers, and scepticism is likely to prevail as the use of the Internet expands. When on the Internet, people communicate, interact and trust it more than the mass media, which may have a detrimental effect on the latter. Information in the offline media may be a partial remedy.

The past two decades have exhibited a number of tendencies. This is the period during which the media have changed from being 'spokespeople for democratic change' to tools in the internal power struggle among the political and business elites, partly reverting to the role they played under Soviet rule, i.e. the government's propaganda machine (Ryabov 2004: 194). On the other hand, audiences and their interests now matter, which was not the case in Soviet times (Mickiewicz 2000: 105). Yet audiences are largely viewed from the advertiser's standpoint – as potential consumers of goods and services.

Russian newspapers have experienced considerable difficulty in finding a new role for themselves. Generally speaking, the media have mostly chosen consumerism, seeing their audiences as a commodity to be offered to advertisers.

Notes

1 In this chapter, we use term 'newspaper' in its Russian context to refer not only to daily papers but also to weekly, and even less frequent, papers, and include free sheets as well.

References

Achkasova, K. (2008) 'Auditoriia neefirnogo TV', in *Materialy konferentsii 'Mediabiznes: strategii razvitiia i diversifikatsiia mediakholdingov'*, (Moskva, 28.2.2008).

Belin, L. (2002) 'The Russian Media in the 1990s', *Journal of Communist Studies and Transition Policies*, 18: 139–60.

Benn, D.W. (1996) 'The Russian Media in Post-Soviet Conditions', *Europe-Asia Studies*, 48: 471–9.

Bolotova, L.D. (2005) 'Osobennosti sovremennogo radioveshchaniia', in Ia. N. Zasurskii (ed.) *Sredstva massovoi informatsii Rossii*, Moskva: Aspekt Press.

City of Moscow sociological survey 2002. Online. Available www.mos.ru/opinion/op021014002.htm (Accessed 29 March 2008).

Dubin, B. (2005) 'Media postsovetskoi epokhi: izmenenie ustanovok, funktsii, otsenok', *Vestnik obshchestvennogo mneniia: dannye, analiz, diskussii*, 2005: 22–9.

Eismont, M. (2007) 'Gazety malykh gorodov', *Pro et Contra*, 11: 43–55.

Eismont, M. (2008) 'Towns without censorship', *Index on Censorship*, 1/2008, 121–30.

Issledovaniia auditorii: Televidenie, radio, Internet (2005), Moskva: Media komitet.

Izuchenie auditorii regionalnoi pressy. Otchet ob issledovatelskom proekte (2005), Moskva: Natsional'nyi institut sotsialno-psikhologicheskikh issledovanii.

Koikkalainen, K. (2007) 'The Local and the International in Russian Business Journalism: Structures and Practices', *Europe-Asia Studies*, 59: 1315–29.

Kozlova, L.A. (2000) 'Infomatsionno-analiticheskie ezhenedel'niki kak novaia tipologicheskaia gruppa zhurnal'noi periodiki postsovetskoi Rossii', *Vestnik Moskovskogo universiteta, seriia 10, zhurnalistika,* 6: 3–13.

Lovell, S. (1996) 'Ogonek: The Crisis of a Genre', *Europe-Asia Studies*, 48: 989–1006.

Mickiewicz, E. (2000) 'Institutional Incapacity, the Attentive Public, and Media Pluralism in Russia', in R. Gunther and A. Mughan (eds) *Democracy and the Media. A Comparative Perspective*, Cambridge: Cambridge University Press.

Nikula, J. (2002) *Restoration of Class Society in Russia?* Aldershot: Ashgate.

Obshchestvennoe mnenie. Ezhegodnik 2007, Moskva: Levada-tsentr, 2007.

Pietiläinen, J. (2002) *The Regional Newspaper in Post-Soviet Russia. Society, Press and Journalism in the Republic of Karelia 1985-2001*, Tampere: Tampere University Press.

Public Opinion Foundation (Fond Obshchestvennoe mnenie) (2009a) *'Internet v Rossii'. Metodika i osnovnye rezul'taty issledovaniia, vypusk 26*, leto 2009.

Public Opinion Foundation (Fond Obshchestvennoe mnenie) (2009b) *Oprosy 'Internet v Rossii'. Spetsial'nyi vypusk*, mart 2009.

Resnianskaia, L., I. Fomicheva (1999) *Gazeta dlia vsei Rossii*, Moskva: IKAR.

Rossiiskii rynok periodicheskoi pechati 2009. *Sostoianie, tendentsii i perspektivy razvitiia*, Moskva: Federal'noe agenstvo po pechati i massovim kommunikatsiiam.

Russian Periodical Press Market 2007. *Situation, Trends and Prospects*, Moscow: Federal Agency for the Press and Mass Communications.

Russian Periodical Press Market 2008. *Situation, Trends and Prospects*, Moscow: Federal Agency for the Press and Mass Communications.

Ryabov, A. (2004) 'The Mass Media', in M. McFaul, N. Petrov and A. Ryabov (eds) *Between Dictatorship and Democracy. Russian Post-Communist Political Reform*, Washington, DC: Carnegie Endowment for International Peace.

Schudson, M. (1978) *Discovering the News. A Social History of American Newspapers*, New York: Basic Books.

Starobakhin, N.N. (2007) 'Transformatsiia programmnoi politiki obshchenatsional'nykh rossiiskikh telekanalov (1999–2006)', *Vestnik Moskovskogo universiteta, seriia 10, zhurnalistika*, 2: 27–31.

Stephenson, S. (2007) 'The Changing Face of Women's Magazines in Russia', *Journalism Studies*, 8: 613–20.

The Post-Soviet Media Law and Policy Newsletter 2, (17 Nov. 1993). Available also at www.vii.org/monroe/issue02/richter.htm.

TNS Web Index (2006) *Proekt 'TNS-Web Index' Osnovnye rezul'taty ustanovochnogo issledovaniia*. Online. Available www.tns-global.ru/media/presentations/webindex_es_may_2006.pdf (Accessed 29 March 2008).

TNS Gallup (2007) *Reitingi SMI – Pressa. Reitingi SMI. Pressa (Dekabr 2006-Aprel' 2007)*. Online. Available http://www.tns-global.ru/rus/data/ratings/ (Accessed 29 March 2008).

Vartanova, E. (2002) 'Media Structures: Changed and Unchanged', in K. Nordenstreng, E. Vartanova and Y. Zassoursky (eds), *Russian Media Challenge*, Helsinki: Kikimora.

Voltmer, K. (2000) 'Constructing Political Reality in Russia. Izvestiya – Between Old and New Journalistic Practices', *European Journal of Communication*, 15: 469–500.

Yandex (2007) *Yandex derzhit ruku na pulse blogosfery*. Online. Available http://company.yandex.ru/news/2007/0427/index.xml (Accessed 29 March 2008).

Zorkaia, N. (2003) 'Chtenie v kontekste massovykh kommunikatsii', *Monitoring obshchestvennogo mneniia*, 2: 60–70.

3 A new generation of journalists

Svetlana Pasti

This chapter explores recent changes in the profession of a journalist by asking who comes into journalism today and how these newcomers perceive the profession. These questions are posed within the context of the paradoxical situation in which journalism in Russia finds itself today. On the one hand, the profession enjoys popularity and prestige as seen in the growth in the number of journalism schools and the large number of applicants, many of them from wealthy families. This is not surprising when journalism shines in public relations (PR) and show business, where big money moves and personal career advancement are achieved, especially in the big cities. On the other hand, people do not respect the profession, not least because of the quality of journalism at present.

The national survey of professions (VCIOM 2007) found that the most respected professionals in Russia are doctors and teachers, whereas the least respected professionals are businessmen and journalists. *The Global Voice of the People Survey* (Gallup International 2008) conducted in 60 countries reveals that the level of trust in businessmen and journalists in Russia is much lower than the average world index: 4 per cent for businessmen and 6 per cent for journalists, whereas the respective figures for the world are 11 and 16. The survey of the elite *Barometer of Trust* conducted in 18 countries reveals that the Russian elite trusts business and the authorities and does not trust the Russian media, with the exception of the business press (*Kommersant* 2008a). The survey of the Russian blogosphere conducted among journalists and PR workers (Mmd Corporate 2007) reveals that, in spite of definite scepticism regarding the information appearing in the blogosphere, every respondent has a certain list of blogs enjoying more trust than the traditional media, and this is particularly true concerning political information.

The paradox affecting journalism at present emerged from an imbalance between the popularity of the functions of entertainment and the PR service on the one hand and the insignificance of the function of public service on the other. There is a conflict of interests in the profession between *commercial journalism and PR journalism* representing self-interest, and *quality journalism* representing public interest. The increasing popularity of the functions of entertainment and the PR service predicts that self-interest in the profession prevails over public interest. This means that journalism increasingly degenerates into business and loses the basic attribute of the profession – the lofty spirit of universal truth and public service.

After the collapse of the USSR, a new Russia started its rapprochement with the West. Westernization was seen as the most appropriate way for the political and economic reforms. Russian journalism experienced two basic trends: the rise of the *quality* press and the rise of the *commercial* press. The first one adopted a pro-Western concept of news based on separation of fact and comment, reference to a source of information, speed and accuracy of its transmission. The journalists began to develop independent reporting, open public discussion and pluralistic coverage - a new genre of journalistic investigation. That is, the situation began qualitatively to change from the Soviet semi-truth in the frames of the political state to truth and integrity as a new human value in the work and conduct. Quality journalism began to become to be the 'fourth estate' in democratising Russia owing to a growing ethical approach to serve the truth and the public interest. The second trend, the rise of commercialism, produced another idea of journalism as entertainment. The media began to indulge mass tastes and reached big audiences. A perception of journalistic publications as commodities identical to other goods on the market had condoned venal journalism for political and commercial ends, and ethics became unwanted (Pasti 2006: 77). McNair (2000) characterises the clientelism of the Russian media of the 1990s with such key words as 'power, profit, corruption, and lies'. Roudakova (2007) argues that the post-Soviet transformation of journalism passed 'from the fourth estate to the second oldest profession'. Bakshtanovskii and Sogomonov (2002) pose a problem of the moral choices of a journalist. It is a fact that the commercialisation of journalism was a part of economic development, as the media assumed the function of advertising agencies. Editors promoted and stimulated journalists who could increase the effectiveness of advertising. Each of the papers, radio and TV channels set up special advertising departments that were an element of pressure upon journalists.

Overall, the first post-Soviet decade of market reforms, metaphorically speaking, split journalism into quality journalism pursuing the public interest and commercial journalism pursuing self-interest. The latter included not only an entertainment function, but also a PR function serving the interests of merging groups of politics and business whose aftermath cemented political corruption. In the mid-1990s, conditions for quality journalism began to deteriorate, the political pressure increased, access to information diminished and assassinations of journalists began as documented in several monitoring reports (Dzialoshinskii 1997; Ratinov and Efremova 1998; *Media in CIS* 1999; Public Expertise 2000). External unfavourable factors were joined by internal factors, when the young pragmatically minded heads of media and journalists made their choice in favour of an alliance with the new political authority (Zorkaia 2005; Dubin 2006: 9).

The next decade, the 2000s, was led by a new president, Putin, who took a new course towards the verticalisation of authority with an idea for re-constructing a Great Russia, i.e. the building of a sovereign democracy with implied resistance to external pressures proceeding from the West and primarily the USA (Trenin 2006). The government increased its control on the economy, policy, culture, media and other areas. Its new political shift from informational openness to informational security narrowed the professional freedom of journalists by returning them to frames of political subordination. The critical function of quality journalism, which had begun to rise in the liberal 1990s, was gradually reduced. In its place a new form of the agreement, 'the Polit.PR contract', between media and the government came into force.

In contemporary Russia the problem of generations serves as a springboard for future prospects (Levada and Shanin 2005; Iasin 2005; Kapitsa 2006; Zaritsky 2006; Omel'chenko 2006). Many writers and publicists expose the characteristics of our time with concepts such as 'Generation Pepsi' (Pelevin 1999), Plastic Boys (Loshak 2005), Spiritless (Minaev 2006) – nowadays also, referring to Putin, 'Generation PU'.

Empirical study

The chapter asks where a new generation of journalists finds its place in the present conflict of interests and what perspectives appear for public service from value orientations of the new generation. The term 'generation' here is taken not in a narrow demographic sense limited to the dates of birth of individuals, but in a broader sense attached to the period of their coming into the profession; in other words, their age in the profession. Earlier research (Pasti 2005; 2007) revealed that the present journalistic population consists of three generations of working journalists: first, the old professionals who started in the Soviet media; second, the new professionals who entered the profession during the transition of the 1990s; and third, those clearly post-Soviet professionals who entered the field after 2000. The differences between the old Soviet and the new post-Soviet practitioners divide their professional subcultures formed in different periods of the political history of Russia: in the epoch of the USSR, after the collapse of the USSR and the rise of liberalisation in the 1990s, with the beginning of Putin's presidency and his new course for the central role of the state.

Sample

The chapter is mainly based on empirical data from a study of St. Petersburg journalists conducted in December 2005. The first study on St. Petersburg journalists was carried out in 1999.[1] The sample of the follow-up study in 2005 also included 30 randomly selected journalists from 11 leading news media outlets.[2] All respondents gave their consent to meet and to talk with an interviewer (postgraduate students of St. Petersburg State University, Faculty of Journalism). The follow-up study used practically the same questionnaire as in 1999. In 2005, the sampling included three generations working in journalism: 11 respondents entered journalism during the Soviet time (until 1991) identified as the Soviet generation, ten respondents entered during the 1990s (1991–9) identified as the transitional generation and nine respondents entered since 2000, identified as the young generation of the 2000s. In these studies, the definition of a journalist includes those specialising in news and working full-time on the dailies and weeklies, in radio, TV and on the Internet. They produce information on political, economic, social, cultural issues, crime and sports news.

The sample shows that the professional structure of journalism is becoming younger and more attractive to females. New post-Soviet journalists outnumbered old, Soviet journalists by two-thirds. Surprisingly, for only the first five years from 2000 did the number of young journalists reach one-third. The news media preferred to employ young people: in the sampling of 2005 the majority came into journalism by age 30 and females prevailed. Thus, among the 30 respondents, there were 13 males and 17 females, with ages ranging from 19 to 59 years, and time spent in the journalistic profession ranging from two to 40 years. Their division on grounds of gender and age was almost equal, except for those aged from 20 to 30 being one male and nine females. In 2005, the respondents were highly educated. However, distinct from 1999 when only one-third of newcomers had professional education, in 2005 practically every young journalist had had journalism education. In this respect, the transitional generation of the 1990s consisting of representatives of various occupations, education and age differs from the old (Soviet) generation as well as the new generation of the 2000s. In 2005, most young journalists worked as reporters and correspondents, and some were employed on temporary contracts. The young females did not have a second job, complaining about the hard basic workloads in contrast to their older colleagues and young males who combined their main job with a second job. In comparison with 1999, the wage significantly increased from the minimum 1,200 rubles in 1999 to the minimum 6,000 rubles in 2005. In 2005, the income (basic job with second job) of half of the respondents was 10,000–30,000 rubles a month. One-third had incomes at the level of the cream of the Russian middle-class.[3] This clearly showed that journalism provided good earnings. The average nominal wage paid in St. Petersburg in the first half of 2006 was 12,024 rubles (354 euro) per month (*Saint Petersburg* 2006: 5).

In 2005 about half of young journalists explained their coming to the profession out of interest and vocation. They used such expressions as ‘devotion’, ‘childhood dream’ and ‘love of literature’. Their choice of journalism was made while still at school or straight after school. In this respect they were reminiscent of the Soviet journalists assessing journalism as a dream vocation and had begun to write for the press straight from school. The other half had rather pragmatic reasons: an easy way of getting an education, parents’ advice, those failing to pass examinations in other faculties and going to the journalism faculty. There were also those who came into the profession by accident. Most of the young journalists started as stringers and succeeded in accumulating experience working in different types of media and jobs. Half arrived in St. Petersburg from other regions (Pskov, Tol’iatti, Volgograd, Murmansk) in search of better offers. They had moved over three or four work-places striving to get to the leading media, for instance for one respondent from a local newspaper in the home city, to St. Petersburg to a local newspaper, then from there to a major channel of the state radio, from there to state TV. Migration of journalists from the provinces to the capital cities Moscow and St. Petersburg began in the 1990s with liberalisation of the labour and housing markets, the media boom and the PR service. The provincial journalists left in search of better opportunities for income, career, professional freedom and simply a job when their local media became bankrupt.

Between self-interest and public interest

Journalists were asked about their work, aims, perceptions of their audience and attitudes to corruption. Significant differences were evident concerning their work values depending on the type of journalism and media in which they worked, whereas an insignificant difference was found regarding their attitudes to corruption. Thus, among the journalists working in the government-oriented media there prevailed value orientations of *workers for hire* or *mercenaries*. In the commercial media the journalists were mostly oriented to creativity by resembling *artists*. In the quality media the journalists strove to be *experts*. However, despite distinguishing work values, practically all respondents approved corruption in the profession. The practice of ordered articles (*zakaz, dzhinsa*) written in the political and commercial interests of clients for money or services in the post-Soviet era became a 'professional norm'. The client made an order to a skilful journalist, a competent professional. Journalism and journalists became commodities in the political market of media services.

Mercenaries

In the state media and the private media oriented towards support for the government, journalists perceived their work as any other sphere of production being implemented under supervision. There it was natural to follow the editor or co-ordinator in defining topics and emphases in the work. Their media was in close contact with the government and the journalists had supposed official sources of information to be reliable ones. They distinguished officials from other people by safeguarding their interests. Thus, to the question: 'Do you disclose the names of rape victims before the court's decision?', one respondent answered: 'It depends who has suffered. If (s)he is some official, so naturally not'. Some used unverified sources of information in order to amplify the official content: 'If I use them, so usually I say that they are unverified, usually this elaborates a story'. Some excerpts from their interviews:

> I am a worker for hire, what the boss wants, the boss gets. Today the bar is lowered. It seems for me, today it is a job among jobs. Somebody is better, somebody is worse.
>
> A usual job, the same as any other work, simply the treatment of some things, the same as in the plant workers make parts of machines every day.

Journalistic perceptions of their professional responsibility were formed under the conditions of officials' interference in their work and power of the 'telephone right' of the officials, under strict editorial control over the content of journalistic materials and corresponding media agenda. The journalists considered that they had a responsibility to themselves, the editorial line and their informants, mostly the official sources:

> I will not comment on a fact if it concerns politics and goes against the line of our broadcasting.
>
> It was pressure when we broadcast information, simply information without comments and the city's authorities demanded "blood" for this information. This was simply the information about a protest action, the people held a mass meeting against one resolution of the authorities and the authorities quickly reacted and demanded that such information should never be given.
>
> Everything depends on the editorial office where you work. Concerning our city TV channel where I worked, there naturally when you came back from a shooting you ask how to write: how it was or the official version? Without ceremony the editor gave up such things as tears from the video already prepared, some intellectual faces in the mass meeting, that is, censorship.

The perceptions of the audience were quite abstract among those working in TV and radio, such as 'a soul of any man', 'an educated man interested in my work'. On the contrary, the young journalists producing texts had concrete perceptions regarding who they write for: 'for city dwellers of 20–40, working in offices, using the Internet and keeping up with affairs', 'for those interested in culture and history, but not politics'. Overall, the young journalists tried to avoid 'dangerous topics', which could cause trouble at the work and even dismissal.

Artists

Creative work and self-expression were the most important things for the young journalists working in the commercially oriented media:

> I think when a young male journalist begins to write for the newspaper for him the most important thing is he himself and his feelings. Is he satisfied with himself, is his editor satisfied? This is primary. That is, will he be published here? In order for him to be satisfied, his friends and those closest to him must be satisfied, and later when time will pass, when he is fed up with this feeling, then he writes for a reader.

As distinct from 'mercenaries', laconically and carefully answering the questions of the interview, these artists looked like extroverts emotionally telling in detail how they succeeded in getting an interview and tracking down the hero of their report. They were like hounds hunting for exclusive information and new topics to attract readers and be interesting for them themselves. But they were also interested in raising social problems, e.g. about the problem of unemployed footballers in St. Petersburg, where football was highly developed and popular. These young journalists perceived the most unprofessional behaviour in their profession as 'when a journalist is not curious'. In their work they used the Internet sources extensively, their circle of informants, acquaintances and friends. To obtain a good story, an exclusive, they used hidden cameras, payment for information, false identity and fabrication. Their perception of responsibility was attached to those people about whom they made their stories:

> Sin – to harm, to betray the trust of those people about whom the material was made.
>
> In my opinion first of all you must have responsibility towards those people about whom you make your materials. It pains them if a journalist garbles something, misrepresents material, exaggerates or otherwise misrepresents the material. You must re-read and think how those people will react and think about them more.

The old journalists in these media were more anxious than the young ones about existing limitations in the selection of the topics, which, as a rule touched on sensitive subjects in the social development of the city (alcoholism, drugs, homeless children, problems of pensioners, social insurance and others). The editorial control distorted the real picture of life in favour of a rosy view of the city authorities' positive agenda. The old journalists were not satisfied with this and would prefer to meet the needs of their readers:

> There is a directive for whom to write but in point of fact there is the audience. The directive is to write for an active reader of 20–40 who works and goes by *Metro*. Since the newspaper is free of charge and has no constant readership, it has been distributed in a short period of time and nobody except pensioners will contrive in order to go to work earlier and take the newspaper. Whoever goes by *Metro* in the morning, takes it, including pensioners. They are a definite type. We write nothing for pensioners, but in the city, they are one fourth by the population. We have a lot of pensioners as readers. Before it was better, because we gave a slice of life, wrote a lot on the economy, and the law, and interpreted them. People liked this very much because they could get this from nowhere else. We gave a picture of city life. We wrote about homeless persons (*bomzh)* and homeless children as if by a short line. Now we do not write about them. It is as if they no longer exist. It is considered that we are a successful newspaper. I am not for such a policy.

The young journalists also experienced editorial censorship and corrected the materials according to the editorial line, but took it indifferently. The well-being of their media depended on many things including the loyalty of the media to the political authorities. Interestingly, in contrast to the young journalists from the government-oriented media, they did not reveal a fear of losing their job, being sure of finding a job anywhere. The journalism staff in their editorial offices had often changed, and they began to combine a staff job here and a second job outside, in this way developing diverse experience and broadening professional contacts in the market. The greatest satisfaction in the work was to get approving feedback from their audience and if their materials enraged officials. They perceived the audience as anybody, all sorts of people, causal readers, as 'the people in *Metro*', and also oriented to their own circle of people, consisting of friends, acquaintances and relatives.

Experts

In the media orienting to quality information, balanced coverage of events, presentation of different points of view including critical opinions regarding the officials and entrepreneurs and not excluding constructive relations with the city authorities, the young journalists strove to become experts. They emphasised the importance of pluralism of facts and opinions to produce quality information and maximisation of those facts to actualise the topic taken by a journalist, and tried to make the situation better:

> I try to do good work. I cannot say that I am a big fighter for democracy. I try my best to get the maximum of information, to get quality information, to be as objective as possible in my view, only neutrally without taking sides as far as it is possible, without marked bias. Always to take consider the opinion of the other side, find as many opinions as possible on any problem, to make the material more informative.
>
> As a rule, I take those materials, those topics which are interesting for me, in which I want something to change for the better, such as humanitarian aims as a whole.

As distinct from the young journalists from the government-oriented media, *experts* had a certain scepticism regarding the statements of the officials and asserted that it is necessary to verify information coming from official sources. They also testified to cases of pressure coming from the city government not to cover certain events and not to publish certain comments. As a rule, such requests had been made by phone. The young journalists followed their editorial line by learning the role of watchdog under the protection of their organisation. For instance, if they know that their article will cause trouble among officials, they publish it, if they are sure they are right. That is, in the frame of their editorial policy they had an opportunity to publish such materials. Dangerous topics, such as political murders, the activities of skinheads or nationalists were written using pseudonyms. The young journalists were very proud of working together with well-known professionals in the media with a good reputation among the residents of the city. This stimulated them to work better in order to reach the level of their senior colleagues. Their responsibility was placed firstly upon the editorial office and their senior colleagues. The main things for them were personal integrity in their work, objectivity and professionalism:

> Not to lie because we are a source of information for people and we must not let the source become dirty or print untrue information. Objectivity is needed, because otherwise a journalist begins to lie, to distort the existing reality. There is no engagement, to select those topics which really are topical for the given time. I mean if in the city a foreign student is killed and the first city channel broadcasts about some wonderful exhibitions, premières, operas, it is wrong. The principle of actuality, importance, importance for a reader, what it is important for people in our city, country first of all.

In contrast to their young colleagues from commercial media and government-oriented media, they perceived the audience not as consumers or a mass, not just as people interested in culture, but as socially active citizens, educated, interested in politics, striving to know more, with income close to the middle-class and needs for expertise in current problems:

> This person is interested in political life, and a person interested in different spheres of life. I consider that (s)he is successful, as a whole such a person interested in the current events in the country and the world.
>
> People around 30. Here are two categories: elderly people call, not very mobile, analyse the situation and mobile people - bank workers, economists, from the city Parliament, the city administration, there our newspaper has been distributed.

Overall, the understanding of their audiences comes from everyday work and type of media, where journalists work and follow the editorial line. Although the journalists working in the press and in online media seemed to know their audiences better than broadcasting journalists, the newspapers continued to lose their readership. Thus, in 2006, the total print run of all the city's daily newspapers was about 100,000 for a population of five million (*St Peterburgskie Vedomosti* 2006). The local experts noted a dwindling interest of the people in the political information provided by the city media.

Attitudes to corruption

In 2005, two-thirds said that they did not produce corrupt materials and hidden advertising, although these practices existed in the media and among journalists. One-third admitted that writing corrupt articles and hidden advertising was normal for earning money and that it was necessary to barter services in their informal networks. However, as the journalists noted, times changed, were stabilised, and the media began to pursue profit by aiming at advertising services and at PR services that required establishment of good relations with their clients, mostly business and the officials. To attract orders and advertising, the media tried to build their image as solid and reliable partners in the market of informational and advertising services in conditions of increasing competition for clients and audience. Some media introduced rules of corporate discipline and corporate ethics, e.g. no disclosure of inside information to outsiders and loyalty to colleagues from other media. The respondents were asked: 'It became commonplace to talk about the corruption of Russian journalists, the widespread practice of writing articles for money. Could professionalism and corruption be connected?'. Most of the young journalists answered positively by perceiving corruption as a private practice of a professional. Among the journalists there was no difference according to what type of journalism they represent. Thus, the journalists from the government-oriented media considered:

> It is quite normal, for the professional it is natural.
>
> Professionalism and corruption are connected. Money is paid to professionals. Professionalism is when you are bought by money. That is, when somebody is ready to pay you do this and that. They want to use your professionalism for their own aims. They do not turn to just anybody but to the professional who competently organises the black PR campaign, who is competently able to raze a character and his business to the ground.
>
> Combined. Material is for money. It is a common practice. A professional does what (s) he knows how to do and he is paid for this. It is combined with professionalism.

Young journalists from the quality media responded:

> It seems to me, yes, corruption and professionalism are combined. There are whole editorial offices where this has been practised and by all the people working there, they are professionals and by passing over in silence they are not allowed to say some things, but in actual fact this is only some names or to name some names more often… Because of this the journalist does not work worse. Although engaged by the editorial office, he is an engaged journalist, he will not work worse. Even he can be objective.
>
> Yes, they could be, yes. I know that some journalists who write very good texts, independent and engaged by nobody, at the same time they can earn additionally by PR. As a rule they do this under pseudonyms and they are right to do so. If they produce successful texts, it right to forgive them additional earnings in PR.

Only two had doubts about corruption – that it contradicts ethics. The first excerpt comes from a young female journalist working in the state media and the second excerpt from a young male from a popular daily:

> Among professionals there are those who will dispute any point of view for money. Tomorrow he will get money from opponents and will change his position and will dispute completely other values for other money. Such

> professionals exist but I consider that it is an infringement of professional ethics. But it is possible to act professionally. I learnt with young males which quite easily said "We will do whatever is asked of us". They managed easily with such unscrupulousness: a good review for a film – for God's sake, to write a bad review – for God's sake!
>
> Here a lot depends on the understanding of the conception of professionalism. If ethics and morality are added to this conception, in this case this is not professionalism, this is anti-professionalism. But if we do not add this, then they are best "*ofigennye*" professionals, they dig up such muck about people. Ordered advertising articles are a private matter, it is possible to advertise, to use some name, as if by chance, a title in the article, but it is loathsome. It seems, I would not do this, I hope that I will not to do this.

Six years earlier, in 1999, practically all journalists accepted corruption in the profession and in life. They considered venality and professionalism as things of the same order. Their arguments were that as everything around was corrupt and dependent, there was no other way to leave poverty behind. Nobody buys unprofessional journalists. Old (pro-state) values had been displaced by new (pro-market) values (Juskevits 2002: 201). In 2005, a typical journalist noted that 'journalists are not from another planet, but take bribes just like doctors and teachers'. Overall, during the 2000s journalists' attitudes to corruption did not change, on the contrary, this remained to be legitimised in journalists' awareness as parts of acting economic and interpersonal relations. Corruption simplified life and work, and success could be achieved at any price.

Self-image

The young journalists in 2005 distinguished their generation from older generations in the profession by being critical of themselves and having a profound respect for Soviet journalists. It was a completely new turn in the relations between the old professionals and young practitioners. In 1999, the newcomers (transitional generation) were establishing their identity via the conflict with the Soviet generation, putting a distance between themselves and 'non-professionals', who for their entire lives only produced brainwashing and Communist propaganda. In turn, their perceptions about themselves were as 'new professionals' introducing new values of Western journalism (objectivity, neutrality, separation of fact and comment, etc). Today, young journalists of the 2000s emphasise the professionalism of the Soviet generation and realise their own imperfections:

> Now everything is more commercialised. We are less ready to work free of charge than our colleagues in the past.
>
> Soviet professionals, they were so educated that they tried to get a result by their publication. They were not satisfied with a simple description, they kept up with the situation, wrote after that report, called, demanded a reaction to their texts. The present journalists write texts for the sake of text. The text is

> not intended to change something, but is simply text for the sake of the text, in order to fill space, time, and preferably, of course, make money.
>
> Today it seems journalism is held up by older people. Among young journalists, unfortunately, I seldom meet individuals who in the first place want to stay in journalism and, secondly, want to be of some use and really will be interesting for readers, listeners and viewers. You understand, the profession of a journalist now is fashionable, it is the worst thing, that the profession is a very fashionable. It became fashionable maybe five years ago and continues to be splendidly fashionable still now, although each began to say that journalists tell lies there and so on. Contemporary youth, such advanced young people, the Pepsi generation burst into journalism. [...] I hope, that in ten years when the number of journalists is smaller and there is a major shortage of them, by that time this profession will not be fashionable. And then in journalism there will be people who actually understand that journalism needs them, because they want to do this work, but not because that they want to say "I am a journalist, I am such a hardboiled journalist". I hope that these young people will become DJs. I do not know what will be in ten years, but I have quite a pessimistic view of the future.
>
> The difference is first of all in ideology. That is, the journalists of the Soviet time aimed at directives from the Communist party and they worked for this idea. Then, in the transitional times of the 1990s there was nothing, vague times, journalists perhaps tried to find their own way. And now, at least I associate myself with the last generation because I came into journalism in 2000, my generation favours independence and freedom, freedom of speech and action. That is, first of all, it is an ideology. If during the 1990s there was a search for ideology, so now there is no search for ideology, as such. Each has his own ideology, each works in his own way, independently.

Future prospects

At the end of 2005, the journalists answering the question 'How do you estimate the profession of journalist today?' described journalism in polar extremes. Some described it as a prestigious and interesting profession, fashionable and attractive to young people, including PR services and well-paid, offering opportunities for access to elite circles. Others described journalism as poorly paid and falling in its social status. Journalism is developing in the direction of diverting the attention of people away from serious problems, the entertainment share is growing while journalists increasingly pursue ratings. As a result, journalism is viewed as having become unimportant to people. Journalists acknowledge that information is being suppressed as their media have been controlled and serve the political interests of the authorities. Journalism has become increasingly accommodating and freedom of speech is diminishing. Ten years ago it was better than it is now:

> This profession in time will cease to be actual because the word "journalist" becomes not very important. If such conception as "Poet in Russia is more

> than poet" had died already and today nobody seriously perceives poets, nobody listens to them, so and time of journalists who could influence by a word social events and create social resonance, it goes away. Information becomes less, we speak about some particulars, like what hotel is opened for homeless people or who gets a free lunch, but that big businessmen become officials, we do not speak about this.

In contrast to 1999, the journalists in 2005 connected their hopes for the future with political rather than economic changes. They said that the future of the profession depends on the development of society. Half of the journalists attached their hopes to the future with technical progress and its influence on journalism, especially the rise of Internet services and online journalism. One-third was pessimistic about the future. There is little hope of change with this regime and with universal globalisation as a whole. The public media are increasingly seen as becoming a part of popular culture, journalism is becoming entertainment. Soon the audience will not need journalism because it has acquired a taste for mass popular genres. Newspapers will die; already today they are useless and unprofitable. Journalism will lose the spirit of humanity, and the capability to narrate about people. The Polit.PR function will increase and the situation in freedom of speech will deteriorate. Journalism will have to move into a special niche for those who are still able to read.

Discussion

Political and economic conditions stabilised in the frame of a new state policy of the verticalisation of power. From the pluralistic agenda of the 1990s, media turned to increasingly uniform instruments constituting an administrative octopus of the state and business. Critical opinions and discussions were relegated behind the mainstream; to less visible media (*Delo*, *Ekho Peterburga*), programmes on TV and radio and also the Internet. For example, after years of publishing, the analytical weekly *Delo* with a readership of intelligentsia was closed down 'for economic reasons'. The local elections for the legislative assembly in 2007 showed St. Petersburg 'as a mirror of Putin's political stabilization', when voters 'put the so-called stability promised by the party "United Russia" far above traditional democratic values, civil rights and market economy' (Lomagin 2007). It did not diverge from the situation in other parts of Russia (*Lenta.ru* 2007). From the individual and collective corrupt practices of the 1990s paid under the table, media moved to a new form of contract, made between the media and the government as well as the media and business. As a whole, it stabilised the agenda and the budget, although the practice of corrupt materials persisted. In 2005, the city's news media remained in the sphere of corporate interests of the state and capital (mostly owned by banks and industrial groups), and some of them had mixed ownership (state and private). In contrast to the 1990s, when foreign capital (mostly from Scandinavia) energetically entered the media market, established and acquired some media outlets (the daily *Delovoi Peterburg*, the free daily *Metro*, radio

Baltika, the popular weekly *Peterburg Express*), in 2005 mainly domestic owners controlled the main news media outlets. That is, the process of internationalisation of media capital was discontinued in the 2000s. On the contrary, corporate control increased: close friends of Vladimir Putin became the main media tycoons in the city.[4] In terms of political economy, the media market modernised slowly, having the same major owners (the state and big business) with their invariable goals concerning the news media (propaganda and social control). Technologically, modernisation of media formats, print, content and working conditions of journalists were in obvious progress. This had a positive impact on the work values of journalists, especially the young generation in their strive to develop multiskilling and mobility, to be economically independent and creatively successful. From strategies of survival (second jobs to feed the family, *sandwich* journalism) during the economically hard 1990s, the journalists moved over to strategies of attainability in the economically favourable 2000s by converting their capital (education, experience, social networks) into new positions among the political and (media) business elite at the peak of the popularity of their profession.[5]

For educated, creatively thinking people, journalism remained an attractive field mostly due to its opportunities for individual freedom and potential for doing things in a personal way. Unemployment was practically non-existent; the level of self-regulation of the journalistic market was high. Journalists freely chose where to work, including the opportunity to combine a staff job with freelance work. Although the news media preferred to employ professionally educated people, access remained open for non-educated individuals and migrants from the provinces. The market for informational and advertising services continued to increase owing to economic growth and the need for skilled workers. The rise of *commercial journalism* and *PR journalism* (self-interest) and the marginalisation of *quality journalism* (public interest) testified that journalism moved increasingly into the media business, where the political and the commercial interests of the state and the capital were merging just as in the economy. The media approached society predominantly as a consumer of goods and services (functions of entertainment, propaganda and advertising), and to a lesser extent as citizens to participate in reforms (functions of information, analysis, critics). Becoming a part of the political–commercial alliance of the state and business, the media lost the trust of the public and, consequently, the ability to organise a dialogue between all parties: state, business and society. It seems that the government began to be aware of the problem and to attempt to find a solution, but in a familiar way by turning journalism increasingly into (pro-)state service. The process began with increasing control of the state over the media, especially TV and the printing houses. The government criticised contemporary journalists for a lack of competence, low professionalism and corrupt conduct (Russian Periodical Press Market 2006: 8–9). Hence, we could expect a new state reform for the regulation of the media and their workers, and modernisation of journalism education by, ultimately, raising the prestige of journalism among the population and the trust in the media as a social institution. Perhaps the role of *social organiser* will be required for support of the state initiatives in society? Overall, the post-Soviet transformation of the media moved from the status of the party-state organisations in the Soviet time to the status of a market freelancer during the 1990s, and in the 2000s to a consolidated partner of the state and business.

The new generation of the 2000s is, in fact, the first generation of journalists of a new Russia. They are its contemporaries who experienced all the changes: born in the romance of the *glasnost* and *perestroika* (1985–90), grew up in the adventure of the 'wild capitalism' (the 1990s) and entered the profession in the 'meek' era of the 2000s, when to criticise or to protest is considered to be unpatriotic, with no need to 'rock the boat'. Their basic distinction from the older generations is that they do not reveal ideals, as it was with journalists of the Soviet epoch (the happy future with communism) and as it was with new journalists of the liberal 1990s (the happy future with capitalism). Their ideology is pragmatic individualism and concern for their own fate, therefore conformism dominates, successfully combining the political order and market supply, as the state and business are the basic clients of their media. They are children of the new post-communist society of consumerism, market values such as individual freedom, personal economic success and self-realisation are central for them, in contrast to those of the older generations with priority in the political values of development of democracy, free media, free elections and human rights. The youth do not appear to be interested in politics, perhaps, because today this includes a high risks. They do not show any interest in the role of adversary and investigator; on the contrary, editorial censorship operates in the frame of the official news. They tend to stay with such topics as culture, the sights of their city, its history and art just as it was with Soviet journalists, who escaped a straight confrontation with the political regime. They rely mostly on themselves, acting competitively with each other as freelancers, changing jobs, combining jobs and developing multiskilling. Their socialization today in the profession proceeds from their individual initiatives for new experience, new contacts, new status, not including any collective interests in establishing solidarity (the question on solidarity was incomprehensible) or joining the professional association (practically nobody). But some corporate loyalties and agreements can be observed in some situations and between some journalists.

Their lifestyle has been profoundly Westernized: high mobility, contract employment, freelance approach, multiskilling, journalism technology (they are competent in the Western 'type' of news). They approach the West as equals, not having such existential experience as the Soviet and transitional journalists – the superiority of the West and the inaccessibility of the West. On the contrary, the West is now a close neighbour, open and accessible to them, often satisfying their needs and demands (the professional exchange programmes, tourism, shopping, recreation, etc.). The young generation does not mythologise the West, owing to free communication and personal experience, but the Soviet past in the general context of the present official discourse and the nostalgia of the old generations have a positive sound for them and does not find grounds for criticism, distinct from the radicalism of the transitional generation, who fiercely criticised the Soviet past. Rather, the new generation of the 2000s is aware of themselves as the successors in the great history of the USSR, and approaches the Soviet generation with profound respect.

In spite of the Westernization of life and work, political consciousness changed slowly, with the Tsar staying in the mind. As it was in 1999, and six years later, in 2005, the city journalists pinned their hopes for change in journalism to a shift of the main national leader, the president of the country. Explicitly, they revealed the same way of thinking as the majority of the population in the country; implicitly, the heterogeneity of their profession tidily attached to the political authority. Paradoxically, the majority were very critical of the present quality of journalism, engaged and commercialised; pessimistic about its 'health' in the near future. However, few protested against the present status quo and the news media in the narrow interests of political and economic power. Indisputably, they knew the price of the protest that could destroy their individual careers, income, personal security and further employment in the profession. The young journalists valued their present with ample opportunities for earnings inside and outside journalism. The majority showed self-interest in the profession preferring to remain atomised and to use the profession mostly as a way of earning income and creating networks, creative ambitions and search for personal better future. Additionally, they were not too poor to enter the protest, on the contrary, the close alliance of the media, the political authority and business guaranteed for them a regular income and future prospects. Karl Mannheim (1950) in his essays wrote about the young generation as a potential, which makes a protest because it is an outsider. Due to its protest, the young generation is able to change the existing state of things; the new generation is a vehicle of social change. In the present Russia young journalists do not want to be losers, they want to be winners and to get all the rewards from life as soon as possible in the frame of their individual freedom. Therefore, they make no protest. This means that they do not reveal the potential to change the conditions of their profession and to reach political independence in journalism. This means that the current situation will persist.

If we seek the roots of conformism, we should look at the society in which the journalists work and live. According to Pitirim Sorokin (2006: 590–1) the type of society is determined by the type of relations there. Sorokin identified three types of relations: agreed or contractual relations inherent in the modern capitalist society, family relations establishing the traditional society and coercive relations inherent in an authoritarian regime. The present Russia appears as the traditional society with the most developed family and coercive relations. The young generation, like their parents who grew up in such relations, perceives the coercive relations as family relations and thus does not protest against the present restrictions, including limits to professional freedoms. The new generation reveals its readiness to serve the present order, like its predecessors the Soviet journalists did in the USSR. Nevertheless, some optimism is shown by those journalists who belong to the outsiders, the losers who had a critical stance to the present quality of the profession and who perceived the present status quo as provisional and had hopes for an alternative way – more integration with the West. In their critical approach and distrust that the present situation would last, we could see a hidden reserve for a change. In other words, the situation of Soviet journalists during *perestroika* may recover when the political freedoms come and the journalists use this opportunity. That is, the present outsiders could unite and fight for the profession.

Notes

1 The sample of the first study included 30 journalists: 14 Soviet practitioners and 16 post-Soviet practitioners randomly selected from eight media representing different types of news journalism in the city: the state Tele Radio Company which includes TV Peterburg 5th Channel and Radio Peterburg, a private radio station Baltika, three dailies – *Sankt-Peterburgskie Vedomosti*, *Smena* and *Vechernii Peterburg*; the St. Petersburg edition of the national leading daily newspaper *Komsomol'skaia Pravda*; and the most popular city weekly *Peterburg Express* (Juskevits 2002).

2 TV Peterburg 5th Channel (on 1 October 2006 it resumed federal broadcasting) and Radio Peterburg, the local dailies *Sankt-Peterburgskie Vedomosti* and *Vechernii Peterburg* and the St. Petersburg edition of the national daily *Komsomol'skaia Pravda*, Sankt Peterburg branch of the All-Russian State Television and Radio Company (VGTRK), Television Channel 100-TV, FM Radio station Ekho Peterburga, the analytical weekly *Delo*, the free daily *Metro* and the Internet daily Fontanka.Ru.

3 Some Russian sociologists define the 'cream' of the middle-class to be young people aged 24–35, with high education and monthly wage per person in Moscow $1500, in St. Petersburg $1000, in other big cities $800 (*Nezavisimaia gazeta* 2008). The average salary in Russia in 2008 was 16,400 rubles (about $500) (*Kommersant* 2008b).

4 NMG (the National Media Group) belonging to the bank Rossiia and its partners (Iurii Koval'chuk, well-known as a close friend of Vladimir Putin) owns Tele-Radio Company which includes TV Peterburg 5th Channel and Radio Peterburg, TV channels REN TV, co-owner daily *Sankt-Peterburgskie Vedomosti*, News Media (with such scandal tabloids as *Tvoi Den'* and *Zhizn'*) and the newspaper *Izvestiia* (www.mediaatlas.ru/news/print.php?id=24807).

The Baltic Media-Group of Oleg Rudnov (also known as a close friend of Vladimir Putin) includes Radio station Baltika, a new interactive TV channel 100-TV, co-owner of TV Peterburg 5th Channel, such city newspapers as: *Nevskoe Vremia*, *Smena*, *Vechernee Vremia*, daily *Vechernii Peterburg* (more information in www.stockmap.ru/company/847/0/).

The media group Azhur includes the Agency of journalistic investigations (Azhur), newspaper *Vash tainyi sovetnik*, the weekly *MK v Pitere*, and the Internet daily Fontanka.Ru (www.fontanka.ru/about.html).

5 St. Petersburg is a good example. Here, former journalists have followed vertiginous careers; some of them occupy leading posts in the city's government (vice-governor, the head of the culture department, press secretary of the governor), while their predecessors moved higher to Moscow. In the opinion of the head of the St. Petersburg Union of Journalists, it was/is pleasant for a journalist working there both during of the rule of the former governor, and now in the period of the present governor (*Sankt Peterburgskie Vedomosti* 2006).

References

Bakshtanovskii, V.I. and Sogomonov J.V. (2002) *Moral'nyi vybor zhurnalista*. T'iumen: Tsentr prikladnoi etiki.

Dubin, B.V. (2006) 'Mass-media i kommunikativnyi mir zhitelei Rossii: plasticheskaia khirurgiia sotsial'noi real'nosti', *Vestnik obshchestvennogo mnenia Levada-Tsentr*, 3 (83): 33–46. Online. Available www.polit.ru/research/2006/09/06/dubin/ (accessed 25 June 2008).

Dzialoshinskii, I.M. (ed.) (1997) *Svoboda dostupa k informatsii v Rossii: Pravovye, organizatsionnye, professional'nye problemy*, Moskva: Komissiia po svobode dostupa k informatsii.

Gallup International (2008) 'The Global Survey in Sixty Countries'. Online. Available www.gipp.ru (accessed 18 January 2008).

Iasin, E. (2005) *Vyzhivet li demokratiia v Rossii?*, Moskva: Fond Liberal'naia missiia.

Juskevits, S. (2002) 'Professional Roles of Russian Journalists at the End of the 1990s. A Case Study of St. Petersburg Media', unpublished licentiate thesis, University of Tampere. Online. Available http://tutkielmat.uta.fi/pdf/lisuri00006.pdf [In Russian Pasti (2004)].

Kapitsa, S.P. (2006) 'V nashikh universitetakh dedy uchat vnukov', *Moskovskie Novosti*, 26 May.

Kommersant (2008a) 'Rossiiskaia elita doveriaet biznessu i vlasti i ne doveriaet media i NKO', 30 January.

Kommersant (2008b) 'Sotsiologi: rosiiskie bednye stanoviatsia eshche bednee'. Online. Available www.polit.ru/news/2008/07/02/bednost (accessed 2 July 2008).

Levada, J. and Shanin, T. (eds) (2005) *Pokolencheskii analiz sovremennoi Rossii,* Moskva: Novoe Literaturnoe Obozrenie.

Lenta.ru (2007) 'Rossiiane gotovy pozhertvovat' svobodoi SMI radi sotsial'noi stabil'nosti'. Online. Available www.lenta.ru (accessed 10 December 2007).

Lomagin, N. (2007) 'Quiet Russia: St. Petersburg as a mirror of Putin's political stabilization', *Expert Article 99 Baltic Rim Economics, Bimonthly Review,* 2. Online. Available www.tse.fi/pei/bre/email/bre2_2007.html (accessed 30 April 2007).

Loshak, V. (2005) 'Plastmassovye mal'chiki', *Izvestiia*, 16 February 2005.

Mannheim, K. (1950) *Diagnosis of Our Time Wartime Essays of a Sociologist*. London: Routledge & Kegan Paul.

McNair, B. (2000) 'Power, profit, corruption, and lies: The Russian media in the 1990s', in J. Curran and M-J. Park (eds) *De-Westernizing Media Studies*, London, New York: Routledge, 79–94.

Media in CIS (1999) 'Russia'. Online. Available www.internews.ras.ru, 188–241. (accessed 25 June 2008).

Minaev, S. (2006) *Dukhless: Povest' o nenastoiashchem cheloveke*, Moskva: AST.

Mmd Corporate, Public Affairs & Public Relations Consultants (2007) 'Agency Mmd published a survey of Russian blogosphere', Guild of Press Publishers. Online. Available www.gipp.ru (accessed 6 April 2007).

Nezavisimaia gazeta (2008) 'Polovina molodykh i uspeshnykh rossiian mechtaet ob emigratsii', 27 June 2008.

Omel'chenko, E. (2006) 'Pop-kul'turnaia revoliutsiia ili perestroechnyi remeik? Sovremennyi kontekst molodezhnogo voprosa, *NZ (Neprikosnovennyi Zapas)*, 1 (45).

Pasti, S. (2004) *Rossiiskii zhurnalist v kontekste peremen. Media Sankt-Peterburga*. Tampere: Tampere University Press.

Pasti, S. (2005) 'Two generations of contemporary Russian journalists', *European Journal of Communication*, 20 (1): 89–115.

Pasti, S. (2006) 'Concepts of professional journalism: Russia after the collapse of communism', in F. Marcinkowski, W.A. Meier and J. Trappel (eds) *Media and Democracy Experience from Europe*, Bern, Stuttgart, Wien: Haupt Verlag, 73–89.

Pasti, S. (2007) *The Changing Profession of a Journalist in Russia*, Tampere: Tampere University Press.

Pelevin, V. (1999) *Generation 'P'*, Moskva: Vagrius.

Public Expertise (2000) *Anatomiia svobody slova*, Moskva: Soiuz zhurnalistov Rossii.

Ratinov, A.P. and Efremova G.H. (1998) 'Analiz dannykh monitoringa 1997 goda Fonda zashchity glasnosti', in A.K. Simonov (ed.) *Chest', dostoinstvo i reputatsiia: Zhurnalistika i iurisprudentsiia v konflikte*, Moskva: Prava cheloveka, 194–236.

Roudakova, N. (2007) *From the Fourth Estate to the Second Oldest Profession: Russia's Journalists in Search of Their Public after Socialism*, unpublished doctoral dissertation, Stanford University, USA.

Russian Periodical Press Market 2006: Condition, Trends, Prospects (2006), Moscow: Federal Agency for the Press and Mass Communication of the Russian Federation. Online. Available www.fapmc.ru/ (accessed 10 June 2006).

Sorokin, P. (2006) *Sotsial'naia i kul'turnaia dinamika*, Moskva: Astrel'.

Saint Petersburg in the first half of 2006, Biannual Review, November (2006) Economic Monitoring of North-West Russia. Online. Available www.economicmonitoring.com/reports/?lang=en (accessed 10 September 2008).

St Peterburgskie Vedomosti (2006) 'Konstantinov Andrei Dmitrievich', 20 May 2006.

Trenin, D. (2006) 'Sdelka Putina s Amerikoi ne sostojalas''. Online. Available www.polit.ru/analytics/2006/07/06/trenin.html (accessed 10 June 2006).

VCIOM (2007) 'Opredelennye samye prestizhnye professii', *Vzgliad Delovaia Gazeta*. Online. Available www.vz.ru/society/2007/9/22/110521.html (accessed 25 June 2008).

Zaritskii, T. (2006) 'Tsennosti i identifikatsia molodogo pokolenia rossiiskoi i pol'skoi intelligentsii (po resul'tatam sravnitel'nogo issledovania studentov vuzov Moskvy i Varshavy)', *Vestnik obshchestvennogo mneniia Levada-Tsentr*, 5 (85): 51–86.

Zorkaia, N. (2005) 'Russkaia pressa: spetsifika publichnosti', *Vestnik obshchestvennogo mnenia Levada-Tsentr*, 5 (79): 58–66.

Part 2

Biopolitics of the media

4 'We must all give birth: That's an order'

The Russian mass media commenting on V.V. Putin's address

Arja Rosenholm and Irina Savkina

> And now for the most important matter. What is most important for our country? The Defence Ministry knows what is most important. Indeed, what I want to talk about is love, women, children. I want to talk about the family, about the most acute problem facing our country today – the demographic problem.
>
> (Putin, accessed 24 October 2009)

With these words President Putin ensured his listeners' attention and shifted his rhetoric to the demographic situation in the country in his annual 'Address to the Federal Assembly of the Russian Federation' on 10 May 2006. Putin took up three issues: the death-rate, the birth-rate and immigration. A special programme was to be initiated to 'stimulate' the birth-rate, including special financial and other measures to 'support young families and women who have decided to have children.'[1] Of the three topics the media picked out the first – the fertility rate. The newspaper *Izvestiia* under the heading 'The country will not die out' writes that the speech was on 'questions of demography, or more specifically, on childbirth and government support for it' (Iz 11 May 2006).

The speech, especially the exhortation to 'have children', was vividly and broadly commented on in the Russian mass media, both the newspapers and the Internet. This chapter focuses on the reaction of the Russian media and on the kind of speech the media discourse constructed. Rather than the demographic policy as such, our main object of interest here is the fact that the speech was eloquently quoted, and the way it was quoted by the media in negotiating itself into competing political positions. We ask how the speech and the media constitute each other. Of special interest is the way the overall linkage between gender and nation constitutes other current discourses. What kinds of positions are offered to readers in public discourse, who is to be addressed and with what kind of rhetoric?

The main body of material comprises 117 articles published between 11 May and 30 September 2006. They were taken from 15 publications – nine daily newspapers,[2] four weekly newspapers[3] and two weekly magazines[4] – that responded to and commented on the demographic section in President Putin's speech. Some of the articles were available as paper copies, but most of the material was retrieved from the databank *Integrum,* using the search term '*rozhdaemost'*' ('birth-rate'). The publications selected for this chapter cover a variety of ideological programmes without particular format, so that they may be said to reflect the view of the media for 'all', 'the people', the 'mass reader'.

The media discourse clearly manifests the political significance of the demographic debate, not least due to its cumulative power: the discourse on demography and reproduction becomes a nodal point, which draws together a wide range of discourses and spheres of life, shedding light on the diverse interpretations of the intensive social, political and cultural transformations under way in Russia today. This chapter analyses the way the rhetoric used by the media on the topic of 'stimulating the birth-rate' helps to (re-)construct the plots that draw together the concepts of gender and nation. The notions are indeed closely intertwined, and, as we shall see, the ways in which they become linked in media discourse confirm what, for example, Rivkin-Fish has already pointed out:

> indeed, the monitoring of fertility rates and attempts to manipulate them constitute a primary vehicle for nationalist revival in contemporary Russia. [...] With discussions of fertility rates closely linked to issues of women's sexual, reproductive, and professional practices on the one hand, and national survival on the other, reproductive politics represents an arena of central importance for analyzing the mutually constitutive entities of gender and nation in contemporary Russia.
>
> (Rivkin-Fish 2006: 152)[5]

Media discourse as rhetoric

Our question of how the implicit linkage between gender and nation is constituted in media discourse underlines the productive power of symbol-creating language and its rhetorical practices. We draw attention to the dialogical contact between reality and language as an autonomous element in the symbolic order of society (Parker 1992; Fairclough 1992; Potter 1996). Media discourse is a speech act characterised by immanent instability. Accordingly, we will focus on the way media discourse creates arguments and (counter) meanings as a part of communication, and by rhetorical positioning places gender and nation – particularly unstable entities – at the centre of negotiation between criticism and justification, discursive matrices of past and present (Billig 1996: 121).

From the rhetorical point of view, as Kenneth Burke (1969a: 26) has pointed out, it is the repetition that is of interest. The current media discourse repeats and reiterates existing meanings and refers to discursive matrices from earlier demographic debates. This clearly emerges when we consider the linguistic conventions and paradigms which Rivkin-Fish brings out in her work on Soviet and post-Soviet demographic research. The familiar terms comprise alarm at the size and quality of the Russian nation from the 1990s, an imagery of impending national 'catastrophe' and 'genocide of the Russian people', the 'marriage of Post-Soviet reproductive politics and vibrant nationalism', and the hegemonic pronatalism of the whole Soviet era in general (Rivkin-Fish 2006: 155–8). Repeated quotations assert the message, or as Burke (1969a: xiii, 20–9) puts it, 'identification', as a key concept in rhetorical persuasion, is established and stabilised by repetition and quotation, which the audience can adopt, deconstruct or demystify. We inquire here into the material of its rhetorical identifications, i.e. what are the plots by which the media attempt to persuade the reading public, what are the views the authors share with the readers that enable rhetorical persuasion to overcome controversies.

The media reviewed here show that for the reader to be convinced of the argumentation, a clear and appealing story must be offered. In the process of persuasion not only rhetorical strategies but also unconscious motives of identification are upheld. Stories are needed to draw complex phenomena together in causal relations, and to ponder the dire prospects predicted for the future, e.g. whether there will be any future for Russia without her children, as '[w]e find ourselves in dangerous proximity to the ultimate limit beyond which depopulization becomes simply inevitable' (RG 18 July 2006).

Narrative plots reinforce belief in causalities and introduce order into the world with agents assigned to roles similar to those in a drama 'treat[ing] language and thought primarily as modes of action' (Burke 1969b: xxii, also 60–1). In our 'media drama', we find three master plots of 'identification', which overlap and compete with each other. The most appealing 'representative anecdotes' (Burke 1969b: 59) create and order the 'facts' in such a way as to gain the readers' acceptance; 1) the story of Russia in danger, 2) the story of the love and marriage of Mother Russia with Father State and 3) the story of doubt and deceit.

Parallel to their political underpinnings, the narratives evince two tendencies, both familiar from Russian cultural grammar: the one interpretation of development is sympathetic to the shift towards a 'Western' and 'European' mentality, whereas the other is of a more fundamental nature, implying that there should be no change at all, or that change should be sought in the glorious but vanished Russian past. Despite their conflicting rhetorical identifications and divisions, both approaches share the significance of gender as a central category of the Russian national identity, which, like all national identities, as Goscilo and Lanoux point out, is 'historically grounded on notions of masculinity and femininity' (Goscilo and Lanoux 2006: 3 and 9, also Yaval-Davis 1997). National identity exists in categories based on the gendered duality of Father-State and *Matushka-Rus'*: the state is equated with historical temporality and its great men, whereas the nation (*narod*) is associated with the amorphous life-giving force of Mother Russia (Goscilo and Lanoux 2006: 4). The media discourse on the birthrate and fertility feeds on a complexity of this gendered distinction between the Father-State and the feminised nation-body, intersecting in symbolical, biological and socio-cultural spheres.

Despite differences in scope, the three plots tell stories of the Motherland (*Rodina*) and the Fatherland (*Otechestvo*). They are 'cultural constructs', as Irina Sandomirskaia (Sandomirskaia 2001: 23, 24) has called the groups thus signified, which have their being in discourse, as do *Rodina* and *Otechestvo*, not so much as geographical or administrative entities but rather as groups of metaphors and plots intimating the social and cultural unity of individuals within a collective state. The space of national unity offered by *Rodina* and *Otechestvo* overlaps with that of a metaphorical family – being constituted in media speech via its negativity, as the lost ideal Russian family of the past (e.g. LG 19 July 2006 and RG 18 July 2006). The connotations of the metaphors 'family' and 'birth' motivate the reader to identify with the territory and its inhabitants. Cultural and physical spaces tend to mingle and the metaphors of (giving) birth and closeness to family and to one's 'own' community offer the reader a country, a land inhabited by *our* people, born by *our* women and not by immigrants: 'In Moscow the population is of course growing. But is this not to a significant extent because of immigrants?', asks the reader (KP 19 May 2006). Another voice answers: 'They will produce children. But look at who and whom... We must induce the Russians to have children, otherwise in ten years or so the Chinese and Vietnamese will easily surpass us' (KP 11 May 2006). The media present the different voices of readers, experts, commentators and journalists; the voices are serious, full of pathos, or else they are ironical, yet for all their differences the rhetorical repetitions reveal that when the authors use the politically correct terms of *Rossiian* (citizen of the Russian Federation) and *Rossiiskii* (Russian), referring to the civic Russian nation, whose members are all citizens of the Federation, they in fact basically imply ethnic 'Russian', indicating that the Russians should not lose out to non-Russians in the fertility race.[6] This grows evident when we look at the media plots, especially that which tells of the suffering nation, living under threat, as Russia is said to be.

A Russian grammar of (dual) motives: Money or love?

The various authors address the project of 'stimulating fertility' via sub-projects by which they emphasise the uniqueness of the Russian nation; they negotiate a new – post-Gorbachevian – gender contract with the wage-earning woman as mother,[7] and discuss the issue of unflagging trust in a strong state. This mediated world is built up of vocabularies that serve as authoritarian terms structuring the scope necessary for adaptation to a world of multiple identifications. We find culturally engaged 'terministic points of view' (Burke 1969a: 91–117), which, as Gusfield (1989: 35) puts it, 'prefigure and typify situations, becoming "ultimate endings" to thought and speech'. Such a prefiguring structure in the media discourse follows the cultural paradigm of duality in selecting vocabularies and organising the world (see Lotman and Uspenskii 1996: 219–53). Worlds depicted in dual terms – inscribed in the central distinctive categories of East and West, old and new, good and bad, and in the binary gender structure of the national identity discourse – seem simpler, more united and coherent than the real world. Accordingly, the discourse on fertility gives us a reduced circumference, which brings about a reduction of motives; the reduction is represented in a competition between 'money' and 'love'. On the one hand, fertility is discussed in a positive context of pragmatic material stimuli such as loans, childcare benefits and the 'basic maternal capital'. On the other, a markedly dubious voice is saying that 'the solution lies not only in money' (Gaz 16 May 2006). Not only pragmatic reforms are important; 'what was most interesting to the majority in the population was, without doubt, that part of Putin's speech where he spoke in poetic vein of the main thing of love' (MK 11 May 2006). 'Love – it is an important word', we read in *Komsomol'skaia Pravda* (KP 22 June 2006). The artist Nonna Mordiukova points out: 'Read the President's order carefully. Yes, he did speak of money. But he began with love' (KP 11 May 2006). Another article aims at a balance, asking: 'Will love and money save Russia?' (KP 11 May 2006). This dual vocabulary of money and love, which pervades the entire media material emphasises, on the one hand, the pragmatic necessities of the global monetary and economic rationalism of socio-political reforms; on the other, however, the semiotic code of love gives rise to a kind of mystic and moral–philosophical discourse. It carries with it ideal Russian values with an implied cultural self-image of reader-citizens as victimised, deceived pawns in state officials' and politicians' corrupt games. It is the contradictory locus of a rhetorical identification that the heterogeneous audience shares, be they liberal-Western oriented, nationalist or gender-consciously motivated: while money is linked to Western values, to rationalism and soullessness, love should represent Russia with its idealised selflessness reflecting orthodox moral values.

In point of fact, this ambivalent media speech focusing simultaneously on money and love bears a character competitive in the sense of Nancy Ries' formulation of the discursive logic of Russian litanising as a speech genre (Ries 1997: 83–8, 105ff.). Although the authors are open to the central notion that money is needed for social reform to 'stimulate fertility', simultaneously money is perceived to be inadequate, even a threat to society's moral self-consciousness: 'The self-esteem of a society may deteriorate by reason of increasing economic indicators' (NG 26 July 2006). What seems to give the discourse its dynamic is what is in fact *not* there, the emphasis on loss, what is lacking, as love is claimed to be. With its mythic connotations retrieved from Russia's 'golden past' (*zolotoi vek*), the lament at the lack of love tends to outweigh pragmatic orientations. This competition between ultimately incompatible entities endows the media discourse with a contradictory and dual character; the political dialogue with its pragmatic scope is partly obscured in a diffuse and vague commentary guided by moral virtues, the 'spiritual-moral coordinates' (*dukhovno-nravstvennye koordinaty*, Iz 30 May 2006), which join love and goodness in the contest against money and worldly evil. Love endows the land with its poetic beauty, its sacred title and the name of a cult, *Rodina*, which appears beside the proper name *Rossiia* (see also Sandomirskaia 2001: 148). The Russian lack of freedom and wealth, the characteristic vocabulary for Western societies, finds compensating power in the specific spiritual values of love, which, as the media discourse proposes, reveals something uniquely Russian.[8]

The dual grammar of motives represented by money and love is also inscribed within the three master plots engaging the terms nation, state and gender. The plots situate readers differently. We would distinguish a) the national locus of 'we Russians feeling threatened', b) the gendered locus with naturalised roles of women as mothers protected by the Father state, and men as sexual heroes, and c) the locus of 'real' readers and groups with different interests who feel deceived by the promises of politicians and state officials.

The story of the endangered Russian gene-pool

The first story is subsumed under one of the culturally implicit pre-agreements, i.e. those unspoken starting-points and value criteria of a *locus*, as Perelman and Olbrecht-Tyteca put it (Perelman and Olbrecht-Tyteca 1971: 67–92 and Perelman 1982: 21–32), which exist beyond the field of rhetorical disagreement. This is the locus where the Russian people (*narod)* appear endangered and the motherland is seen as a victim:[9] the future of the land is under threat via the Russian gene-pool, and it is thus a patriotic duty to rescue the *Rodina* and the *Otechestvo*-state by producing more children in the sense envisaged in the fertility programme; the article 'Russia is emptying' in *Moskovskii Komsomolets* (MK 30 June 2006) underscores that 'there is no alternative for the patriotic-minded Russian citizen. If you wish to help Russia (*Rossiia*, A.R., I.S.) – have children!' This is the tone and vocabulary of many slogan-like newspaper headlines calling the citizen to battle on behalf of Russia's future children, to save the *Rodina*: 'Have Three Children – Save the Motherland!' (KP 15 May 2006), 'Let's Give Birth to a Patriot' (NI 27 October 2006), 'All Must Give Birth' (Gaz 16 May 2006), 'Only One Solution – Have More Children!'(NV, No. 23, 2006).

The *locus* of this threat draws its historical currency from the repository of the Russian awareness. In this tradition the Fatherland is in constant danger, and it is precisely the state of being under threat that confers a residual vestige of legitimacy on the existence of the Fatherland. According to this ideological tradition it is normal to be threatened. The discourse on the nation becomes a mythological narrative of 'a local apocalypse'.[10] Being in jeopardy is a generally accepted cultural code with values appealing to the collective memory of the Russian audience 'imagined' (Anderson 1983) as a nation of 'we Russians', 'unique' and 'under threat'.

The *locus* of uniqueness implies Russia's geopolitical and cultural position between East and West and is reinforced by an emphasis on the genetic continuity of the Russian people under threat from hostile forces, both within and outside the country. This national self-image of uniqueness draws upon the Russian cultural memory and is permanently reinforced by rhetorical repetitions that embrace the paradigm of 'negative identity', a concept that the Russian sociologist Lev Gudkov (Gudkov 2004) has coined as being one of the Russian auto-stereotypes. Contemporary readers are reminded of wars, sacrifices, sufferings and victories as an exhortation to a united nation faced with an enemy – a stranger; internal and external threat. The lexicon of defence and defiance in the face of enemies revives 'facts' from the Russian and Soviet history of turmoil (revolutions, wars, *perestroikas*), as well as rhetorical slogans exhorting to collective mobilisation, familiar from the Soviet jargon: Member of Parliament E. Lakhova has said at a press conference: 'Lenin said: 'learn, learn and learn', and Putin said: Give birth, give birth, give birth!' (MK 22 May 2006). Alongside the fields of war and revolution, an analogue for the current demographic struggle is to be found in the great but challenging conquest of the Cosmos:

> There are no analogues to the measures which have to be taken in Russia today, neither in the past nor in the world. The costs and difficulties are not comparable even with those of conquering the cosmos in the Soviet era.
>
> (MK 30 May 2006)

These implicit assumptions are constructed by reproduction and repetition of national, religious, cultural and mythical elements, which appeal to readers' tacit motivations and stimulate their belief in a better future for which one should be ready to fight – men as virile warriors (*bogatyry*), women as intuitive and potential mothers. 'Russia', in this discourse, is not only a territory but rather a symbolic system, a 'rhetorical machine' (Sandomirskaia 2001: 157), which circulates a universal imagery of time and power into figures and symbols that make 'us' imagine 'ourselves' as part of the nation.

The discourse on the nation is imbued with a mythical and moral rhetoric. It includes the central metaphor of *narod* (people, folk, populace), pointing to the collective consciousness of Russianness as a source of national and ethnic virtues. The eternal battle between the moral values of good and evil, genuine and artificial – '*istinnoe*' and '*lozhnoe*' (MN, No. 20, 2006) – is complemented by other familiar Russian dichotomies such as past versus future, spirit versus body, high versus low, East versus West, we and the others. The dual pattern contains, on the one hand, an entire chronicle of the suffering and poverty of the people, and on the other the *narod* is also rewarded, in the form of a recompense of moral wealth: if Russia is poor compared to 'well-nourished Europe', Putin is claimed to have given his people the 'energy of self-dignity' (Iz 25 May 2006).

Analogically to the cultural dynamics of 'lamentation', the present life is seldom valued as anything positive or adequate. Instead, the perspective more often reverts to the past, notwithstanding lost ideals and resources; the pragmatism of social reforms is not sufficient and cannot bring about positive results if national self-dignity (*dostoinstvo*), with its genuine sources in the Russian people and their spiritual values, is overlooked. The perspective activates an anachronistic parlance born of victorious national traditions: the problem of fertility will be solved, as 'We will succeed in this because there is a special Russian mentality and tradition'. As one official asserts:

> Because of the Russian (*rossiiskii*, A.R., I.S.) mentality – which is a special one. Time moves on, but overall we have to return to what has made Russia (*Rossiia, A.R., I.S.*) strong – her traditions. It was not by chance that the President spoke of family values, of a family.
>
> (MK 25 May 2006)

The media insistently claim that the Russian people have already begun the process of 'dying out' (*vymiranie*): the key words are 'national catastrophe', 'threat to national security' (*ugroza natsional'noi bezopasnosti*), 'annihilation of the population', depopulation (*ubyl'*), degeneration (*degradatsiia*) and 'moral catastrophe'. It is not only communist and nationalist supporters who are inclined to the most alarmist reporting; the discourse is quite widely conducted in an apocalyptic parlance, which motivates the majority's task to 'save' the nation. The call of Solzhenitsyn to 'save the nation' is quoted both by President Putin and in media discourse (e.g. Iz 11 May 2006, also Iz 25 May 2006).

What Goscilo and Lanoux (2006: 10) have called the 'irresistible pull of tradition', invoked by titles such as 'Russian Cross Over Russia' (*Rossiia*, A.R., I.S.) (RG 18 July 2006), 'Children We Lose?' (Iz 31 May 2006), 'Russia (*Rossiia*, A.R., I.S.) is becoming empty' (MK 30 June 2006), 'That the candle would not go out' (AiF, No. 20, 2006) and 'Good and Evil Changing Places' (MN, No. 20. 2006), consists in abstract religious–philosophical concepts of the great spiritual strength of the Russian people. The rhetorical perspective of high spirituality tends to close the discourse even before social–political arguments are developed. Parallel to the pragmatism of the demography discourse, the *locus* of 'saving the nation' draws on morally oriented arguments. This intermingling of motifs makes for an effect of diffuse and highly loaded discourse deployed by cultural stereotypes, which together resist analysis of the political consequences of imperial and socially elitist distinctions in the population. The national identification brings with it an imagery of enemies; external and internal, foreign and Other, as, to follow Gudkov's conception, it is the foreigner (*chuzhoe*) who will mark the outer border of what is 'our own', the boundaries of the understanding and identification of the group, while simultaneously the function of the Other (*drugoe*) is to point from within, i.e. from the point of view of values common to the group, to the cultural limits of the 'we group', of the zone of 'ours', of 'our kind' (Gudkov 2005: 14–15).

External enemies are those who bear various liberal–pragmatic and foreign values not in harmony with Russian spiritual tradition, and seek to destroy the 'buttresses' (*ustoi*) of society and to 'spoil' (*razvrashchaiut*) potential Russian mothers with emancipatorian ideas and a taste for the easy life. The 'foreigners' are represented by a symbolical America, Europe, the West *in toto*, and the 'fifth column' within the country, i.e. the liberals and the feminists. The threat is suspected to emanate from a conspiracy of the Western countries to introduce their secularised family values and sex education into Russia, supported by their Russian counterparts, the Bolsheviks and the 'liberals' – as we read in the article 'The Great October Sexual Revolution' (in AiF No. 21, 2006).

The internal 'foreigners' in this demographic discourse are shaped by the concepts of 'islamisation' (also '*kitaizatsiia*', 'Chinaisation') and 'lumpenisation'. The word '*islamizatsiia*' (IZ 25 May 2006) manifests the anxiety felt in the face of ethnic Others, above all the Islamic population in the Caucasus, with their large families posing a threat to Russian preeminence, as do also the Chinese population and other migrants into Russian territory. This is pointed out in an article asking 'Must We Beseech Tadzhiks to work here?' (MK 30 June 2006), implicitly suggesting that this is one of those 'desperate means' in the situation of 'demographic suicide' of the Russian population (e.g. NI 1 June 2006).[11] The other term '*lumpenizatsiia*' (Iz 25 May 2006), familiar from Marxist and Soviet jargon, is used to exclude the Others within, the poorest Russians, the alcoholics and 'outsiders'. Their contribution to the 'genuine' and 'clean' biogenetic entity of Russian 'blood' is not desired. A young reader answers the question of a journalist: 'The Caucasus has become quite impudent. They also breed like rabbits... There will be no Russians left, that's what you will achieve' (MK 15 May 2006). Physicians from a Moscow gynaecological clinic state: 'We expect rather a flood of alcoholics and migrants from the Caucasus and from Central-Asia. Yet the indigenous Moscow population will produce children as it has until now' (KP 11 May 2006). The usage of the word '*lumpenizatsiia*' reveals an immanent contradiction in the nation discourse; whereas the *narod* is offered as a sacred unity on the one hand, the same discourse, leaning on the tenets of biology, reproduces its Others as excluded from the national unity. There should be more Russians, but only of good 'quality'.

The moral debate appears in media discourse as a hegemonic strategy. It emphasises the spirituality and religious–philosophical style shared by specialists and scholars alike, invited to make an unbiased or 'scientific' analysis of the declining birth-rate, as here in the article 'Support Does no Harm', by the Director of the Centre for Demographic Research:

> The problem of childbirth lies on another level [not economic, AR, IS] which is closely connected with the system of spiritual and moral coordinates and social values, and no economic stimulation is able to repair a poor birthrate.
> (Iz 30 May 2006)

The media specialists use an abstract discourse based on hegemonic concepts such as genuine national values, Russian spirituality and moralistic criteria. This 'spiritualised' rhetoric, harking back to the genuine 'Russian Soul', brings with it a dualism of secularisation and sanctification; of money and of love, of Western pragmatism and Russian spiritual uniqueness. The very embodiment of this cultural dualism is a Russian woman who is to be saved for her own good from her earthly and 'free' yearnings into the collective unity of traditional Russian values.

Holy matrimony: Russian mother and state-husband

The litany reproduces the cultural salience of Russia as long-suffering, enduring and tragic. In the cultural memory this uniqueness is associated with the feminine, including the country (*strana*) and the motherland (*rodina*), values from Old Russia allegorised in the person of a genuine Russian woman. Woman's role in the media drama is limited. She is to be saved, as mother and moral inspirer. Simultaneously, the rival grammars of money and love also define women's identification as contradictory: on the one hand, pragmatic support with a developed infrastructure (with kindergarten facilities etc.) should encourage women to combine maternal and professional duties; on the other, we may ask whether Russian women, if involved by the cultural memory that legitimates the Fatherland only in its 'negative identification', as existing under threat, can be anything more than mothers giving birth to future soldiers. Both options emphasise the role of the state, or rather of a hybrid of State and *Rodina*, to both of which citizens must pay their duties, simultaneously. Rather than being heirs to their own parents, children belong to the state. In complete analogy with Soviet rhetoric, the post-socialist discursive state acts as a surrogate body harnessing for its purposes idioms of feminine and masculine, metaphors of childhood, and symbolic constructions of home and family (Sandomirskaia 2001: 116; Buckley 1989: 171–82).

Obviously a variety of bodies are involved. The media texts play, both explicitly and implicitly, upon the lexica of 'birth' – of giving birth (*rozhat'*), woman in labour (*rozhenitsa)* and the native land, i.e. the Motherland (*Rodina*) – visualised e.g. as a pregnant Motherland, '*Rodina-Mat'* calling' (AiF No. 20, 2006). A woman's body is metaphorised as the Motherland and, accordingly, is subsumed under the interests of the state, which also motivate the sanctification of maternity. We find that the main responsibility for increasing the birth-rate is assigned to women, whereas men are absent, not part of the family, not trusted as partners in the home: 'I think that women do not have children because they don't trust their men', says engineer Verbin in the article 'Everybody should be given a Sex Passport' (RG 30 June 2006). A rare article, 'Thing-Children-Thing' points out that for a happy life a child also needs a father, but that hardly anything is said about the fathers (MK 12 May 2006).

Men being thus absent, it is logical to find the state in the role of the father, creating a family with a Russian mother. The state is appealed to, as it is rewarded: 'if the state will help us, women say. The main thing is that the state remembers us, values us and reaches out its helping hand', notes the article 'No Mercy on our Bellies' (RG 12 May 2006), and in another article, 'Bless the Woman', we read: 'Material support from the state, I think, plays a colossal role in a woman's decision to have not only one, but two children' (RG 12 May 2006). The alliance between the Russian woman and the Father-state is, as we see it, no new phenomenon. It rather confirms the thesis of Oleg Riabov, who emphasises hierogamy – the holy marriage of the Ruler with the Earth – a significant cultural phenomenon in Russian national discourse (Riabov 2007: 56, 119). Various rhetorical strategies attribute to the state the role of father in the current family, in accordance with the old Russian imagery of *Batiushka*-Tsar and *Matushka-Rus'*. We find this in various idiomatic combinations such as 'children of the state' (RG 18 July 2006), the 'President's children' (MK 26 July 2006), 'children of P' – in the double meaning of children of Putin's '*Poslanie'* (official document of V.V. Putin, A.R. and I.S.) (MK 12 May 2006), or titles like 'Medvedev's Children' (NI 22 May 2006). The metonymic shift in many titles replaces the state with the name of a well-known state official, e.g. governors in titles like 'Father-Hero Georgii Boss' (NG 19 June 2006) or 'Rossel' is expecting an addition' (NG 19 June 2006), and in male status such as 'Boris Nemtsov, Standard-bearer of the Fatherland's fertility' (Iz 16 May 2006).There are several episodes with the president or a state official acting in the role of 'father': in an article headed 'No Baby Boom yet' (NI 13 October 2006), we may read how President Putin visited a maternity hospital in the town of Kurgan with mothers presenting him their new babies to share their happiness with him, and, as the vaguely suggestive tone gives to understand, 'both mums promised the president to go on working on the demographic problem'. The article on 'Medvedev's Children' calls Dimitrii Medvedev 'the chief welfare officer for fertility', assuming that the title may be a sign of his becoming the future father of the nation (NI 22 May 2006). State power and its metonymic representatives, politicians and officials, replace biological fathers, form the family with women who are subjected to the patriotic duty to give birth. Whereas woman is symbolically represented by the mothers of the nation, the father-state and power are masculinised, acting out the role of defender, patron and teacher. Most articles approach the topic from a playful or ironic angle, yet their rhetorical constructions imply the idea of both men and women as predestined to biological roles – women as birth-giving bodies subjected to the state, and men begetting for the state. There is, however, a clear difference between the mother speech (of love) and eroticised male sexual heroism: men may be absent as fathers of the family but emerge in the role of sexual giants.

Men's absence from the family is explained thus: the context where men appear in the discourse deals with the problem of mortality caused by alcoholism. When debate turns to mortality and men, there is no admonition of men's responsibility to refrain from drinking or to look after themselves; rather women are urged to induce their men to unlearn their bad drinking habits: 'In order to draw men away from alcohol, they have to be kept busy', thus the article 'Women Fighting for their Men's Health' (KP 22 May 2006) quotes from a speech by the president of the 'Ural Association of Women', Vera Sokolkina. Men are not regarded as autonomous subjects responsible for their own health. In the demography discourse they are given a more 'pleasurable' part. *Komsomol'skaia Pravda* (11 May 2006) notes: 'In women's consultations all the talk was – about Putin'; the President inspires mythical atamans to command their fellows to fulfil the virile 'order', as also suggested by the title 'The Ataman Ordered: All Have to Produce Children' (RG 11 July 2006). Male participation becomes eroticised by ambiguous imagery and suggestive connotations playing on pleasure: 'new organs are created by officials, this time a child-creating organ' (NI 22 May 2006), 'each man should get his own "sex passport"' (RG 30 June 2006), 'men are to be called to fight for a higher birth-rate' (KP 18 May 2006), the imagery of 'skirt as our rudder' (NG 31 May 2006), playfully parodying the Soviet slogan 'the party is our rudder', points out what is essential; implying a male perspective it claims that women should not wear unisex clothes but rather skirts to stimulate male participants. The male 'fight' for higher birth-rates is a heroic competition for power, imbued with erotic pleasure: *Argumenty i fakty* (AiF No. 20, 2006) quotes Vladimir Zhirinovskii: 'I will challenge Ziuganov to a duel, and promise that in 10 years I will have four children as my private contribution, but with him, nothing will change'.

A proper man should be an 'ataman', 'a regular guy and patriot' endowed with virility: 'Honour to Russia (*Rossiia*, A.R., I.S.)! Forward! For the Male Act!' (KP 20 May 2006).

At the same time, however, this glorification also glosses over some of the instability of the male sexual identity: 'Give a Strong Family', 'More Children – Beautiful and Clever!', 'Are there still Men in Russia or only *pediki*?' (KP 22 May 2006). The question of whether there are any real men left or only 'poofters', challenges 'real men' to take distance from what are called 'pederasts' ('*pediki*'). Naturalisation of gender by the binarities male versus female, natural versus unnatural, produces heterosexuality as a normative discourse, and homosexuality – here identified in *pediki* – as unnatural. Whereas 'maternal instinct' implies women's 'virtuous nature', the opposite is produced by 'unnatural' homosexuality, as demonstrated by a homophobic article on a planned gay parade in Moscow in *Moskovskie novosti* (No. 20, 2006). The demography discourses exert an immanently two-sided effect; while seeking to make sense of the problems, they also marginalise other discourses. Both sides of the discourse, production and suppression, exist in parallel: in order for there to be something, there must be something which is not: What should be is 'normal' heterosexuality, as against 'abnormal' homosexuality and women's refusal to bear children. The sexuality debate is made public in contradictory approaches, highly eroticised imagery intersecting with a suspicious and body-abnegating anti-attitude to sex education. *Argumenty i fakty* (No. 20, 2006) published an article on 'The War against Russia', in which the author opposes any programmes of sex education. Accordingly, enlightenment on safe sex, contraception and family planning is a Western plot against Russia. Women who find that there is something like 'safe sex' will consequently not give birth to children. The Director of the Centre for Demographic Research, Igor Chindin, maintains the modern sexuality dispositive with other experts – scholars, medical specialists, gynaecologists and political authorities – who produce an ensemble of discourses representing powerful institutions (Government, Church, institutions for demographic research, etc.) and leave their mark on laws – on abortion, adoption, etc.

'But where is the mother, where the madonna and the child?'

The media discourse constitutes sexuality as a utilitarian and functional performance imbued with an anti-individual character. When readers are addressed in general, sexuality is 'purged' of eroticism, 'free love' belongs to the Soviet era and is morally frowned upon. 'Genuine' moral values should be sought in the utopian past, which glorifies virginity (*tselomudrennost'*) at the expense of sexual pleasures. This renunciation, however, is expected only of women. The author of an article in the journal *Moskovskie novosti* (MN No. 20. 2006) argues that girls who do not protect their virginity until after marriage are guilty of reversing 'the places of good and bad' in the modern world. The female body becomes an object of control. As female sexual identity is exclusively associated with reproduction, woman as mother symbol represents, accordingly, 'a means of homogenizing the otherwise differentiated national consciousness in the post-Soviet states, and has proved to be a useful instrument in nationalist conflicts', as Rosalind Marsh (Marsh 1998: 94) has written.

An important aspect of the demography campaign and comment on Putin's speech is that the very audience represented as the agent responsible for success in the campaign comprises women. Women – as mothers – are required as social and moral guardians to redeem their responsibilities vis-à-vis the state. The discourse on fertility concerns almost exclusively women. 'What did Putin offer the Russians, or rather, the female citizens of Russia?' (*rossiianki*, A.R, I.S.) asks *Moskovskii Komsomolets* (MK 11 May 2006). And another article answers: 'there is a serious obstacle – so little desire for children among the female residents in the capital'. 'Moscow women take marriage and divorce very liberally', writes *Komsomol'skaia pravda* (KP 19 May 2006). Women and childbirth are linked together both by religious–mythological ideologemes and by essentialist categories such as women's 'natural predetermination', 'women's responsibility before nature and state'.

The media discourse reconfigures the relations between citizens and the state and the assertion of political and moral legitimacy. Women and men are depicted as particular kinds of citizen whose roles and responsibilities are defined on the basis of politically useful categories such as biology/nature, social norms and the ideologies of the rational subject. The central social constructs – gender and nation – are subjected to naturalisation, turning normative heterosexuality into a hegemonic paradigm and women into potential mothers. In the great majority of the articles in question the word 'woman' is used as a synonym for 'mother'; *Rossiiskaia gazeta* (RG 12 May 2006) writes:

> Bless the Woman [...] for the land to overcome the crisis, the women of Russia (*Rossiia*, A.R., I.S.) need to give birth to more than two children [...]. If a woman in her twenties with intervals of one and a half to two years gives birth to three, four children, it will be useful both to her and to the children's health.

In numerous statements made at various press conferences, Ekaterina Lakhova, Chairwoman of the *Duma* committee for women's affairs, family and children, speaks for a fashionable mode of pregnancy; she advocates showing pregnant women on television with their 'beautiful pregnant bellies' (MK 25 May 2006). *Izvestiia* ran a headline: 'Make Pregnancy Fashionable' (Iz 17 May 2006). Women are somatised through the 'instinct to give birth', which should be stimulated. Titles such as 'Nine Months', 'What Comes into being in 9 Months' (PG 6 July 2006), 'It is Fashionable to be Pregnant' (MK 31 May 2006), 'We Must All Produce Children – that's an Order' (*Ogonek*, No. 20, 2006) form an important part of the 'body-making' naturalisation techniques.

How do women then lose their 'natural' virtues? The binarity of natural versus unnatural, good versus bad, is completed by the dualism of self-sacrifice versus egoism. American and Swedish feminists (e.g. *Ogonek* No. 45, 2006) represent the negative values of implicit and explicit Western egoism and careerism, turning women's 'self-realisation' (*samorealizatsiia*) into an irony. Women are blamed for the demographic problem in their desire for emancipation; moreover, feminism is a threat to the 'natural' heterosexual norm, equally to the various media, irrespective of their political orientation.

The gender discourse reorganises itself as a counterimage to what is regarded as 'Soviet': women now wishing to make a career forget their maternal sense of duty (*dolg*) and take an excessively liberal attitude to divorce and unregistered marriages. The attribute 'free' – a synonym for both the Soviet and the Western morale – is to be condemned and brought under control if women forget their maternal duty before the state. The ambitions of women to make a career is subverted as a pseudo-achievement after the years of (Soviet) equality ideology. An article on the 'Great Sexual Revolution' in *Argumenty i fakty* (AiF No. 21, 2006) explains what untold harm the Soviet period did to women with its policies of equality, free abortion and divorce, and the propaganda of 'free love'. Igor Beloborodov, Director of the Centre for Demographic Research, puts the problem quite clearly in an article headed 'The main thing would be for a desire to awaken in society to have children':

> the decree carries with it a positive contribution in the sense of creating a warmer attitude to family, motherhood and fatherhood. This is very important after decades of destructive policies which the Bolsheviks and their successors brought with them regarding family. Legalization of abortions and divorces, detachment of women from families and their integration into the process of production, the destruction of the Church – all this resulted in [...] a decrease in the birth-rate.
>
> (Gaz 16 May 2006)

Almost all the achievements of women's emancipation – education, participation in production, and the possibility of earning one's own money, planning the family, self-realisation, control over one's own body – are mistrusted, being seen as obstacles to women to accomplish their maternal and patriotic 'duty' – these being in the context one and the same thing: 'It is rather much to expect women, after being given the opportunity to enjoy higher education, to have 8–10 children, as did our grandmothers', notes the expert Irina Zbarskaia in the article 'Will Money or Love save Russia?' in *Komsomol'skaia pravda* (11 May 2006). 'What kinds of images of women are being circulated today?', asks the author of the article 'I will forget the image of mother' (KP 22 June 2006). There are many negative images of a woman who is

> either slave of her sex or a sexless mannish creature. [...] Either a tough business-woman, an avid careerist, or simply a feminist bent on celebrating with crazy Americans of similar mind [...] in the struggle against men – not for equality with them. [...] But where is the mother, the madonna with a child?
>
> (KP 22 June 2006)

Here to our mind is the key question in the whole discourse: 'But where is the mother, the madonna with the child?' (KP 22 June 2006). Idealisation – sanctification – is harnessed to producing a dualism of the good versus the bad woman. The 'good woman' is constituted by quotations from high culture and the moral resources of Russian female images. She is a Russian patriot who prefers 'self-sacrifice' to 'self-realisation' (*samorealizatsiia*). Positive values are morally 'genuine', values that can be found in the lost but ideal Russian past: motherhood, love, happiness with a child – on the one hand there is the religiously oriented rhetoric with its sentimental images of a mother bending over her child, as the holiest of configurations; on the other, condemnation and contempt for modern women's everyday dreams of professional success, travel or even having enough to eat (LG No. 23, 2006). The good Russian woman is 'Mother of God', she is Sophia, the spiritualised, eternal Woman, Mother Russia. She is positioned within nationally significant events from the past (e.g. victories in wars) and the history of great 'cultural–spiritual' and moral achievements. 'Woman's happiness' is embedded in traditional Russian family values; to 'save' the nation is 'to revert to the family values of our grandmothers and grandfathers [...], marriage should be registered and be forever', thus *Komsomol'skaia pravda* (KP 19 May 2006). In motherhood women find genuine happiness:

> "A woman's happiness" – the greatest happiness of all – is to be loved. In rejecting maternity, we reject love. Our future. Happiness and beauty. What can be more touching than a rounding belly with a new life beating? Or the first cry, the first smile, taking a baby to breast? No successful career, no journey to exotic places can give that magic feeling that awakens when the child shows his joy solely in the fact that his mother is bending over him. Yes, you can be rich, nourished and successful today. We can show our success, and hide our happiness...In order to solve the demographic problem, not only money is needed, but propaganda advocating a sound family, pregnancy, parenthood, normal human happiness.
>
> (LG No. 23, 2006)

As many other quotations show, here we also have the duality of love against money, not to be reconciled, not even in motherhood. Success, self-realisation and well-being emerge as antonyms to happiness and love, as not adaptable to the joys of self-denying motherhood. Simultaneously, the ideas of contraception, family planning and legalisation of abortion on social criteria are products brought to Russia by Western feminists in the 'War Against Russia' (AiF, No. 20, 06); thus warns Igor Chindin, Executive Director of the Centre for Demographic Research, that 'these criteria – poverty, bad living conditions, lack of a permanent job, divorce etc. – are shared by practically all women'. Accordingly, the opposition of good and bad women is supplemented by that of Russia versus the West, and the presentation of social problems in this context only appears as the pretext of a bad feminist-oriented woman anxious to avoid fulfilling her natural and patriotic duty.

The story of doubt and deceit: A counterposition?

The stories of childbirth give explanations and help to elucidate – at least for a moment – a complexity of social challenges; the narratives combine various phenomena by means of a causal logic, which creates order in the world in defining positions for friends and foes. For all the familiar narrative plots, however, the discourse on childbirth involves contradictory voices: many journalists, specialists and readers cannot accept that the state and the power invested in officials are convincingly cast in the role of a caring father to the mother-nation. At the same time, a large number of articles place their hopes in the state; as in Soviet times, many readers agree that they would be ready to have two or more children if only the state would guarantee them social benefits. We thus have both voices trusting in the 'helping hand' of the strong state and, equally strong, the voices of scepticism, irony, even cynicism. A third media plot involves the voices of doubt and mistrust.

Marked scepticism and distrust in the powers and their promises are heard, especially in readers' letters and comments on specialists' views, particularly in journals with a special readership and a special concept, either professionally, socially or on some specific topic. The sceptics quite explicitly name the social misery of families with children, particularly of women bringing their children up alone; the tone is disillusioned: 'Why produce children for a state which does not need us, [...] you give birth and the only thing you hear is that the State owes you nothing' (KP 20 May 2006). And, 'Nothing will be given to us! Personally, I see nothing good given by our state' (MK 15 June 2006).

Irony often pervades the tone on how to approach subjects of power and undermine the authority of those aiming to become symbolic fathers – of Putin or Medvedev, and the parties, usually of state officials of lower status. What is common among the diverse critical positions is the view that money is disappearing into officials' pockets, that bureaucrats only turn any problem into empty campaigning, 'a fashionable mode'; 'we are served only three menus: "*Code da Vinci*", childbirth in whose increase nobody believes, and Dima Bilan' (NG 2 June 2006). The quotation reveals the aesthetisation of politics as a rhetorical means of depoliticised discourse, and criticises the policy that seeks to convince the readers that there is no disagreement concerning the birth-rate campaign. Another critic comments: 'The absence of politics – is also politics' (Iz 11 May 2006). We find sceptical voices complaining that there is only empty talk without real action, that money is being misused only to increase the officials' own childbirth rate, as suggested in the article 'Lessons in Demagogy' in *Novye Izvestiia* (NI 23 May 2006, also NI 22 May 2006):

> The main problem is that in this broad struggle to increase the birth-rate we perceive a feature deeply rooted in official bureaucracy – the tendency to please the leaders rather than a striving for real change.

Nezavisimaia gazeta (30 May 2006) writes: 'The broad masses are still discussing the demographic theses of the President, while the officials are already beginning to breed like rabbits', pointing critically to the increase in the number of officials in general. An author from *Moskovskii Komsomolets* (12 May 2006) asks:

> how to avoid money meant for children being taken by bandits, stolen by officials, drunk by licentious parents. [...] Corrupt officials and those educated by television and beer will find a way to steal and waste the wealth. The officials are channelling the money into their own pockets.

The sceptical discourse of 'real' readers prefers a more realistic style with a tone free of idealising, openly laughing at the slogans urging us all to have children, and at the various somewhat diffuse *ad hoc* campaigns organised by officials, as in Ul'ianovsk with the campaign advocating giving birth to patriots on the day of the Russian Federation (NI 13 September 2007). Many of the voices are cynical: there is suspicion of promises, and disappointment and betrayal are also among expressions used. The speakers seek to bypass the nationalistic rhetoric and raise the problems they want to discuss, for example, the situation of homeless children, questions of adoption, mortality, the values of the individual, social–political reorganisation to help families and women to combine profession, career and childcare. Many speakers also tend to interpret the President's speech as part of a larger political game:

> Why does a country where children's homes are already overfilled need more children? Why give children to a society riddled with indifference, swindling and envy of others' good fortune, pathological xenophobia and drunkenness? These are things we need to save the Motherland (*Rodina*, AR, IS) from. And we are told only: have children, have children.
>
> (KP 20 May 2006)

> There is already a new generation [...] with life values totally other than to produce soldiers and workers for the country [...] people are different, they want to enjoy themselves, have a career, gather material goods in their lives, not give birth to children... There is no point in juggling with populist slogans.
>
> (Iz 17 May 2006)

The media seems to cultivate a kind of 'carnevalistic' dialogue; whereas the elite in their idealising, diffuse and abstract speech tend to banish reality and the individual female body from discourse, there are other voices attempting to restore 'reality', to deconstruct the images of ideal motherhood. There are opposing voices that distrust abstraction and visionary images. The hegemony of trust in the state is disturbed by fragmentary and individual voices of experience, by concrete and detailed narratives of people's lives. The most disillusioned voices belong to women who express their suspicion that, if there are no changes in women's everyday lives – including the socio-political infrastructure (kindergartens, healthcare, living conditions, combination of motherhood and profession, etc.) – women will refuse to have children. The official exhortations to 'Russian mothers' to give birth to new patriots are disparaged by women answering that they will not give birth to children whom the 'Fatherland' will only send as 'cannon fodder' in defence of nationalistic policies (NovG 15 May 2006).

Although the media discourse tends to devolve into appealing cultural narratives, it is by no means homogeneous, as shown above. There are conflicting voices, even if, as we see it, the critical potential of the diversity of ironic and sceptical positions does not evolve into productive criticism. The rhetoric of cultural stereotypes tends to close the door to social–political discourse. The discursive logic of irony and cynicism, even as it brings out pragmatic orientations, is not capable of developing any mediation between 'bad' state officials and 'good' citizens. Quite in line with the logics of litany, as Ries has pointed out (Ries 1997: 113–15), the logic of scepticism and cynicism will structure a contradictory logic between criticism and avoidance of confrontation between competing political ideas. Current issues of pragmatic socio-political reform become encoded by the rhetoric into mythical notions from the past, which will force the birth-rate discourse into the field of national identity. Drawing its legitimation from the national identity, the rhetoric can hardly offer a neutral forum for productive negotiation. Rather, as Michael Urban[12] has pointed out regarding the post-socialist political discourse, the logics of demonising the Other – politicians, the corrupt, the West, the feminists and finally, Russian women – also brand them as the 'aliens' responsible for Russia's troubles.

What characterises the media dialogue is that when readers criticise the impasses, voids and errors for which they blame politicians, state officials, bureaucrats and specialists, their litany also reaffirms a discursive logic, which does not encourage negotiation or mediation between different positions but rather reinforces the chasm of duality between good and evil others. The discursive logic, which, although implying cynicism, irony and despair, tends to separate the citizenry from political processes (Ries 1997: 115). The rhetoric of irony and distrust is directed against state proposals, yet simultaneously reinforces the belief that despite the proposed benefits, the ordinary people will ultimately be deceived, will become the hapless victims of selfish and crafty politicians. This position of reduced power does not encourage speakers to engage in political negotiation, but is more likely to reproduce the dual paradigm of villain and victim, ordinary and powerless citizens seeing themselves in the role of losers – and handing over to the state its legitimate role as a patron of the nation.

The latest reactions: What about love?

Has the media changed in its narratives on the demographic crisis? The latest reflections in the media follow the plot lines we already know from the year 2006.[13] The most popular is the story of success. A large number of articles loudly celebrates the increase in the birth-rate; the tone of the rhetoric resembles that of applause for the socialist achievements attained under the regime of the former communist party, and the technique of reporting from a particular locality gives the feeling of authenticity, as do the figures documenting the fulfilment of the task in 'Children's Arithmetic' (RG 12 March 2008). The emphasis on local success – in the Perm district, the Saratov district, in Arkhangel'sk, Irkutsk, Izhev or Udmurtia – depicts a vast land united, following the voice of Moscow and the Father-State: 'Children are born – the country becomes stronger', thus the journal *Edinaia Rossiia* (24 March 2008). The dual motives of pragmatism and sentimental imagery are again mingled; the rhetoric of 'demographic quartiles' (RG 10 April 2008) and the money talk in titles like 'Human capital – the main wealth of the region' (RG 5 March 2008) and 'Money for Mum' (RG 3 April 2008) aim to project an image of a future dynamic capitalist country, which, nevertheless, remembers to cherish its Russian values, couched in anachronistic and sentimental imagery of 'the maternal lot' (RG 18 April 2008) and how 'every little one is worth its weight in gold' (RG 25 April 2008).

Another leitmotif might be entitled 'Hurrah, But!'; it points out that concrete improvements, not noisy action, are needed. Many articles agree that the birth-rate is increasing, but lament that the infrastructure is not ready: there are not enough maternity clinics or qualified specialists, the system of healthcare is far from complete, there is a lack of nursery schools and kindergartens, young families cannot get cheap apartments (e.g. *Vedomosti* 29 April 2008, NovG 10 April 2008, NI 1 April 2008 and 26 March 2008; RG 9 April 2008 and RG 29 March 2008). The style of the criticism is neutral, avoids high rhetoric, authors merely list the shortcomings.

Deeply sceptical voices with the same arguments as two years earlier constitute the third approach: the reform is not going to be a success, quite the opposite. The tone of these voices is more disillusioned, even to the point of titles like 'Russia will die out' (*Vedomosti* 29April 2008) or 'False calculation indicators' (MK 26 March 2008), and articles accusing officials of 'cheating' and misleading the people, giving them false figures and nurturing expectations of a bright future.

We would like to close this chapter on the note struck by ex-president Putin when he asked what has become of the 'love, the women and children', which he mentioned in his speech in 2006. The topic of love is an essential part of the demography discourse – which has in the meantime crossed genre borders into the realm of fiction with the overawing family topic – not least because of the proclaimed 'year of the family' in 2008. The discourse on the birth-rate has shifted to that on the family. Much as in 2006 with the call to restore love to current values, in the year 2008 love offers one of the main fields of negotiation. Consequently, with love, meanings and values are given to family and gender: good love means family and children, bad love is 'childless and egoistic', to be resisted, as in the campaign against the advertising of contraceptives in Novosibirsk, mediated and encouraged by *Nezavisimaia gazeta* (7 April 2008). Good love is embodied by mothers whose 'lot' does not aim at any 'maternal capital', this being sooner a low thought, 'some feminist thing', as evaluated by a professor at Moscow State University, forcefully advocating families with several children (RG 5 March 2008). When love and family, as central 'indicators', are implied in the 'national idea', the country could be born united, and consequently, 'induce its many peoples to say "yes" to children' (LG 9 April 2008).

Putin emphasised love, family and children as elemental lexica in the demographic discourse, and the media take up this emphasis on love, which should infuse the demographic discourse. Yet in the Russian media context of the last two years, love is far from being inspiring, pleasurable or to be enjoyed 'egoistically' – not least for women. Rather, it is to be joined to the long list of litanies of Russia's human losses. It is still the lack of love that gives stimulus to the lament on 'moral decay' and the attempt to compensate the complex socio-political discourse challenged by the 'demographic crisis'. 'Love is in the air', and those concerned to say something new also end up quoting old identifications; thus Alla Kuz'mina, President of the interregional charity fund for the 'Russian family':

> What do we tell people today? Give birth! Here is money for it! But no-one talks about feelings. About what is called love, or perhaps honour [...]. No-one speaks of the spiritual and moral basis of man. All we can talk of today is statistics and marshalling facts. But a human being needs a home, because there it is warm and cosy, because there he is expected, there he can share his thoughts, he will find compassion. If Putin or Medvedev were to stand up on a podium today and begin to speak of love – they would not be understood. [...] Hence we need a society to take this up, to cry out for family values, and to create for the family a spiritual-moral relation.
>
> (NG 25 March 2008)

Love is upheld as the 'source and ground of being, making all else comprehensible',[14] analogous to other 'terministic screens' that direct their users to the ultimate end. Once action has been accounted for in terms of love and 'spiritual–moral' aspirations, there is scarcely an argument to be brought against them. Love, spirituality and high moral values constitute the Russian rhetorical strategy, which by reason of its abstractness and flexibility draws different readers together in the cultural memory, which can be adapted to a wide range of political discourses. Moral values and the ideal of spirituality entail those highly positive memories of which there remain but few from the past – after the victory in the Great War of the Fatherland and the contest for the Cosmos – to be adapted as a resource for the national identity.

But what will become of the political screen? Will not its users be carried to an ultimate end where the socio-political rhetoric is lost and gives place to mythical ideals of reality, for example those of absolute love and high spiritual values, which can hardly sustain an active subject in the pragmatic socio-political dialogue? Rather, the people are identified as subjected to those in power and their bureaucratic representatives as active agents of demographic policy with its clear-cut gendered roles: women as the audience addressed, to be persuaded into motherhood, forming the core of the Russian family, whereas men totally fail to fulfil the role of father in this future family unity.

Notes

1 The main focus of the speech was on childcare policies, which should stimulate fertility and encourage particularly the having of a second child. The speech's approach to demographic problems was economic and of a pragmatic nature: 1,500 rubles should be given as monthly childcare benefits for the first child under 18 months, and 3,000 rubles for the second. Wage-earning mothers should receive at least 40 per cent of their wages until the child reached 18 months. A new concept of benefit was introduced in the form of a 'basic maternal capital', consisting of a larger sum to be given to a mother when her second child turns three, whereby the money should be invested in loans, housing, the mother's pension or education of the child. The total amount of maternal capital for a mother of two children would be 250,000 rubles. Putin 2006.

2 *Gazeta* (Gaz), *Izvestiia* (Iz), *Komsomol'skaia pravda* (KP), *Moskovskii komsomolets* (MK), *Nezavisimaia gazeta* (NG), *Novaia gazeta* (NovG), *Novye izvestiia* (NI), *Parlamentskaia gazeta* (PG), *Rossiiskaia gazeta* (RG).

3 *Argumenty i fakty* (AiF), *Literaturnaia gazeta* (LG), *Moskovskie novosti* (MN), *Novoe vremia* (NV).

4 *Itogi*, *Ogonek*.

5 See also the work of Gal and Kligman on the issue of control over fertility and reproduction in reconstituting political agency and legitimacy for the political elite in post-socialist countries. Gal and Kligman 2000.

6 As to the differences between the predicates 'Russian' – *russkii* – and *rossiiskii* the historian Vera Tolz (1998) has identified five ways in which the Russian nation was defined in public discourse during the late 1990s: 1) '"Union" identity (the Russians as an imperial people, based on their mission to create a supranatural state); 2) the Russians as a nation of all eastern Slavs (including Belorussians and Ukrainians); 3) the Russians as a community of Russian speakers, regardless of their ethnic origin; 4) the Russians as defined racially; and finally 5) a civic Russian (*rossiiskaia*) nation, whose members are all citizens of the Russian Federation, regardless of their ethnic and cultural background, united by loyalty to the state and its constitution'. We thank Elena Trubina for drawing our attention to this article.

7 Our reading corresponds to that of Rotkirch, Temkina and Zravomyslova, who see President Putin's speech as representing a change to the Gorbachevian model appealing to women's 'essential' values as mothers and wives. Rotkirch, Temkina, Zdravomyslova 2007.

8 Discussing nationalism and tolerance in the Russian pro-regime mass media Tolkacheva and Akifieva also found that 'love' plays a role in the nationalistic discourse. While connected with certain spiritual values, love in this discourse signifies a Russian specificity, quite opposite to the assumed Western understanding of it as 'only sex'. For this reason those – non-Russian – others are to be pitied, despite their freedom and wealth. Tolkacheva and Akifieva 2008: 389.

9 In this sense the story is reminiscent of what Nancy Ries has identified as a 'Russophile Litany', Ries 1997: 102–5.

10 Sandomirskaia refers to the writings of A.S. Shishkov on the eve of the war of 1812, and how the speech of the Fatherland is constructed in the tradition of the Fatherland under threat, Sandomirskaia 2001: 166, 179.

11 See also the article by Mikhailovskaia, op.cit., pp. 63–8, who also points out how openly the view of 'ethnic purity' is discussed among the political elite. She shows how the members of the faction *Rodina* discussed in 2005 the legislative project of financial support for the third and the fourth child, the main idea of the discussants being that it is important to support the birth-rate among ethnic Russians, not among the whole population of the Russian Federation, as in regions such as the Caucasus, Kalmykiia, Chechniia or Karachaevo-Cherkessiia.

12 According to Urban, there is a parallel conception of the political dialogue: 'pragmatic orientations are overwhelmed by mythic notions retrieved from the past and the possibilities for political dialogue become lost in antipathetic claims pitched around competing ideas of national identity', Urban 1994: 737. See also Ries 1997: 113–4.
13 We studied a body of material including about 114 articles on the topic from the year 2008. The publications are *Argumenty i fakty*, *Vedomosti*, *Gazeta*, *Edinaia Rossiia*, *Izvestiia*, *Komsomol'skaia Pravda*, *Literaturnaia gazeta*, *Nezavisimaia gazeta*, *Novaia gazeta*, *Novye izvestiia*, *Rossiiskaia gazeta*, *Trud* and *Ogonek*. The latest material includes 114 articles from 1 March to 22 April 2008.
14 Gusfield discusses Burke's use of 'God-terms' such as money in modern Western societies in Burke's *Grammar of Motives*. Gusfield 1989: 35.

References

Material

Argumenty i fakty (AiF)
Edinaia Rossiia
Gazeta (Gaz)
Itogi
Izvestiia (Iz)
Komsomol'skaia pravda (KP)
Literaturnaia gazeta (LG)
Moskovskie novosti (MN)
Moskovskii komsomolets (MK)
Nezavisimaia gazeta (NG)
Novoe vremia (NV)
Novaia gazeta (NovG)
Novye izvestiia (NI)
Ogonek
Parlamentskaia gazeta (PG)
Rossiiskaia gazeta (RG)
Vedomosti

Anderson, B. (1983) *Imagined Communities: Reflections on the Origin and Spread of Nationalism*, London: Verso.
Billig, M. (1996) *Arguing and Thinking. A Rhetorical Approach to Social Psychology*, Cambridge: Cambridge UP.
Burke, K. (1969a) *A Rhetoric of Motives*, Berkeley, Los Angeles, London: University of California Press.
Burke, K.(1969b) *A Grammar of Motives*, Berkeley, Los Angeles, London: University of California Press.
Buckley, M. (1989) *Women and Ideology in the Soviet Union*, New York: Harvester Wheatsheaf.
Fairclough, N. (1992) *Discourse and the Social Change*, Cambridge: Polity Press.
Gal, S. and Kligman, G. (2000) *The Politics of Gender after Socialism: A Comparative-Historical Essay*, Princeton, NJ: Princeton UP.
Goscilo, H. and Lanoux, A. (2006) 'Introduction. Lost in the Myths', in H. Goscilo and A. Lanoux (eds) *Gender and National Identity in Twentieth-Century Russian Culture*. Northern Illinois: Northern Illinois University Press, 3–29.

Gudkov, L. (2004) *Negativnaia identichnost'. Stat'i 1997–2002*, Moscow: Novoe literaturnoe obozrenie, VTSIOM-A.

Gudkov, L. (2005) 'Ideologema "vraga". Vragi kak massovyi sindrom i mekhanizm sotsiokul'turnoi interpretatsii', in (eds) L. Gudkov and N. Konradova *Obraz vraga*, Moscow: OGI, 7–79.

Gusfield, J.R. (1989) 'The Bridge over Separated Lands: Kenneth Burke's Significance for the Study of Social Action' in H.W. Simons and T. Melia (eds) *The Legacy of Kenneth Burke*, London: The University of Wisconsin Press, 28–54.

Lotman, Iu., Uspenskii, B. (1996) " Rol' dual'nykh modelei v dinamike russkoi kul'tury (do kontsa XVIII veka), in B.A. Uspenskii, *Izbrannye trudy I*. Semiotika istorii. Semiotika kul'tury. Moscow: Iaziki russkoi kul'tury, 219–53.

Marsh, R. (1998) 'Women in Contemporary Russia and the Former Soviet Union', in R. Wilford and R.L. Miller (eds) *Women, Ethnicity and Nationalism,* London: Routledge, 87–119.

Mikhailovskaia, E. (2008) 'Fraktsiia "Rodina" v kontekste natsionalisticheskogo diskursa v Gosudarstvennoi Dume' in M. Lariuel' (ed.) *Russkii natsionalizm. Sotsial'nyi i kul'turnyi kontekst*, Moscow: NLO, 33–72.

Parker, I. (1992) *Discourse Dynamics. Critical Analysis for Social and Individual Psychology*, London: Routledge.

Perelman, C. (1982) *The Realm of Rhetoric*, Notre Dame, IN: The University of Notre Dame.

Perelman, C. and Olbrecht-Tyteca, L. (1971) *The New Rhetoric. A Treatise on Argumentation,* Notre Dame, IN: The University of Notre Dame Press, 67–92.

Potter, J. (1996) *Representing Reality. Discourse, Rhetoric and Social Construction*, London: Sage.

Putin, V. (2006) 'Annual Address to the Federal Assembly of the Russian Federation', 10 May, Marble Hall, the Kremlin. Online. Available http://eng.kremlin.ru/speeches/2006/05/10/1823_type70029type82912_105566.shtml (accessed 24 October 2009).

Riabov, O. (2007) *Rossiia Matushka. Natsionalizm, gender i voina v Rossii XX veka*, Stuttgart: Ibidem-Verlag.

Ries, N. (1997) *Russian Talk. Culture and Conversation During Perestroika*, Ithaca, NY and London: Cornell University Press.

Rivkin-Fish, M. (2006) 'From "Demographic Crisis" to "Dying Nation" – The Politics of Language and Reproduction in Russia', in H. Goscilo and A. Lanoux (eds) *Gender and National Identity in Twentieth-Century Russian Culture*, Northern Illinois: Northern Illinois University Press, 151–74.

Rotkirch, A., Temkina, A., Zdravomyslova, E. (2007) 'Who Helps the Degraded Housewife? Comments of Vladimir Putin's Demographic Speech', *European Journal of Women's Studies* 14(4): 349–57.

Sandomirskaia, I. (2001) *Kniga o Rodine (Opyt analiza diskursivnykh praktik*), Wien: Wiener Slawistischer Almanach, Sbd. 50.

Tolkacheva, A. and Akifieva, R. (2008) 'Natsionalizm i tolerantnost' v propravitel'stvennoi presse Sankt-Peterburga', in M. Lariuel'(ed.) *Russkii natsionalizm. Sotsial'nyi i kul'turnyi kontekst,* Moscow: NLO, 371–400.

Tolz, V. (1998) 'Conflicting "Home-Land Myths" and Nation-State Building in post-Communist Russia', *Slavic Review* 57(2): 267–94.

Urban, M. (1994) 'The Politics of Identity in Russia's Post-Communist Transition: The Nation Against Itself', *Slavic Review* 53(3): 733–65.

Yaval-Davis, N. (1997) *Gender & Nation*, London: Sage Publications.

5 Portrayal of health policy in Russian newspapers[1]

Marina Bondarik

Introduction

This chapter examines how federal health policy is addressed in the most widely circulated newspapers in Russia and reviews the current developments in welfare policy, focusing specifically on the National Project 'Health' launched by Vladimir Putin, the current Prime Minister and former President of the Russian Federation (2000–8). The two-year National Project 'Health' (2006–7) outlines the policy priorities of the president and the government and is the most important health project implemented in Russia since the collapse of the Soviet Union.

Furthermore, the chapter discusses reasons for the deterioration of the health situation during the transition period and the future challenges in improving public health and well-being in Russia.

Health is recognised to be one of the most important correlates of well-being (Graham 2008). The health status of the Russian population is severely impaired, and Russia continues to struggle with a health and mortality crisis. The deterioration in basic indicators of health and human welfare that began in the Soviet period and accelerated after the Soviet collapse has yet to be overcome. Life expectancy at birth has not recovered to an acceptable level, and this is caused by high levels of avoidable deaths from non-infectious diseases and exogenous causes of death. As of 2005, the average Russian life expectancy of 65.3 years at birth is 12.5 years shorter than the overall figure for the old EU-15 countries (Rosstat 2007). The main factor contributing to the relatively low life expectancy is high mortality among working-age males as a result of preventable causes, such as accidents, alcohol poisoning, violent crime, heart disease and smoking. As a result, the mortality of males of working age exceeds the average level for the EU-15 by 4.5 times. Almost half of 20-year-old men in Russia will die before retirement – this is the highest rate in the world (WHO 2008). The country is facing a demographic crisis: mortality is high and fertility is low. However, there has been no direct federal intervention until recently.

Implementation of the priority national projects is oriented to the legal strategic position laid down in Article 7 of the Constitution of the Russian Federation on the social state, 'whose policy is aimed at creating conditions ensuring a worthwhile life and the free development of Man' (*Konstitutsiia Rossiiskoi Federatsii* 1997: 6). National priorities are tied to the solution of problems that concern Russians most: health, education, housing and agribusiness. The goal of all national projects is to improve Russian citizens' quality of life. They are orientated towards spheres that directly concern every person, determining the quality of life and comfort and creating 'human capital' – an educated and healthy people. The state of these aspects of public welfare largely dictates the social health of society, the demographic well-being of the country and its competitiveness in the global economy. In other words, a vital government task is the development of a high quality of life for Russian society.

Within contemporary society, people construct their understandings of events such as health reforms from a multiplicity of mediated and interpersonal sources (Hodgetts and Chamberlain 2003). According to Brodie *et al.* (2001), people learn about health issues from the mass media. Until recently, as a topic in the Russian mass media, health has attracted very little interest among both media and health researchers (Seale 2003). Consequently, there are no studies available on how the post-Soviet media presents health matters.

This chapter reports the results of research on the media publicity gained by the National Project 'Health', and draws conclusions on the role of print media in influencing the government welfare policies in Russia. The aim is to explore the dominant cultural and political frames and to reveal different interests related to health system development articulated in the newspapers in Russia reporting on the National Project 'Health' (NPH), which was announced by the Russian government in September 2005.

The priority NPH was intended to bring about tangible improvements in the healthcare system during the period 2006–7. The health project is by far the largest of four projects undertaken by the government in 2005. It channelled an additional US$7.5 billion from federal and regional budgets into healthcare during the course of 2006–7, the bulk of which was spent on increased salaries for primary care physicians, the creation of 15 new high-tech medical centres and expanded immunisation and disease-prevention efforts (Tompson 2007). This represents a substantial increase in expenditure focused on a limited number of priorities and was administered under a high degree of political direction. It should, therefore, have had a positive impact on healthcare in Russia. The project also marked a long-overdue resumption of active policy-making in healthcare, following a period in which little was done.

Data and method

Five national newspapers were selected to represent the views of publications targeted at the general public, and one professional medical paper to represent views aimed at the medical community. Newspapers were chosen first because they provide readers with a 'more accurate source of information, explanations, and argumentation' compared to television or radio media (Collins *et al.* 2006: 92). Here, the aim was to reveal possible disparate interests in the portrayal of the NPH.

The criteria for selection of the newspapers were their circulation and socio-political views, whereas for the professional publications the criterion was their importance among health professionals. In our sample, we named all *general* newspapers, except for one professional publication. The *Argumenty i Fakty* is the weekly newspaper with the highest circulation, enjoying great popularity throughout Russia by maintaining a developed system of regional branches. The other four newspapers are national dailies. The *Izvestiia* and the *Trud* position themselves as quality mainstream broadsheets, and the *Rossiiskaia Gazeta* is published by the Russian government. The *Komsomol'skaia Pravda* is a tabloid paper that closely resembles Western periodicals (Khineyko 2005). The *Trud* and the *Komsomol'skaia Pravda* are the most popular papers after the *Argumenty i Fakty*. The *Meditsinskaia Gazeta*, one of the oldest professional nationwide medical newspapers, is issued twice a week.

The research data comprise 403 articles collected during a one-year period (5 September 2005–5 September 2006). The speech given by Vladimir Putin to launch the project (Putin 2005) was considered to be the starting point of the data collection, because media attention was already focused on the project in the four months leading up to its commencement. The texts were selected using the Integrum database, the largest online full-text database in the Russian press. All articles with the search item 'National Project Health' in its various grammatical forms were included in the analysis.

The actantial framing

For the quantitative and qualitative analysis of the texts, we incorporated ideas from semiotic actantial theory (Greimas 1983, 1987, 1990) and framing theory (Entman 1993; Pan and Kosicki 1993). The underlying assumptions were that the articles are presented in the media following the general narrative structure with key actants, and the framing defines how the actants are discussed. An actant is a role, a structural unit, or a function of any story. It may be a person, a concept, a state of affairs (e.g. well-being) or an institution (e.g. the health insurance system).

Developed in the 1960s, Greimas' narrative semiotics was derived from Propp's morphology of the folktale and was initially intended to map the structure of the narrative. Greimas claimed that the actantial model possesses universal features and is universally applicable (Greimas 1983). For instance, Greimas (1983) used it to study a soup recipe. In these terms, narrative semiotics has been accused of imperialism, and it has also been charged with being outdated. Indeed, the utilisation of an analytical model should not be determined by fashion but by epistemological relevance. It will be seen that the actantial model has proven very useful in terms of highlighting key actors of the NPH and their relations in the studied print media texts.

Here, I will outline some components of the theory to be used in the analysis of the newspaper articles. Essentially Greimas' argument is this: all stories can be reduced to a deep narrative structure, a kind of transcultural and universal grammar of storytelling. This deep structure has three axes: an axis of knowledge, an axis of desire and an axis of power. These three axes are basic plot functions. The axis of knowledge is the commission; someone tells someone else to undertake

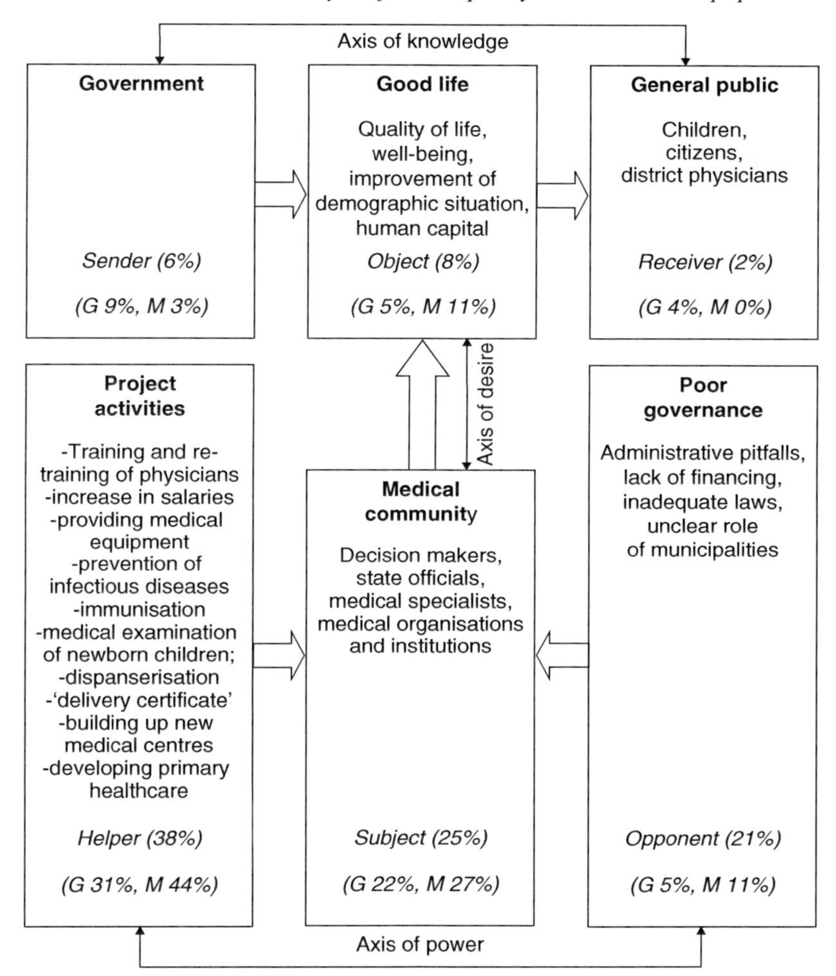

Figure 5.1 The six actants of the National Project 'Health' (NPH) derived from newspaper texts September 2005–September 2006.

a task. The axis of desire is the quest; the hero undertakes a particular assignment to fulfil a particular mission. The axis of power is the conflict experienced by this quester. These three axes have six character-types or actants associated with them. The first is the *Sender*. S/he gives a commission to a second actant, the *Receiver*. The Receiver in turn comes into conflict with the third actant, the *Opponent*. However, s/he receives assistance from the fourth actant, the *Helper*. Throughout all of this, the Receiver is involved in a quest. This Receiver is the *Subject* and the quest itself is the *Object* (ibid.) (in Figure 5.1, the key actants are presented in italics).

Despite the simplicity of the model, this scheme can be usefully applied to a range of texts. For example, Vestergaard and Schrøder (1985) utilised it in studying advertisements for vitamins, Stribbe (1994) in the analysis of John's Plot, Munizaga (as cited in Davies 1999) in the analysis of Pinochet's public discourse, Søderberg (2003) in organisational studies, Demers, Giroux and Chreim (2003) into corporate wedding narratives, Wang and Roberts (2005) in the analysis of self-narratives, and Aarva and Pakarinen (2006) in the analysis of health promotion cultures.

In this chapter, I have treated the term 'actantial framing' as referring to the way in which the actants, i.e. the dominating actors and issues of newspaper headlines and head-notes, are discussed and presented to readers.

Data analysis

Actantial framings were revealed by the following procedure. First, we used Putin's speech as a methodological tool for the construction of the preliminary actants of the NPH. Based on the actantial model of Greimas (1983), we split the speech of President Putin (Putin 2005) into six actants (Box 5.1).

For the analysis, we derived the key actants of the newspaper texts by coding them according to the main characters derived from Putin's speech. The headline and the head-note (the first two paragraphs or first 100 words) of each of the 403 newspaper articles were chosen as the primary units for analysis. For the framing analysis, we then read through the analysis units to qualitatively assess the ways in which the actants were discussed. Furthermore, we read through the full texts to enrich the analysis with possible additional findings related to the key protagonists identified for each article. Finally, we assessed the interrelationships of the actantial framing within the axes of desire, knowledge and power.

Box 5.1

In his speech to introduce the NPH, the President declared *himself* as the *Sender* as he authorised *the government, the state officials, and the medical community (the Subject)* to work for *a better life (the Object)*, which includes *quality of life, well-being, demographic situation and the human capital* of the Russian Federation. The position of the *Receiver* was assigned to the *general public* in terms of enhancing general well-being and to *the primary healthcare staff* and, in particular, district physicians, because they were seen as a target of organisational improvements, such as the increase of salaries. The planned *activities of the NPH*, which included training of medical personnel, wage increases, provision of medical equipment, new medical centres and various methods to strengthen primary healthcare, earned the position of the *Helper* in Putin's speech, where *the poor service delivery system, lack of funding, present laws, and the unclear role of the municipalities* were seen as the *Opponent*.

Actants of the National Project 'Health' in the newspapers

Actants derived from the newspaper texts differed slightly from those in Putin's speech. This is understandable because the newspapers reported a significantly wider range of project issues than the key ideas present in the NPH itself. As Greimas (1983) pointed out, actants may change places (e.g. from *Subject* to *Receiver*) during the narrative process. This is what happened when the presidential speech was transformed into newspaper narratives after 5 September 2005. The summary of the actants is given in Figure 5.1, and their distribution by month is provided in Figures 5.2 and 5.3.

Besides the President, the key decision-makers, such as the state officials, were given the highest importance – the position of *Sender* in the newspaper texts. However, some newspaper texts assigned the *Subject* role to the government officials. As in Putin's speech, medical personnel appeared to have not only the key role of implementing the NPH according to the instructions from the federal decision-makers, but also the position of the *general public* in the texts discussing the consequences of the salary increase for district physicians (the largest group of primary healthcare physicians in Russia). The general population was assigned the *Receiver*'s place in the actantial model. The views and opinions of the population received very little focus in the texts analysed.

The portrayal of the NPH in the newspapers studied indicates the great importance of the expected concrete tasks and actions of the project (the *Helper* – 38 per cent of all actants). The project objectives published in the official documents of the NPH were repeated in the medical newspaper, which devoted a great deal of space to listing the numerous project tasks and activities (44 per cent of all

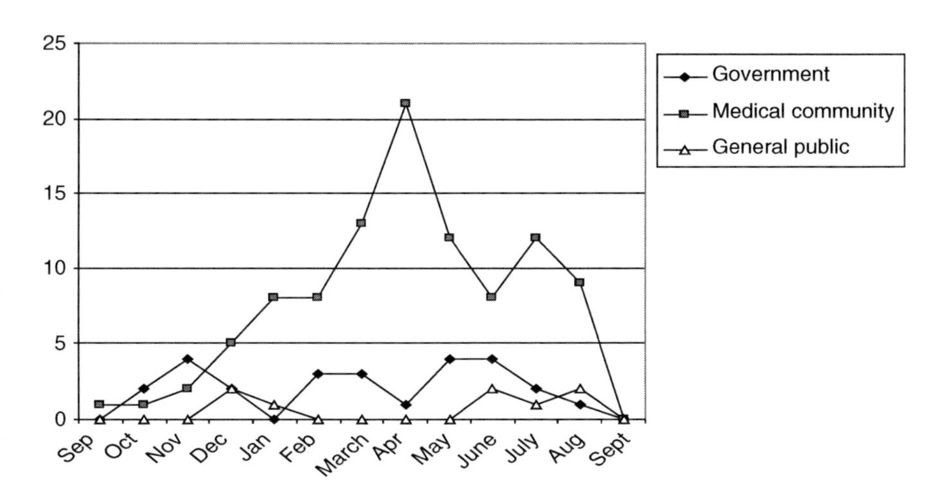

Figure 5.2 The number of key actants (government, medical community and general public) in newspaper articles on the National Project 'Health' by month, September 2005–September 2006.

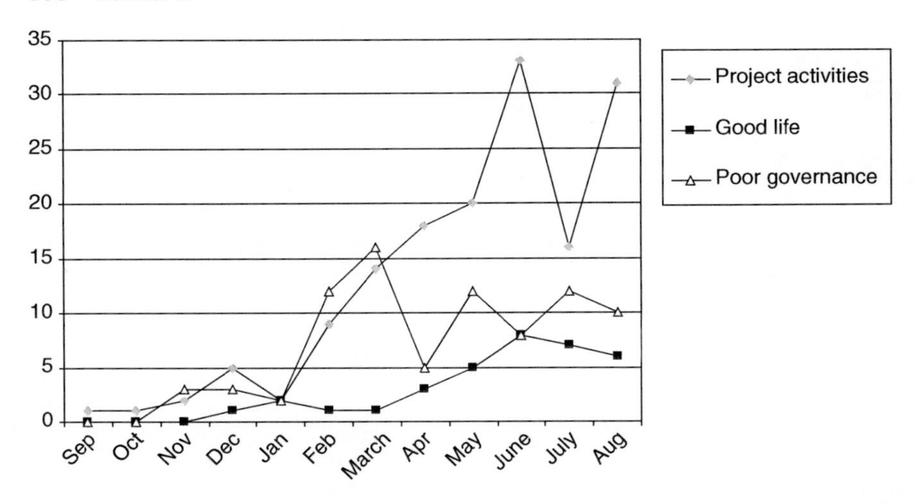

Figure 5.3 The number of key actants (good life, project activities and poor governance) in newspaper articles on the National Project 'Health' by month, September 2005–September 2006.

its articles). The critical approach to the legislative and financial organisation of health services (the *Opponent* – 21 per cent of all actants) was also observed to be a key issue in framing the NPH, particularly in the general newspapers. The government publication and the professional newspaper were less critical than the other general newspapers. Their articles framed the project aims (the *Object*) in a positive tone, actually expressing their wishes for the future and describing an idealised development of the health system (Figures 5.1–5.3).

The axis of knowledge: From the government to the general public

When framing the NPH from the government (the *Sender*) position, the main issues were the political pronouncements of the President, ministers and the state officials about the overall goals of the project. The pronouncements were mostly related to the requests for improvement in the quality of medical services, targeting overall health improvement in the general population.

The second topic was reports on the meetings conducted by the federal and regional state officials to adopt the NPH strategic plans, and to agree upon the objectives and the expected results of the project. The major message from the high-level authorities to the population appeared to focus on convincing people of the importance of the project, which was presented in the form of a solemn promise to improve the performance of the healthcare system. This promise was conveyed to the readers in a positive tone by all the publications we examined. The medical newspaper created positive expectations of the forthcoming project implementation with a headline 'Clinical check-ups: the plan is ready, finances have been calculated' (*Meditsinskaia Gazeta* 27 January 2006)[2]. This message refers to the fact that the government is seen to finally appreciate the necessity of distributing a considerable amount of money to support the health of Russian citizens. It is interesting that this kind of financial discourse was not present in the President's speech; journalists, however, offered readers a new image of the project, with the addition of state financing for the healthcare system.

Both the government framing and the framing of the general public appeared more often than other actantial framing in the first months of NPH implementation (Figure 5.2), and only 2 per cent of all the 403 texts had the general public as a focus of attention in the headline and the head-note.

Axis of desire: The medical community for public well-being

The analysis of our material showed that the key actors in the realisation of the project are the politicians, and, to some extent, the medical community. The task of the department heads is to make correct and co-ordinated decisions on the implementation of the project, whereas the task of the medical specialists is to provide medical services for the population. The results of these actors' work will achieve the desired result of a better quality of life and well-being (the *Object*).

A quarter of all research items (n=100) presented within this framing are the activities of the medical community (the *Subject*). The main actors here were the directors of the medical institutions and organisations and medical specialists. The following topics were discussed in the newspapers:

- various working seminars – co-ordination meetings, panels, discussions of medical representatives about the implementation processes of the NPH and its initial results (this topic appeared in the first half of the given timeframe);
- the working conditions of medical specialists – their well-being and vocation.

The second theme that is strongly present in this actantial frame is the work of medical specialists. There was a positive slant to the description of the medical personnel's duties: 'During a two-month period, "the train of health" will examine the inhabitants of 35 settlements located along the Trans-Siberian railway' (*Trud* 17 February 2006)[3]. The content of this text is reminiscent of the practices of the old Soviet healthcare system – medical specialists reaching people living in remote areas by train. In the remainder of the articles in the medical community's frame, we found descriptions of the role of the medical personnel (the *Subject*) in achieving the population's well-being (the *Object*).

The print media did not pay any significant attention to the idea or goals of the project's implementation. In our research material, the following frames began to be discussed only eight months after the project was announced to the public. Newspapers presented the following topics within well-being frames: children's health, public health, the current high mortality rate and the impending demographic crisis. In other words, the readers are thought to understand the entire aim of the project as a whole, and to negatively view the chances of its success. Within this frame, there was a large number of publications on different kinds of public health problems. For example, 'Teenagers up to the age of 14 years become ill twice a year on average' (*Argumenty i Fakty* 18 January 2006)[4].

The framing of the medical community appeared more often during the spring months (Figure 5.2), when the role of medical specialists in providing medical services was widely discussed. 'The good life' frame appeared marginally (8 per cent of all texts) in newspaper discourse for the whole period of our study (Figure 5.1).

The axis of power: project tasks and activities versus poor governance

In our study units, the NPH tasks and activities were predominantly discussed in a very positive light, referring to a hypothetical better future. Conversely, the current shortcomings of the healthcare system were generally reported in a negative tone, with emphasis on the poor performance of those people or institutions deemed responsible.

The most popular project task mentioned in the research material concerning the implementation of the NPH was the topic of funding. This was discussed widely at both the federal and regional levels. A second popular topic was the provision of new diagnostic equipment to medical centres and medical-prevention establishments in all regions of the country.

The print media also discussed all the specific objectives declared by the government. These included such matters as the construction of medical centres, the training and re-training of medical staff, immunisation of the general public, the introduction of a programme of check-ups for newborns, as well as the provision of high-technology medical care. The actant frames in this group were presented in a large proportion of our research material – up to 38 per cent (n=153) (Figure 5.1).

This part of the research material shows the acute problems endemic in the Russian public healthcare system. Poor governance of the NPH is widely presented in one-fifth of all newspaper articles (21 per cent). We analysed these character frames thematically to obtain a precise representation of the results.

The most widespread theme for the discussion is the difficulties in implementing the project. Here, we refer to both specific problems (e.g. 'Only a quarter of all medical establishments are ready to conduct medical check-ups on the population', *Rossiiskaia Gazeta* 2 March 2006)[5] and more general problems ('The NPH has sometimes received criticism from the mass media, and dissatisfaction with how the funds provided for it are distributed has been declared' *Meditsinskaia Gazeta*, 12 July 2006)[6].

In a quantitative sense, the NPH tasks and activities appear in our study units as the largest actantial frame. The print media has paid a great deal of attention to the implementation of project activities since the NPH launch. The shortcomings of the present healthcare system were widely discussed, especially during the first months after the NPH commenced (Figure 5.3).

Actantial framing: Public media versus medical media

The differences between general newspapers and the medical newspaper lie mostly on the axis of power: public general newspapers presented more text material about 'opponent' forces than medical newspapers and *vice versa* with the NPH tasks and activities (the *Helper*) (Figure 5.1).

Along the axis of desire, we can see that the medical newspaper paid considerable attention (15 per cent of its material) to the activities of medical society and medical institutions (the *Subject*). This actantial framing in the *Meditsinskaia Gazeta* had a mostly positive tone. On the other hand, the general newspapers tended to analyse the present state of affairs in a more negative way. The government newspaper and the medical newspaper wrote considerably more about the NPH than the other general newspapers.

The research material described the NPH at the initial stages of its realisation; however, it enabled us to gather the main condensed framing issues as the key implementation points receiving exclusive attention in the media we studied.

Discussion and conclusion

As the print media representation of health policy issues is an under-researched area (Seale 2003), this study makes a new contribution to the field of health communication. Healthcare reform issues are likely to remain at the top of policy agendas for the foreseeable future and will continue to garner coverage from the news media. This is especially true as there has just been a 15-year period in which there were no political attempts to improve the healthcare system in Russia (Ivanov *et al.* 2007). Our findings contribute to a developing understanding of how the news media are framing the health project, reinforcing some assumptions, such as salary increase or the amount of funding, and challenging others.

Using the Greimasian actantial model to guide our exploration of the NPH in print media, we showed the dominant relationships and functions of key actors in planning and implementing health policy in the Russian Federation. Government and state officials, as well as the medical community, were the most common actors, being represented in 6 per cent and 25 per cent of all study units respectively. The general population had the lowest mention rate in the print media framing. Project tasks and activities and framings of the poor governance of the medical system (38 per cent and 21 per cent respectively) tended to reflect positive and critical approaches to healthcare reform. The dominance of government actors (including projects, tasks and activities) in the newspaper coverage supports Soroka's (2002) point that the media merely act as a conduit for policy agendas. The lack of framing about the general public can be attributed to our observation of only the initial implementation stage of the NPH when media content presented readers with particular actions and activities without discussing the project goals per se.

The NPH has been portrayed in newspapers in a supportive tone, and the government has been praised for its efforts to achieve a good life for ordinary people by strengthening various medical services and implementing project tasks and activities. The important 'health knowledge' seems to come from the top down – from the government, which announces great promises down to the general public (axis of knowledge in Figure 5.1). The government declared improvement of the quality of life as the main goal of the NPH; however, the print media frames presented improvement of the quality of medical services (axis of desire in Figure 5.1) as the main goal. Those print media frames depicted public issues in terms of particular instances or specific events – descriptions of various working seminars, medical specialists' work and so forth. Thus, the central idea – the development of human capital and society's well-being – has often been overlooked in reporting on the project's individual steps (Ivanov *et al.* 2007).

This actantial scheme shows us the ideological framing of health policy in Russia. According to the NPH model, there are attempts to improve the healthcare system itself. For instance, one of the most represented key actors is the medical community, and its goal is to improve medical services. Figure 5.1 shows that the authorities and medical staff have a dominant function in people's health and well-being (axis of desire). Thus, the prevailing policy orientation was to shift responsibility for health to the government rather than to individuals. As mentioned above, the actantial framing of the general population represented only 2 per cent of all newspaper texts, so the health project was not presented in the context of a wider effort to educate ordinary Russians and stimulate them to take greater responsibility for their own health.

One-third of the texts examined are devoted to expenditure-based frames, which are largely related to the amount of funds allocated for the NPH and to the costs of medical services rendered. This kind of discourse reflects the government intention to reclaim the health sector mainly by financial means, without emphasising the investment in the health of the population as was declared in the initial stages of the project.

Generally, health is considered to be a functional characteristic, not a value. In our research, we discovered that the aim of the NPH is often portrayed as 'ill-being', e.g. as a demographic crisis or catastrophe. As Greimas pointed out, every subject (object) has its anti-subject (anti-object). Thus, in our case, the printed media offered the public a state of 'ill-being' when translating the actual well-being goals defined by NPH. Such a negative actantial framing referred the reader to the actual health policy problems instead of outcome-based results of health reform.

According to our findings, it seems that the central idea of the NPH – the development of human capital and creating a high quality of life – became more a declaration of intentions in the field of social policy, a sign to society that the authorities understand health issues. Print media, in their turn, offered readers challenging information rather than good results.

Notes

1 This research was funded by the project 'Making a "Good Life": Post-Soviet Selves in the Russian Mass Media 1980–2006' from the Academy of Finland (Grant no. 214255). The support is gratefully acknowledged. Special thanks go to Dr. Pauliina Aarva for

being so collaborative, for supervising my efforts from the very beginning, and providing very useful comments on the draft of this chapter.

2 Dispanserizatsiia: plan gotov, sredstva opredeleny. (Clinical check-ups: the plan is ready, finances have been calculated) (27 January 2006). *Meditsinskaia Gazeta*, p. 2.
3 Ivanova, O. (February 17 2006). Vracham – zelenyi (The green light to physicians). *Trud*, p. 3.
4 Martynkina, D. (January 18 2006). Sovershenno nezdorov (Particularly unhealthy). *Argumenty i Fakty*, p. 11.
5 Krasnopolskaia, I. (2 March 2006). A pro ushi zabyli (And forgot about ears). *Rossiiskaia Gazeta*, March 2, p. 7.
6 Kartashov, V. (2006) Zigzag, eshche zigzag (A zigzag, one more zigzag). *Meditsinskaia Gazeta*, 12 July, p. 4.

References

Aarva, P. and Pakarinen, M. (2006) 'Studying the striving and opposing forces in newspaper journalism: the actantial model of health promotion', *Health Promotion International* 21(2): 160–8.

Brodie, M., Foehr, U., Rideout, V. and Baer, N. (2001) 'Communicating health information through the entertainment media', *Health Affairs* 20(1): 192–9.

Collins, P., Abelson, J., Pyman, H. and Lavis, J. (2006) 'Are we expecting too much from print media? An analysis of newspaper coverage of the 2002 Canadian healthcare reform debate', *Social Sciences & Medicine* 63(1): 89–102.

Davies, M. (1999) *International political economy and mass communication in Chile*, New York: Palgrave publishers.

Demers, C., Giroux, N. and Chreim, S. (2003) 'Merger and acquisition announcements as corporate wedding narratives', *Journal of Organizational Change Management*, 16: 223–42.

Entman, R. (1993) 'Framing: towards clarification of a fractured paradigm', *Journal of Communication* 43(4): 51–8.

Graham, C. (2008) 'Happiness and health: lessons and questions for public policy' *Health Affairs* 27(1): 72–87.

Greimas, A.J. (1983) *Structural Semantics: An Attempt at a Method*, trans. D. McDowell, R. Schleifer and A. Velie, Lincoln, NE: University of Nebraska Press.

Greimas, A.-J. (1987) *On Meaning: Selected Writings in Semiotic Theory*, trans. P. J. Perron and F. H. Collins, Minneapolis, MI: University of Minnesota Press.

Greimas, A.-J. (1990) *The social sciences: a semiotic view*, trans. P.J. Perron and F.H. Collins, Minneapolis, MI: University of Minnesota Press.

Hodgetts, D. and Chamberlain, K. (2003) 'Narrativity and the mediation of health reform agendas', *Sociology of Health & Illness* 25(6): 553–70.

Ivanov, A., Kazantsev, V., Meier , M. and Karpenko, M. (2007) Prioritetnye natsional'nye proekty – ideologiia proryva v budushchee. Collected articles. Moscow: Evropa.

Khineyko, I. (2005) 'The view from Russia: Russian press coverage of the 2004 presidential elections in Ukraine', *Canadian Slavonic Papers*, Vol. XLVII, Nos. 3–4, September–December: 265–92.

Konstitutsiia Rossiiskoi Federatsii. (1997) Official issue. Moscow: Iuridicheskaia literatura.

Pan, Zh. and Kosicki, G. (1993) 'Framing analysis: an approach to news discourse', *Political Communication* 10: 55–75.

Putin, V. (2005) Speech at the Meeting with the Cabinet Members, the Heads of the Federal Assembly and State Council Members. September, 5, 2005. Grand Kremlin Palace, Moscow. Online. Available www.president.kremlin.ru/eng/speeches/2005/09/05/1101_type82912type82913_93335.shtml (accessed 6 June 2008).

Rosstat. (2007) Rossiiskii statisticheskii ezhegodnik 2007. Ofitsial'noe izdanie.

Seale, C. (2003) 'Health and media: an overview', *Sociology of Health & Illness* 25: 513–31.

Søderberg, A.-M. (2003) Sensegiving and sensemaking in an integration process: A narrative approach to the study of an international acquisition. In Czarniawska, B. (Ed). *Narratives We Organize By* (pp. 3–37). Philadelphia, PA: John Benjamins Publishing Company.

Soroka, S. (2002) *Agenda-setting dynamics in Canada*, Vancouver, British Columbia: UBS Press.

Stribbe, M. (1994) *John's Gospel*, Florens, KY: Routledge.

Tompson, W. (2007) 'Healthcare reform in Russia: problems and prospects', *OECD Economics Department Working Papers*, No. 538, OECD Publishing.

Vestergaard, T. and Schrøder, K. (1985) *The Language of advertising*. Oxford: Blackwell.

Wang, Y. and Roberts, C. (2005) 'Greimas's structural approach to the analysis of self-narratives', *Narrative Inquiry* 15(1): 51–74.

WHO. (2008) *World Health Organization Statistical Information System (WHOSIS)*, Available www.who.int/whosis/en/index.html (accessed 6 June 2008).

6 Eastern cowboys

Masculine selves and coping with stressful life in the Russian edition of *Men's Health* magazine[1]

Ilkka Pietilä

Men's Health magazine and the transformation of masculinities

Men's Health has been a research object of several studies in Western social science over the past decade for two main reasons. First, as an 'elite' magazine, it is assumed to have a role in the reproduction and transformation of idealised masculinity, which is particularly interesting in relation to discussions of a 'crisis' of masculinity in Western societies (e.g. Kimmel 1987; Brittan 1989; Petersen 1998). Second, the magazine combines in an interesting manner the topic of health, traditionally considered feminine, with a male readership. From the perspective of health research, *Men's Health* has been studied as a popular magazine that offers men new, 'pro-health' messages. This interest has been grounded on the idea of traditional forms of masculinity being in conflict with a healthy lifestyle. Men's lower life-expectancy, chronic illness and premature death have been called the 'cost of masculinity' (Messner 1997), representing one of the most significant 'risk factors' for men's health (Harrison, Chin and Ficarrotto 1989). As a health magazine intended for a male readership, *Men's Health* has thus been considered an interesting cultural phenomenon, having a potential influence on the health of the male population through the reformulation of masculine ideals. Accordingly, researchers have analysed how *Men's Health* conceptualises and discusses health, particularly a healthy lifestyle (Stibbe 2004; Crashaw 2007), and how masculinity is constructed in the magazine (Toerien and Durrheim 2001; Kulinka 2004).

Both themes studied in *Men's Health* magazine in the West are also relevant in Russia. The transformation of society has changed gender relations and gendered ideals in Russia. Some researchers have also claimed that the societal changes have influenced men's position in society even more than that of women (Kiblitskaya 2000: 94; Rotkirch 2000: 264–73). The researchers have used terms like the 'man question' (Rotkirch 2000) and the 'crisis of men' (Ashwin and Lytkina 2004), concluding that particularly changes in the Russian labour market have caused many men, especially at the lower end of the labour market, to encounter a crisis in their masculine identities. Unemployment, possibly lower salaries than women and part-time and fixed-term jobs have challenged men's traditionally strong position as the breadwinner of the family. In addition to structural changes, the ideological shifts have reformed ideals of masculinity. As Zdravomyslova and Temkina

(2002) have pointed out, the Soviet masculine ideals, such as loyalty to the Soviet state, constant devotion to its collective goals and sacrifice of individual aspirations to achieve those goals, have to a large extent lost their relevance in post-Soviet Russia. Therefore, new Russian masculinities are largely being produced on the basis of characteristics similar to Western hegemonic masculinity, such as individualism, rationality, professionalism and independence. In this transformation of masculinities, magazines such as *Men's Health* play a role in offering Western ideals to the readers, as well as adjusting these new ideals to fit locally dominant images of manhood.

In addition to changes in gender relations and ideals of masculinity, the fall of the Soviet Union resulted in the deterioration of Russian public health, which was manifested in increasing mortality and morbidity and also in a widening gender gap in life-expectancy. The post-Soviet 'health crisis' has notably concerned men, and among them especially working-aged men (e.g. Watson 1995; Bobak and Marmot 1996; Chen, Wittgenstein and McKeon 1996). The primary social determinants of the decline in male life-expectancy are unhealthy lifestyles, excessive alcohol consumption in particular (Ryan 1995; Cockerham 1997; Nemtsov 2002), accompanied by injuries and violence (Notzon *et al.* 1998; *Dying too young* 2005). Therefore, given the strikingly gendered characteristics of the Russian health crisis, analyses of publications such as *Men's Health* provide complementary perspectives on current discourses relating to masculinity and health in contemporary Russia.

The magazine, the reader and communication of ideals

A brief look at how *Men's Health* discusses men's health issues reveals that it tends to conceptualise health and healthy lifestyle largely in terms of healthy diet and physical exercise, whereas other topics, such as smoking and drinking, safe driving, occupational safety, etc., are rarely considered. Another key feature of the magazine, as noted by Crashaw (2007), is that it approaches health from a highly individualised perspective, thus lacking considerations of the *societal context of health*. *Men's Health* is currently the largest men's brand in the world, with 31 editions in 39 countries around the world[2]. Despite this, there is limited variation in cultural characteristics between national editions. This is because, as Machin and Thornborrow (2003) note, lifestyle magazines sell a globalised 'fantasy world' through weakly localised discourse, which enables readers to feel themselves part of a certain cross-national identity. Due to the globalised nature of *Men's Health*, particular Russian features are far from being omnipresent in the magazine.

The construction of masculinity in magazines such as *Men's Health* concerns both ideals of 'good life' and masculine identities, i.e. what is considered desirable and valued in life in general, and which kinds of men achieve such goals. The lifestyles, ideals of good life and idealised characteristics of the masculine self that the magazine markets are most clearly articulated in the contexts where the magazine makes direct appeals to its readers. Typical of lifestyle magazines, *Men's Health* addresses its readers in direct and explicit ways telling them what 'you' should do or avoid, and how 'you' should think and act. This type of 'advertising style', which uses direct addresses personally to 'you', transcends 'its nature a mass medium' (Machin and van Leeuwen 2005: 589), which is a strong persuader to adopt the ideas. In addition to direct communications, the magazine also constructs its assumed reader (or 'implied', 'model' reader, Kress and van Leeuwen 2002) indirectly and implicitly by making assumptions about the topics discussed in the magazine, the social environment, and the readers' reactions and preferences.

To explore the idealised masculine characteristics presented in the Russian edition of *Men's Health*, I focus my analysis on the assumptions made about the reader. Thus, in analysing masculinity, the focus of my analysis is on communication between the magazine and the 'model' reader covering both implicit and explicit references to the reader. Relating to the 'Russianness' of the local edition of the magazine, I also study depictions of (social) environment and life-events attributed to the reader. Bearing in mind that *Men's Health* is primarily intended for upper middle-class readers, analysing the social contexts of texts is also useful for outlining class-based characteristics attached to the reader.

Empirically, in analysing the masculine ideals of *Men's Health*, I focus on its monthly column *Stress*. There are several reasons for this. Given the weakly localised discourse of the magazine, the topic of stress is an interesting one because it is the only permanent health-related topic, which, conceptually, links health with the social and cultural environment, and physical health with psychological and social well-being. According to a classic definition, stress is thought to be the 'condition that results when person/environment transactions lead the individual to perceive a discrepancy between the demands of a situation and his or her resources' (Sarafino 1994: 490). Accordingly, the context of stress makes it, at least to some extent, possible to read the 'Russianness' of the local edition of the magazine. Stress may be interpreted as the opposite of well-being, both as a state of an individual and as a determinant of future health. Conceptualised this way, texts describing stressful life and stressful events thus implicitly construct a negative version of 'good life': if stress is a central element of a hard and unhealthy life, then non-stressful life, by definition, represents a life that is pursued and valued. Therefore, analysing constructions of stressful life and events as a particular context of *self* offers a means to approach culture-specific characteristics of good life, which might otherwise be difficult in a magazine that lacks, or even avoids, considerations of its social context.

Bearing in mind the 'health crisis' of men in post-socialist Russia, stress is an important topic as several studies have attributed the deteriorating health situation in Russia to 'chronic' psychosocial stress caused by the socio-economic changes after the fall of communism, especially concerning men (e.g. Leon and Shkolnikov 1998; Gavrilova *et al.* 2000; Pridemore 2004). The idea of stress being a major determinant of Russian public health, and men's poor health in particular, has been found to be widely echoed in Russian newspapers (Pietilä and Shek 2008) and lay people's interviews (Pietilä and Rytkönen 2008a, 2008b). The gendered attributions attached to stress thus offer an interesting starting point for analysing gendered health in *Men's Health*.

This chapter has three objectives. First, to outline the gendered ideals and values in the magazine, I analyse the characteristics attributed to the reader in the context of stress. Second, in relation to the previous objective, I also explore how the reader's social environment and Russian society are described in this context. Third, throughout the analyses, I draw attention to how stress itself is conceptualised in the articles, as earlier studies have shown that there is substantial variation in how the word is used in newspapers (Pietilä and Shek 2008) and lay people's interviews (Pietilä and Rytkönen 2008a). Before proceeding to the analyses, I introduce the materials and methods of the study and describe variations of themes and writing styles within the material.

'Reading the reader' in *Men's Health* – material and method

Stress is one of the permanent topics of the *Men's Health* magazine and is – with few exceptions – discussed in every issue in the column called *Stress*. Other similar continuous topics are columns *Ratsion* (nutrition), *Forma* (focused on physical exercise), *Kar'era* (career) to mention a few. For the purposes of this study, I collected 16 issues of *Men's Health* magazine, eight each issues from 2005 and 2007, and analysed texts in the column *Stress*. The topics of the articles are presented in Table 6.1.

I approached the texts from the perspective of critical discourse analysis. The main idea of critical discourse analysis is that the detailed analysis of language is located in a larger social and cultural framework by reflecting the discourse against other discourses (e.g. Parker 1992; Wodak and Meyer 2001). In the detailed analysis of text I have paid special attention to how the assumed reader is addressed and, consequently, described. As Kress and van Leeuwen (2002) have pointed out, in addressing the readers, the texts construct, intentionally or not, their 'implied' or 'model' readers. These addresses may be direct or indirect, explicit and implicit, but the common feature of all those strategies is to create certain 'us-ness' between

Table 6.1 Topics of articles in the column *Stress* in eight issues of *Men's Health* from 2005 and 2007

2005		*2007*	
Jan	Returning to work after holiday	Mar	Hypochondria
Feb	Moving to another city or country	Apr	–
Mar	Driving a car in traffic jams	May	–
Apr	Adapting to girlfriend's/wife's pregnancy	June	Sexually abused men
May	Avoiding street violence	July	Men's suicides in Russia
June	Living without 'big money'	Sept	Psycho-motor practices for reducing stress
July	Loneliness caused by lack of social skills	Oct	Lack of motivation to work
Aug	Doing night work	Nov	Threat of serial killers

the magazine and the reader, for instance by making a distinction between 'us' and 'them' (see Crashaw 2007). In critical studies on men and masculinities, the basic distinctions between 'us' and 'them' have been considered to be those between men and women, as well as those between heterosexual and homosexual men (Garlick 2003). Some recent discourse analytical studies on men's self-identification practices, however, have paid attention to the fact that in many cases the distinctions are more subtle regarding, for instance, differences between 'real men' and 'sissies' or 'modern men' and 'machos' (e.g. Wetherell and Edley 1999).

Arran Stibbe (2004) noted in his study on the Australian edition of *Men's Health* that the health-related articles of the magazine were characterised by the interplay of two distinct discourses. Although medical discourse reports the health-related news to the reader in factualised terms, the 'buddy' discourse translates this information into the language of the male reader and gives instructions on interpreting the facts. Whereas parts of the medical information might be threatening to the male reader due to possible restrictions on his behaviour, the buddy discourse absolves the reader from these restrictions by offering an interpretation that relocates the information in the broader context of the man's life. This kind of 'conversational style' may be generally typical of lifestyle magazines, bringing a sense of informality to the writing style: this is because 'conversation is essentially private speech, dialogue between equals' (Machin and van Leeuwen 2005: 596). In some cases the relationship between reader and writer might also be interpreted as a relationship between brothers, where the big brother (the writer) tells the younger brother (the reader) how he should think and act in different situations. What is common to both is that they mitigate the potentially threatening information by offering a friendly and compassionate interpretation of the information.

It is, therefore, important to note that there is variation in the communication distance between the magazine and the reader: in some cases the 'buddy' or 'big brother' discourse brings the reader very close to the writer, whereas in other contexts the reader is located outside the text. Accordingly, in the analysis I pay attention to the production of the communication distance and its contextual variations.

Variation of themes and writing styles of stress articles

After a brief reading of the columns, I soon noticed that there was substantial variation in stress articles both in terms of topics of texts and in the writing style. Some of the texts concerned very serious phenomena in Russian society, such as young men's suicides and sexually abused men, and were written in a serious, factual and objective style, even involving critical views of Russian society. Other texts, on the contrary, discussed substantially less serious events of everyday life, such as driving a car in congested traffic and returning to work from holiday, and were often written, at least partly, in a humoristic way.

A notable feature in the articles on stress is that the relationship between the issues discussed and their consequences, i.e. stress, was not explicated. Typically the articles concerned situations that are usually considered to be stress-causing, but the ways in which these situations or issues lead to stress remained unexplained. In many cases, the introduction of the story referred to the topic as a cause of stress but the rest of the text did not consider the stressful effects at all. A good example of this is the article about moving to another apartment, town or country (*MH* February 2005: 174–8). The introduction of the story states:

> Changing the place of living considerably cuts down the sum of money in your wallet and reduces the healthy neural cells in your organism. Often it is not possible to prevent the change, but you can reduce stress and the financial damage to a minimum.
>
> (*Men's Health*, February 2005: 174)

Although the introduction claims that moving to another place causes people substantial stress (even damage to neuro-cells), the text itself does not describe these effects. Instead, it focuses on practical tips on how to organise a house move in a way that reduces possible damage to belongings paying special attention to packing things correctly and safely. This kind of *problem–solution* approach was characteristic of the majority of stories, where an event or issue was first claimed to cause stress after which the text introduces methods for resolving the problems.

Another, implicit way of introducing stress-effects related to the topic of the article was presented in a story about serial killers, which starts with a dramatic introduction superimposed on a horrifying picture where a black, shadowy hand attacks the reader with a knife, with an all-red, dark background.

> We all have girlfriends, children or grandmothers. We are certain that you have read our journal long enough to be able to protect them. But you are not always beside them. Autumn has come – maniacs are becoming active.
>
> (*Men's Health*, November 2007: 328)

This four-page story is illustrated with pictures of a knife, an axe and a chainsaw, all blades being covered in blood. Although the word stress is not even mentioned once in the text (except for the heading of the column), the introduction gives the reader an idea that the existence of serial killers is an issue that causes people stress, particularly due to concern about their relatives' security. In contrast to the previous example, the story on serial killers does not discuss the topic from the *problem–solution* approach, but focuses mainly on reasons why some people become 'maniacs'. What is notable, however, is that the topic of the story is treated as if it were a concrete threat, and, accordingly, a major cause of stress to the readers.

The texts considering the stressful effects of more or less daily events (such as returning to work after a holiday) were most often written 'tongue in cheek' and spiced with humour, whereas the articles on the most serious and extreme topics (such as sexually abused men or men's suicides) were dominated by more detached and serious language. It may be concluded that *the more closely the topic is assumed to concern the implied reader's everyday life, the more humoristic expressions are used to soften the text.* The articles thus varied in terms of the seriousness of topics and writing styles (humoristic, ironic, neutral and dramatic styles), as well as in the extent to which the reasons and consequences of stress were articulated. In addition, there was variation in the extent to which the societal context and environment were described, which will be discussed in a later section of this chapter.

Who is the model reader? What is he like?

A notable characteristic of the writing style of *Men's Health* is that the magazine often addresses the reader directly as 'you'. This expression was used in all 14 articles included in the analysis. Due to this, it is relatively easy to outline some of the main characteristics attached to 'you', the reader. In explicit communications between the magazine and the reader, one of the most common features is that the reader is addressed as a heterosexual man who is, with only few exceptions, assumed to be single without children and family. This is mainly achieved by excluding other themes, such as those regarding family, children or homosexual relationships[3], from the text. He is expected to live in a big city, which is fostered by recurrent references to 'provincial towns' depicted as negative counterpoints to the reader's own environment and lifestyle.

The reader is equally consistently expected to work in business, which was manifest in frequent references to 'business plans', meetings with 'business partners' and so forth. In only one article were other occupations mentioned. In a story about working nights (*Men's Health*, August 2005: 156–9), the text notes that sometimes people are eager to make money to the extent that they no longer realise the negative effects of night work on their physiology. In this context, the reader is addressed directly.

> In short, exactly this proposal [to earn money – IP] you could not refuse and you started, for instance, to unload coal trucks. Or to arrange manufactured goods on shelves. We wouldn't like to distress you, but from just this moment on big problems may start to occur in your organism.
>
> (*Men's Health*, August 2005: 156)

It is worth noting that these jobs are mentioned as bad examples of night work, whereas other jobs related to business are not criticised. It might thus be claimed that work related to business is presumed to include tasks that need to be accomplished irrespective of time, where other jobs represent foolish and unjustified examples of night work. In other words, whereas working at night is considered a normal part of work in business, putting too much effort to other, not so glamorous work, is regarded as mindless and irresponsible.

Interestingly, although the implied reader is consistently described as having a rather stable and well-paid job in business, he is not depicted as being in a senior position with a number of subordinates. In my view, there is good reason for this. By locating the male reader in a middle management position, the reader is also exempted from the responsibilities related to higher positions. The middle management position gives the assumed reader relatively high wages and a respected status, but does not limit his freedom to do whatever he wants.

That the model reader of *Men's Health* is assumed to be wealthy and be relatively well paid is noticeable in recurrent references to travelling abroad as well as to unusual and expensive hobbies. Having stable and sufficient earnings is also an assumed means to resolve problems in daily choices. In a story about re-locating to another place, the text discusses how belongings should be sent to the new home and considers, among other things, that it may be easier to leave some belongings and buy new ones in the new place, especially if moving to another town or country.

> Don't take tableware or other household utensils with you. Household appliances are not even worth consideration.
>
> (*Men's Health*, February 2005: 178)

In addition to the implicit assumption that the reader can afford new tableware and utensils, the text takes it for granted that the reader is familiar with the new town abroad to which he is moving. The text notes this by saying that 'you have been there on business-trips and holidays a hundred thousand times'. Both these references to the reader's economic status place him in wealthy business world, where holidaying abroad and renewing household appliances when needed is a part of the lifestyle.

One of the stories illustrates well most of the qualities of the implied reader. In an article discussing stress related to money, the text considers the possibility that the reader may be temporarily unemployed. As the overall assumption is that the reader has a good job with sufficient wages, this exceptional situation raises the main expectations attached to the implied reader. The excerpt below serves as an introduction to the situation where lack of money becomes an issue in the reader's life.

> You refused your female chief, who had been soliciting you at many evening parties. You said all you had wanted to say for many years to the general manager in front of everyone, and as a result you lost your job without severance pay.
>
> (*Men's Health*, June 2005: 172)

Becoming unemployed is notably described, to some extent, as the reader's own decision. Despite this, unemployment, accompanied with financial problems, is assumed to be a shattering idea to the reader, which is manifested in crystallised advice about what to do first: 'Even though this may sound banal to you, you simply have to cut down on your expenses'. The advice given is interesting in the indications of choices and actions that the reader is expected to avoid in his normal life.

> In addition to cutting down on the number of parties, you can buy provisions in supermarkets (considerable savings), give your girlfriend jewellery less often and so on. If the shortage of money gets a bit prolonged, and for this

> you must be prepared from the very beginning, you can sell your car and temporarily take the metro (it is possible, that after this you will need to be dragged out of it: so many beautiful girls you will never see from the car). Besides, you can rent your apartment for a while and stay with your friends or with your mother. She will surely understand everything and forgive you.
>
> (*Men's Health*, June 2005: 172)

This excerpt is full of expectations relating to the reader's normal life: the reader is assumed to arrange parties often, do his shopping in specialised shops, buy jewellery regularly for his girlfriend, own a car and prefer to use it instead of public transport, as well as own an apartment, which he can rent when in need of money. In addition to an affluent way of life, the text repeats the general assumptions of the magazine in taking the reader's heterosexual desires for granted: although the reader is assumed to have a girlfriend, it is considered somewhat natural that seeing 'so many beautiful girls' in the metro is a collectively convincing argument for taking the metro instead of car.

In this context, skirt-chasing serves as a softening element, which lightens the descriptions about a tough situation where the reader is threatened by the possibility of losing so many important things in his life. In addition, the text is one of the rare examples where the reader's mother is brought into the picture. In the story, she is the person whom the reader can trust even in a dire situation, as she 'will surely understand everything and forgive you'. Together with the alleviating component of empathy, the mother serves as an external conscious of the reader who absolves him from feelings of guilt and shame around him. If the mother will understand and forgive everything, then the reader should not feel too discouraged.

Possible unemployment and lack of money is a threat to the reader's masculine identity, which is managed, among others, with humour as discussed above. In addition, the text mitigates the reader's anxiety by referring to his superior talents. Regardless of advice even to be prepared for prolonged unemployment, the text considers this as more or less irrelevant in 'your' case. This is because the reader of *Men's Health* is endowed with exceptional capabilities and should not, therefore, be worried about his future after all.

> If you didn't receive a call and weren't offered the job of a top manager in a trans-national corporation within two days, don't worry. It is likely that they are simply carried away by your experience and are searching for the adequate place for you. [...] You are a versatile personality, and your talents are not restricted to the ability of tapping the keyboard in the office.
>
> (*Men's Health*, June 2005: 173)

The description of the reader is based on the idea that he is a young urban professional oriented to economic success and promoting his personal career. The softening elements of the text are interesting, as typically the reader's emotions are almost completely excluded from articles. In the previous excerpts, the feelings of fear, guilt, shame and anxiety are there between the lines but concealed under enhanced emphasis of rationality and cognitive skills. Throughout the texts, the reader is portrayed as a rational and controlled person who avoids emotional reactions. The reader is also expected to assess other people in his social circles in terms of their IQ, which refers to the idea that a core valued feature of a person is intelligence (*Men's Health*, July 2005: 177). In difficult life situations the reader is urged to have 'rational therapy' by thinking of his relations, motives and actions critically. The reader is assumed to be well-educated and to set great store by science and 'facts' typically presented in numerical form.

Although the reader is generally depicted as independent and critical in his own thinking, sometimes the 'buddy' enters the discussion and negotiates with the reader about the proper interpretation of the information delivered. This is because the reader is expected to share the values of the magazine. Sometimes the 'buddy' is not the writer addressing the reader but, instead, the 'right' interpretations are introduced to the reader by respected interviewees quoted by the magazine. In the story on street violence a self-defence trainer interviewed for the article states that sometimes one has no other choice but to use physical force, especially with those people who are essentially aggressive. With those people attempts to avoid conflict may even make things worse. In this case, 'you' should not feel sorry for them.

> And I never felt sorry for those whom I've hit or kicked. I've had no doubts. In general I'm not aggressive by nature, and that's why I use force only in those situations when there's no other option. And I never have any doubts.
> (*Men's Health* May 2005: 196)

The 'buddy' interpretation provided by the self-defence trainer is necessary in this context where the general advice to avoid violence poses certain challenges to the reader's masculine identity: should a real man really turn the other cheek to an assailant? Avoiding violence and controlled, rational conduct are surely characteristics attached to the model reader, but there are obviously limits to abstaining from violence. Therefore, the buddy helps the reader to overcome this conflict by convincing him of the necessity of using force when 'there's no other option'. When attacked one should not feel sorry for hitting or kicking the offender. As the attacker himself is the aggressor, he is also, justly, the one who has to take the consequences.

The buddy comes on the scene in a situation where contradictory expectations for the male reader's motives and behaviour emerge. The masculine qualities of the reader are not problematised as such, as the reader is assumed – and even urged – to share the values and conceptions of manhood with the magazine. Instead, the contradictory expectations arise from a particular situation, which calls for adjustment of those qualities to situational demands. In a similar way, although the masculine preferences are generally taken for granted, in certain explicitly gendered contexts some components of the idealised life of the male reader need to be reinterpreted, particularly regarding events that fundamentally change his life. One of those changes is fatherhood.

The reader in explicitly gendered contexts

As mentioned above, sex and new conquests are very often included in the stories, often as softening and humorous elements. By references to girl-watching, the 'buddy' redirects potentially threatening discussions in a direction that unites 'us', writer and reader. In stories about stress, women generally play a minor part in men's lives as women – or just 'girls' – are normally described merely in terms of amusement and fun. As the reader is typically portrayed as a single man without family and other relationships restricting his life, women are similarly depicted as people whom the Man takes to fulfil his desires and fantasies only when he wants to. An exception to this rule is the article considering the stressful effects of future fatherhood.

The story is entitled '9 months after orgasm' (*Men's Health*, April 2005: 166–72). The heading of the article about a man's adaptation to a wife's/ girlfriend's pregnancy gives a good introduction to the tone in which the topic is discussed in the article. The starting point of the article is that getting to know about a pregnancy is an unexpected and shocking situation for a man. Despite noting that some pregnancies are planned and welcome, throughout the article pregnancy and future fatherhood are discussed in terms of threats and fears, and described as shocking news for a man. Therefore, the theme of the article is how to adapt to this new life situation and all the changes it brings to everyday life. As the text points out, pregnancy is 'a stressful situation of the highest level'. According to the article, pregnancy changes everything in a man's life because the dishes and laundry no longer do themselves and the man has to make the breakfast for his wife/partner, too. He fears the loss of his freedom because he has to support and take care of the mother and the child. Thus, the man has to adapt to the situation, to the changes caused by the woman's pregnancy. The article ends with a positive future scenario by stating that after the birth of the child everything will be much better than expected.

The article approaches pregnancy from the man's point of view, while simultaneously taking women's assumed needs and ways of thinking into account. According to the text, written in the typical tongue-in-cheek manner, the pregnant partner causes stress in a man's life with her expectations regarding his behaviour:

> Women have invented an unbelievable amount of exotic methods of announcing the happy news. Sending an e-mail message with an ultrasound picture taken in the morning at the doctor's is by no means the cruelest alternative. In that case at least you have time to prepare a reaction which is very important for the girl. You have to come earlier from work and run into the apartment with a bunch of flowers and say happily: "Well look who's pregnant here?!"
>
> (*Men's Health*, April 2005: 166)

In this excerpt, the word 'women' (*zhenshchiny*) implies a generic category, which is not under control (cf. 'women have invented'), whereas the word 'girl' (*devushka*) in this case implies a concrete female partner, whom the man, it is assumed in the text, is capable of manipulating by preparing a desired reaction to the news. It is clear that the woman also manipulates the man to a similar degree: she has several 'alternatives' from which to choose in order to announce the 'happy news'. Thus, the article describes a certain game between the spouses or partners where each is participating and playing their part. Simultaneously, descriptions of women's peculiarities in a way act as 'a collective means of defining oneself, relationally, as a man ('not a woman')' (Toerien and Durrheim 2001: 43).

Women in general are depicted as strange creatures, whose peculiarities become even more incomprehensible during pregnancy. The article addresses several of these 'new problems' by discussing, among others, rapid changes in a woman's mood, changes in her appearance, and also heightened sense of smell, such that 'you cannot even think of drinking beer after work' (p. 170). Most often women's peculiarities are softened by humorous ideas and using 'ironic discourse', which Benwell (2004) concludes to be typical of 'magazine masculinity'. Using this type of language was notable, for instance, in the case of physiological changes. When telling the reader that after four months of pregnancy a woman's belly and breasts start to grow, the text notes that the latter is an 'anti-stress bonus for you'. In descriptions of women, it is also worth noting that the exact words used to denote them vary across the text from the 'wife' (*zhena*), to a 'girlfriend' (*podruga*) and further to just a 'girl' (*devushka*). This variation illustrates that discussion of pregnancy is by no means limited to marriage, which further strengthens the core message of the text: *all this can happen to you!*

Taking women's needs and demands into account by addressing their peculiar behaviour and explaining it to the readers also serves to create a feeling of solidarity among 'us men'. The 'us-ness' of men, and the relationship between the writer and reader, is created by both direct and indirect addresses, as Crashaw (2007) has shown in his study. The indirect addresses concern, first of all, the formulation of topics of discussions and 'shared' assumptions about men's desires, needs and fears. As noted above, the whole text is based on several generalised assumptions about men's desire for free living and the carefree life of a single wealthy professional, where pregnancy is an undesired reversal. The previous examples have also shown that the text addresses the reader directly. The text is full of advice on what 'you' should do in different situations, often accompanied by 'buddy discourse' (Stibbe 2004), which brings the writer closer to the reader and creates an atmosphere of camaraderie between the magazine and readership.

In addition, direct modes of address are also used to describe the reader. The article discusses the five most often feared things (fear of losing freedom, fear of not being able to take the responsibility of fatherhood, fear of losing one's wife, jealousy and fear of ageing), and gives advice on how to cope with these fears. In giving advice on how to cope with the fear of losing one's wife when she is devoted to caring for the child, the text notes that the fear that your place could be taken by a child is not characteristic of 'independent people', and asks the reader: 'But you are not that kind of a person, right?'. This direct address suggests a certain mutual trust between the writer and reader, where the writer apparently wants to be sure that the reader acts in accordance with shared norms.

A notable feature of the text is the *real man discourse*, which, according to Toerien and Durrheim (2001: 42), 'provides a collective solution to a core problematic for today's man: how to essentialize his masculinity and still ward off the critique of men as traditionally macho'. 'Real man' is thus defined not only in contrast to the 'new man', a softer and emotional form of masculinity (Rutherford 1988), but also in contrast to the 'macho man'. In the case of pregnancy, the man is accordingly advised to be sensitive to a woman's wishes and desires, however peculiar, while simultaneously maintaining his assumed essential preferences in sex, football and beer-drinking.

The societal context of the articles on stress

The material made very few explicit references to Russian society. In most cases the stories could have been located in any metropolis where life is organised around business and Western values of competition, economic success and consumption. One of the topics where Russian culture and society were mentioned was heavy alcohol-drinking, which was mentioned in articles a few times. Drinking was in all cases described in a negative manner, typically with references to the socialist heritage and the societal changes of past decades. In a story about serial killers, one of the reasons for 'maniac syndrome' was claimed to be mothers' drinking, which, in turn, was attributed to the social transformation from *perestroika* to market economy: 'taking into account that today's 15–20 year olds were born in the gloomy years of total alcoholization, it is not difficult to conclude that the number of maniacs will only grow'. The reader, however, is strictly dissociated from irresponsible drinking. In an article about street violence, outrages are explained by immoderate drinking, which is actively detached from the reader:

> It's obvious that you yourself don't abuse spirits, since you're reading this magazine.
>
> (*Men's Health*, May 2005: 194)

In a story about traffic jams, corruption of policemen, a phenomenon claimed to be typical of Russian everyday life, is introduced as a stressful issue in traffic. This is because the *militsiia* is described as entirely corrupt, who do whatever they want to find any reason for fining the reader and, consequently, get a bribe from him to avoid the fine. The reader is told that the police often suggest paying bribes in a circuitous way, asking the driver they have stopped about the way he wants to pay the fine: does he want to come to the police station 'or how'? The text actively distances the reader from all such activity by stating that '"or how" is not our method'. Instead, the reader is advised to remain patient and calm whatever the police do or ask. By not being provoked he can convince them of the irrelevance of all accusations.

An exception to the rule of a writing style unconnected to any specific society is the article on sexually abused men. The article is written in a critical tone, where the starting point is that it is a phenomenon that is not discussed in Russian society despite its importance. The article introduces stories of men who have been sexually abused and takes a critical stand to how the problem is treated in Russian society. The legislation is criticised for not acknowledging the abused men, and the procedures of courts and policemen are condemned for their inability to protect the victims.

> Even in civilized countries the rape of a man was recognized by law only in 1994. Can you imagine, who would turn to our policemen to make an accusation about a rape?
>
> (*Men's Health*, June 2007: 144)

Thus, although the problem itself is not depicted as a particularly Russian phenomenon, the text expresses severe criticism of how the issue is handled in Russian society. The article includes none of the humour typical of other articles, and the cases of sexually abused men introduced do not fit the general model reader of the magazine: they represent the range of 'ordinary' Russian men, some of them having children and spouses. In fact, the Russian hegemonic masculinity is taken as a part of the problem.

> Why do men usually keep silent? Because society crudely demands that we should "be strong and able to stand up for ourselves". We are not supposed to show weaknesses and not supposed to become victims. From the moment of birth we enter into a competition with each other, and that prevents us from showing our defenselessness.
>
> (*Men's Health*, June 2007: 143)

It is worth noting that the text does not address the reader directly when discussing the topic, as in other articles in my research material. The only address to the reader is at the end of the story, where the reader is given advice on whom to contact in case 'you have encountered such difficulties'. Without this exception, the communication distance is great compared to the close communication distances in most articles. The reader is not included in the story. The same applies to the story of men's suicide in Russia. The issue is not introduced as a specifically Russian problem and the reader is, to a large extent, detached from the text.

Concerning references to the societal context, two important conclusions can be drawn. First, these references are generally extremely rare, which highlights the timeless and placeless characteristics of the magazine. Particularly considering the topic of stress, it is striking that such societal issues as unemployment, poverty, social inequalities, political instability, terrorism or threat of war, which are often mentioned to be among the issues causing chronic stress to Russians, are not discussed in the column. As a consequence, the social conditions and phenomena are not criticised either. Second, in the rare mentions of the societal context, the reader is described as somewhat above these negative conditions due to his superior cross-cultural global identity. In the most extreme example of sexually abused men, the reader is simply excluded from the text. These issues obviously relate to the genre of the magazine; lifestyle magazines are generally not oriented to social problems, their focus is, instead, on the individual.

Causes and consequences of stress

A notable feature in the articles on stress is that the relationship between the issues discussed and their consequences, i.e. stress, was not explicated. Typically the articles concerned situations that are usually considered to be stress-causing without, however, contemplating the concrete consequences, i.e. feelings or physical ailments resulting from these stressful situations. In the articles included in the research material, the only exception to this rule was the article on working at night, where stress caused by night work was claimed to result in various physiological problems, with many references to metabolism and hormones, and an inability to concentrate. Other concrete consequences of stress were laconic and blurred references, for instance, to damage to neuro-cells, which were represented as taken-for-granted 'facts' that needed no specification or problematisation. It was common to all stories that they focused on discussing the assumed reasons for stress in the model reader's life, and ways of processing the problems, rather than the reader's experiences of stress. Thus, the concept of stress remained vague, often mixed with 'problem', 'bother' or just 'bad feeling'.

What is striking in all the articles covered by this study is that the topics of the articles were not considered in terms of social relations, with the exception of the article on pregnancy. As discussed above, there was notable variation in the topics related to stress, as well as in how seriously the topics were discussed. 'Stress' was typically caused by external factors creating 'stressful situations' and not by people. Human relations were not discussed either as reasons for stress or in relation to coping with it. This was most notable in the article on loneliness, where close relationships within the family were not included in the considerations, although the reader might expect this kind of perspective, too. Similarly, emotions related to stress, such as fear, guilt, shame, anxiety, and anger, were likewise not discussed. Given that stress is primarily a psycho-social phenomenon, absence of emotions and social relations in articles on stress seems strange.

Conclusion

In light of earlier analyses, it could be stated that the articles on stress in *Men's Health* were primarily characterised by a certain triviality. This was most evident in the weak explication for the topics of stories and their assumed links to feelings of stress. The lack, or even deliberate avoidance, of a social context was also evident in that several important social problems, such as poverty or social insecurity, not to mention marital problems, worries about children's future and other relations with people close to the reader, were not included in the topics. Given the wide variation in the topics of the articles, 'stress' might be interpreted as a certain prism through which several and different kinds of issues are projected onto the public screen. As several articles were at least slightly humorous, they may be taken mostly to represent entertainment rather than enlightenment of the readers.

That stress discussed in the articles remains unresolvable might also refer to the idea that stress is thought to be an essential element of the young, urban professional's, i.e. the model reader's, life. Stress is often associated with responsibility, power and importance in the labour market, which contributes to the idea of stress being a part of a business man's life. Interpreted this way, stress may not even be something that should be avoided, as it matches and supports other important qualities attached to the implied reader and thus strengthens his identity.

The infrequent references to Russian society were mostly expressed in implicit ways. The most explicit cases were those dealing with heavy alcohol-drinking, which was attributed to the harmful legacy of the Soviet past. On the other hand, the omnipresent emphasis on sex might also be interpreted as an indirect distinction from the Soviet times, namely Soviet Puritanism. Thus, it seems that the magazine simultaneously avoids explicit discussions on Russian society while implicitly distancing itself from the Soviet past. Taking distance from Soviet Russia follows the general line of the magazine to construct new market-oriented, global, masculine identities.

A striking feature of the texts was the absence of emotions and social relationships. The putative reader is portrayed as a lonely rider who has no close relationships to tie him down. Even when certain people close to the reader are mentioned in the texts, such as friends or 'girls', they occupy the supporting roles in the construction of the heroic Self of the reader. Some of the articles evinced an idea that, in the model reader's life, the mother is the person who supports him when times get rough, although this was mentioned explicitly in only two texts. It is worth noting that despite these references to a mother, who helps the reader, the existence of a father was not mentioned once in articles. It is tempting to draw the conclusion that whereas 'mother' is sometimes needed as a person who is capable of solving the reader's emotional problems, the absence of 'father' underlines the notion of the reader as an independent person whose life is not controlled by outside authorities.

In an earlier study on *Men's Health*, Kulinka (2004) analysed how the magazine produces new masculine identities for its Russian and Belarussian readers. Regarding the values attributed to the new identities, she refers to an editor's formulation: 'No geographical or political divergences make any difference to the essential values of a modern man. In any country in the world, we want the same: to be healthy and strong, to know how to enjoy life, and to have an interesting job and harmonious relationships with women' (ibid: 45). Thus, the magazine intentionally promotes trans-national values for building and strengthening globally dominant masculine ideals and identities. In this process, the local characteristics of readers and their environments represent disturbing trivialities that need to be obscured to make way for a modern male Russian cosmopolitan.

In her analyses of the magazine, Kulinka (2004) shows that the main emphases of texts are on physical strength, economic success through respected and well-paid jobs and, most importantly, sex and sexual prowess. Therefore, she concludes that the formation of a 'new masculine ideology' in Russian version of *Men's Health* is based on the reproduction of traditional masculine values (ibid: 47). Following previous deliberations it might be concluded that most important in the reproduction of masculine values in *Men's Health* is not necessarily the values as such, but rather the ways in which those traditional values are translated into modern form. This is most obvious in the articulation of the status of work in terms of private business and affluent way of life, and conceptualising freedom primarily in terms of overly individualist choices that are not restricted by any external forces. The values are thus largely rooted in the neo-liberal individualism widely promoted in the magazine (Crashaw 2007).

As noted above, in many contexts the magazine offers the reader advice not only on what to do and how to behave but also on how things should be valued. This way the lifestyle magazine promotes certain preferences and tastes considered to fit its readers' social status. In Bourdieaun terms, the magazine markets a certain *habitus* to its readers where preferences, particularly in consumption, but taste in everything men do is an essential element of their identity. The contemporary upper class has a short history in Russia. It is by no means a homogeneous group, consisting of the old *intelligentsiia*, members of the communist party *nomenklatura* as well as the *nouveau riches*, whose values may differ radically from each other. It could thus be interpreted that there is an order for a certain hidden agenda for the contemporary Russian upper class, which the magazine promotes on its pages. This was most obvious in the continuous appeals to the reader where he was advised, even taught, to think in a certain proper way about the issues under consideration. Thus, the reader is assumed, persuaded and taught to share the values of the magazine. *Men's Health* as a lifestyle magazine produces both ideals of life and its ideal readers, and represents a particular context of the construction of a globalised modern masculine self.

Notes

1 I am grateful to Dr. Marja Rytkönen for her help in translating the excerpts as well as several invaluable suggestions she made for improving the manuscript.

2 In some countries, the magazine does not have its own journalists or even editorial office, and the magazine is translated from other versions into the local language. The Russian edition of the magazine is, however, produced in Moscow. The circulation of *Men's Health* is around 240,000 of which 60 per cent is sold in Moscow and 11 per cent in St. Petersburg (www.mhealth.ru/about/magazine/audience.php, accessed 8 December 2008).

3 In the articles on stress, anything other than heterosexual orientation of the reader was not explicitly discussed. There were, however, examples of this elsewhere in the issues included in the study material. In an article on group sex (*MH,* June 2005: 60) the text considers, as a curiosity, the possibility of sex between males, but concludes briefly that this does not 'concern you and me in any way, so we won't discuss them'.

References

Ashwin, S. and Lytkina, T. (2004) 'Men in crisis in Russia. The role of domestic marginalization', *Gender & Society* 18: 189–206.

Benwell, B. (2004) 'Ironic Discourse. Evasive masculinity in men's lifestyle magazines', *Men and Masculinities* 7: 3–21.

Bobak, M. and Marmot, M. (1996) 'East-West mortality divide and its potential explanations: proposed research agenda', *British Medical Journal* 312: 421–5.

Brittan, A. (1989) *Masculinity and power*, Oxford: Basil Blackwell.

Chen, L.C., Wittgenstein, F. and McKeon, E. (1996) 'The upsurge of mortality in Russia: causes and policy implications', *Population and Development Review* 22: 517–30.

Cockerham, W.C. (1997) 'The social determinants of the decline of life expectancy in Russia and Eastern Europe: A lifestyle explanation', *Journal of Health and Social Behavior* 38: 117–30.

Crashaw, P. (2007) 'Governing the healthy male citizen: men, masculinity and popular health in *Men's Health* magazine', *Social Science & Medicine* 65: 1606–18.

Dying Too Young. Addressing Premature Mortality and Ill Health Due to Non-Communicable Diseases and Injuries in the Russian Federation (2005), Washington: The World Bank.

Garlick, S. (2003) 'What is a man? Heterosexuality and the technology of masculinity', *Men and Masculinities* 6: 156–72.

Gavrilova, N.S., Semyonova, V.G., Evdokushina, G.N. and Gavrilov, L.A. (2000) 'The response of violent mortality to economic crisis in Russia', *Population Research and Policy Review* 19: 397–419.

Harrison, J., Chin, J. and Ficarrotto, T. (1989) 'Warning: masculinity may be dangerous to your health', in M.S. Kimmel and M.A. Messner (eds) *Men's lives*, New York: Macmillan Publishing Company.

Kiblitskaya, M. (2000) '"Once we were kings". Male experiences of loss of status at work in post-communist Russia', in S. Ashwin (ed.) *Gender, state and society in Soviet and post-Soviet Russia*, London and New York: Routledge.

Kimmel, M.S. (1987) 'The contemporary "crisis" of masculinity in historical perspective', in H. Brod (ed.) *The Making of Masculinities. The New Men's Studies*, Boston, MA: Allen & Unwin.

Kress, G. and van Leeuwen, T. (2002) 'Representation and interaction: designing the position of the viewer', in A. Jaworski and N. Coupland (eds) *The Discourse Reader*, London and New York: Routledge.

Kulinka, N. (2004) 'Zdorov'e i krasota: krug "muzhskikh" tem popolnilsja. Zhurnal "*Men's Health*" kak instrument prodvizheniia "novogo" stilia zhizni', *Acta Universitatis Latviensis* 666: 43–9.

Leon, D.A. and Shkolnikov, V.M. (1998) 'Social stress and the Russian mortality crisis', *The Journal of the American Medical Association* 279: 790–1.

Machin, D. and van Leeuwen, T. (2005) 'Language style and lifestyle: the case of a global magazine', *Media, Culture & Society* 27: 577–600.

Machin, D. and Thornborrow, J. (2003) 'Branding and Discourse: The Case of Cosmopolitan', *Discourse & Society* 14: 453–71.

Messner, M.A. (1997) *Politics of masculinities: men in movements*, Thousand Oaks, CA: SAGE Publications.

Nemtsov, A.V. (2002) 'Alcohol-related human losses in Russia in the 1980s and 1990s', *Addiction* 97: 1413–25.

Notzon, F.C., Komarov, Y.M., Ermakov, S.P., Sempos, C.T., Marks, J.S. and Sempos, E.V. (1998) 'Causes of declining life expectancy in Russia', *The Journal of the American Medical Association* 279: 793–800.

Parker, I. (1992) *Discourse Dynamics. Critical analysis for social and individual psychology*, London: Routledge.

Petersen, A. (1998) *Unmasking the masculine. 'Men' and 'identity' in a skeptical age*, London: SAGE Publications.

Pietilä, I. and Rytkönen, M. (2008a) 'Coping with stress and by stress: Russian men and women talking about transition, stress and health', *Social Science & Medicine* 66: 327–38.

Pietilä, I. and Rytkönen, M. (2008b) '"Health is a not a man's domain." Lay accounts on gender difference in life-expectancy in Russia', *Sociology of Health and Illness* 30: 1070–85.

Pietilä, I. and Shek, O. (2008) '"Vse my – pod ogromnym stressom". Representatsii stressa v postsovetskom obshchestve: analiz gazetnykh publikatsii 1992, 1997, 2002 i 2007 gg.', in M. Litovskaia, A. Rosenholm, I. Savkina and E. Trubina (eds) *Obraz dostoinoi zhizni v sovremennykh rossiiskikh SMI*, Ekaterinburg: Isdatel'stvo Ural'skogo Universiteta.

Pridemore, W.A. (2004) 'Weekend effects on binge drinking and homicide: the social connection between alcohol and violence in Russia', *Addiction* 99: 1034–41.

Rotkirch, A. (2000) *The man question. Loves and lives in late 20th century Russia*, Helsinki: University of Helsinki.

Rutherford, J. (1988) 'Who's that man?', in R. Chapman and J. Rutherford (eds) *Male Order: Unwrapping Masculinity*, London: Lawrence and Wishart.

Ryan, M. (1995) 'Alcoholism and Rising Mortality in the Russian Federation', *British Medical Journal* 310: 646–8.

Sarafino, E.P. (1994) *Health psychology. Biopsychosocial interactions* (2nd edition), New York: John Wiley & Sons.

Stibbe, A. (2004) 'Health and the social construction of masculinity in Men's Health magazine', *Men and Masculinities* 7: 31–51.

Toerien, M. and Durrheim, K. (2001) 'Power through knowledge: ignorance and the "real man"', *Feminism & Psychology* 11: 35–54.

Watson, P. (1995) Explaining rising mortality among men in Eastern Europe. *Social Science & Medicine* 41: 923–34.

Wetherell, M. and Edley, N. (1999) 'Negotiating Hegemonic Masculinity: Imaginary positions and psycho-discursive practices', *Feminism & Psychology* 9: 335–56.

Wodak, R. and Meyer, M. (eds) (2001) *Methods of Critical Discourse Analysis*, London: SAGE Publications.

Zdravomyslova, E. and Temkina, A. (2002) 'Krizis maskulinnosti v pozdnesovetskom diskurse' in S. Ushakin (ed.) *O muzhe(N)stvennosti,* Moscow: Novoe literaturnoe obozrenie.

7 In search of a 'new (wo)man'

Gender and sexuality in contemporary Russian self-help literature[1]

Suvi Salmenniemi

Introduction

This chapter examines representations of gender and sexuality in contemporary Russian self-help literature.[2] Through a case study of two bestselling authors, Nataliia Pravdina and Gennadii Malakhov, it traces, first, those textual strategies and categories through which self-help books produce gender and sexual identities and gendered patterns of subjectivity. Second, it seeks to identify the sources that the authors draw on in constructing and legitimating their messages.

I approach self-help literature as a 'technology of the self' (Foucault 1988: 1998) that offers cultural tools for individuals to work on their selves; their bodies, souls, conduct and ways of being. Self-help books seek to guide, evaluate and problematise the self, morality and behaviour, and introduce concepts and categories through which they can be made sense of and transformed. In this way they shape the process of subjectivation. Following Teresa de Lauretis (1987: 2–3), we can also conceptualise self-help as a 'technology of gender' that produces representations of femininity and masculinity.

Owing to its prescriptive nature, self-help literature opens a particularly intriguing window for investigating conceptions of gender and sexuality and their shifting meanings in contemporary Russian society. Self-help books provide models of how 'things should be' in order for one to be happy and healthy, and shape and reflect cultural values and ideals. The collapse of the Soviet Union has entailed a radical re-evaluation of many fundamental categories and conceptions in Russia, including the Soviet ideological construction of the 'New Man and Woman'. Popular culture, including self-help guides, functions as an important site in which the symbolic contention about gender, sexuality and subjectivity take place in Russia.

I begin this chapter by discussing the background and context of self-help literature in Russia. In the next section I discuss the data and the method, after which I examine the discourses that Malakhov and Pravdina draw on in their texts. The remaining sections analyse in detail how gender and sexuality are represented in these authors' texts.

Helping the self in Soviet and contemporary Russia

Self-help literature is very popular in today's Russia, but it is an unexplored terrain in academic research.[3] Unlike Western societies, which have witnessed the rise of the 'therapeutic culture' and 'psy' knowledges and techniques, in the Soviet Union such a development did not take root.[4] Psycho-analysis flourished in Russia and the USSR during the first decades of the twentieth century, but it was suppressed during the 1930s (Etkind 1997). Psychiatry in Soviet society gained a notorious reputation owing to its abuse in punishing dissidents. Psycho-therapeutic practices were officially met with suspicion and treated as a bourgeois phenomenon not suitable for the new Soviet society. Consequently, therapeutic language and techniques occupied a marginal position in Soviet society until *perestroika* and the social transformation of the 1990s.

However, popular advice manuals did exist in both Imperial and Soviet Russia, offering advice on how to manage one's self, human relationships, body and conduct.[5] During the Soviet era, advice literature played an important role in campaigns for *kul'turnost'*, i.e. in 'civilising' and making the Soviet masses cultured (Kelly 2001: 244–9). It propagated the new Soviet moral order and sought to inculcate in the population the ideals and norms of the Soviet way of life. Soviet advice literature can be categorised roughly into two main genres. First, the Soviet state promoted individual self-training (*samovospitanie*), which encouraged citizens to work on their selves and shape their consciousness in order to become better communists (for more details, see Kharkhordin 1999).[6] Second, more 'practically oriented' advice books were also published, for example, in the fields of nutrition, hygiene and health (Kelly 2001), which partly helped to compensate for the inadequate supply of consumer goods and services in Soviet society.

In the aftermath of the Soviet Union the centralised publishing industry was privatised and censorship was lifted. As a result, the genres and the number of titles in self-help literature grew rapidly. A casual visit to any bookstore in Russia today reveals the vast range of various types of self-help books on offer. Self-help titles also frequently figure in bestseller lists (see, for example, bestseller lists in *Knizhnoe Obozrenie*) and they are advertised on bookstores' bestseller stands. Self-help literature can be bought at many outlets; for example, Pravdina's and Malakhov's books can be purchased at newsstands in railway stations.

I suggest that the popularity of self-help literature in today's Russia stems at least from three sources. First, the social welfare system has undergone significant changes since the displacement of the Soviet statist model. Social and health services are inadequate and, in particular, the official healthcare system suffers from widespread distrust among the population (Rivkin-Fish 2005). This makes alternative sources of support, such as reliance on informal networks, civic organisations and alternative medical and practical psychological literature, popular.[7] Self-help books are also presumably used for prophylactic purposes, that is, people seek to prevent problems with the help of the advice offered in these books.

Second, the collapse of the ideological framework of state socialism has prompted a quest for new ideals and values. Self-help books tap into this demand by introducing new concepts and techniques for making sense of 'who we are' and 'who we should become'. It seems that the middle classes, in particular, show increasing interest in physical and mental health and self-fashioning (Gladarev and Tsinman 2009), which creates markets for self-help technologies.

Third, one can also expect the appeal of self-help literature to be linked with the structural distrust prevailing in Russian society. Social institutions, such as the government, parliament and law enforcement bodies suffer from an extremely low level of trust (Shlapentokh 2006) and there is a widespread feeling of inability among the population to influence political outcomes (Petukhov 2005). Perhaps this distrust and sense of political powerlessness encourage people to work on what they think could be changed: themselves.

Data and method

The self-help authors chosen for closer analysis in this chapter represent two key genres of self-help: popular psychology (Pravdina) and popular medicine (Malakhov). By focusing on these two different genres, the chapter seeks to trace the potentially divergent interpretation of gender and sexuality emerging in self-help literature. Clearly, the analysis of the books of two authors cannot highlight all interpretations in the self-help genre, but it can offer insights into those that are particularly popular and widely circulating.

Nataliia Pravdina is a feng shui consultant[8] and, as her books advertise, has developed 'a unique system of positive transformation of consciousness' (*unikal'naia sistema pozitivnoi transformatsii soznaniia*). She lived in Los Angeles for some time and began her publishing career in Russia in the 1990s. Gennadii Malakhov began practising folk medicine, or 'natural methods of healing' (*estestvennye metody ozdorovleniia*) as he himself characterises his activities, during the Soviet era by founding a club, *Bodrost'* (Fitness). His first book on this theme appeared in 1989. (*Trud* 1996.) He is a graduate of a sports academy; he does not have a medical degree (*Argumenty i Fakty* 2002). Both authors offer the audience a multifaceted 'self-help package' with a range of media products. Alongside books, they offer advice in the form of CDs, DVDs and seminars. Both authors have websites that include interactive discussion forums and information about their products. Malakhov also hosts a talk show on health issues, *Malakhov Plus*, on national television.

I have chosen three books by Pravdina for the analysis: *Ia privlekaiu liubov' i schast'e* (henceforth IP; I invite love and happiness), *Ideal'nyi muzhchina dlia ideal'noi zhenshchiny* (IM; An ideal man for an ideal woman) and *Chego khotiat zhenshchiny?* (CK; What do women want?). From Malakhov I have chosen four books: *Krasota tela v sile dukha* (KT; Beauty of the body in the strength of the spirit), *Zdorov'e muzhchiny: Lechenie i preduprezhdenie zabolevanii* (ZM; Man's health: treatment and prevention of illnesses), *Zdorov'e zhenshchiny: Eto dolzhno znat' kazhdaia zhenshchina* (ZZh; Woman's health: what every woman must know) and *Zdorov'e obshchestva v zdorov'e zhenshchiny* (ZO; Society's health in a woman's health).[9] These books were chosen on the basis of two criteria: they address happiness and well-being in a comprehensive manner and their titles and descriptions suggest that they address gender relations. I read these books from a discourse analytical viewpoint. I am interested in analysing how gender and sexuality are signified. In which contexts do gender and sexuality appear and how, and when do they remain unarticulated? How are gender and sexuality textually constructed in the context of health and happiness, and why in this particular way?

Pravdina and Malakhov address both female and male readers in their books and offer detailed advice on how to become healthy and happy, and find love and harmony.[10] Gender and sexuality operate as important prisms through which these themes are contemplated. Pravdina seeks to construct a dialogical relationship with her readers, especially women. She addresses them with expressions such as 'dear sisters' and 'my dear women', which convey an impression of confidential interaction between 'girl friends'. By contrast, Malakhov's writings have a more didactic and educational undertone familiar from Soviet advice materials and tend to give advice as exhortations (e.g. 'one should always keep in mind'). Both authors also employ the established convention of self-help writing, that is, they draw on the life stories and experiences of their readers and acquaintances, and occasionally on their own lives, to elucidate their advice and convince the readers that the methods proposed actually work.

Self-made (wo)men and the natural order

Pravdina and Malakhov draw their ideological and philosophical inspiration from multiple sources. Both rely on Christianity (Bible, God, Christ) and Indian and Chinese religious and philosophical traditions (such as karma, reincarnation, feng shui). In this sense, they can be located in the framework of 'New Age alternative spirituality'[11] (York 2001), or 'hybrid spirituality' (Woodstock 2005), characteristic of which is a self-constructed philosophical worldview encompassing elements from a range of belief systems.[12] For both authors the idea of a 'Universe' (*Vselennaia*), a metaphysical Higher Power guiding life, is central. They endorse the idea that all human beings are part of and linked to each other through the Universe, which functions as one single coherent organism. Religious tenets, particularly Orthodox Christianity, occupy a more central position in Malakhov's writings, whereas Pravdina's texts are strongly influenced by Anglo-American self-help discourse with New Age and post-feminist features.[13] Pravdina draws on the specific 'prosperity stream' of the New Age thought, focusing on gaining wealth through personal growth (Heelas 1996), and often cites its famous representative Louise Hay. Positive thinking (*pozitivnoe myshlenie*), the core notion of the American self-help genre (Woodstock 2005), also plays a key role in her books.

Pravdina and Malakhov also circulate scientific discourse – research, statistics and experts' views – in order to legitimise their messages. References to research are, as a rule, formulated vaguely; for example, 'many specialists are of the opinion' or 'scientific research has shown'. The most commonly mentioned experts are sexologists, psychologists and medical doctors. Malakhov draws extensively on medical and physiological discourse and combines it with folk medicine. Physiological discourse, with its key concept of 'organism', was highly influential in Soviet Russia in explaining mental processes and gender relations (Attwood 1990; Riordan 1978), and it is also the framework through which Malakhov makes sense of health and well-being. Although he often refers to medical knowledge, he also takes a critical stand towards it. He characterises medicine as a profit-driven industry: 'The more ill people, the more the sector flourishes and the more it receives profit' (ZZh: 8). As an alternative to this selfish industry he proposes reliance on natural self-healing, which is presented as altruistic and moral activity.[14] What is noteworthy, both Pravdina and Malakhov question the Soviet authority-driven tradition in which a person's health and well-being were seen as guided by medical institutions and specialists of various kinds. Both authors, although invoking expert knowledge, strongly emphasise individual responsibility: people can and should take care of their health and happiness by themselves.

The New Age and post-feminist self-help discourses that Pravdina introduces to the Russian audience promote an individualist self-made (wo)man ideology. Pravdina's ontological stand is based upon the premise that social reality is a direct consequence of our words and thoughts, without any corporeal and structural conditions intervening. The key words here are 'free choice' (*vybor*) and 'individual responsibility' (*otvetstvennost'*), which are 'master norms' of the therapeutic culture characterising contemporary Western societies (Rose 1998). Pravdina stresses that everyone is solely responsible for his/her happiness. We all are free to make choices, from which it logically follows that we choose to be happy or unhappy. This discourse of individual responsibility and free choice offers a countermodel to the official Soviet social order, which endorsed collectivism and paternalist relations between the people and the authorities. With this discourse a new ideal subject is envisioned: instead of being dependent on the state, the new Russian subject should be an active, free-choosing and responsible agent of his/her life. This idea fits neatly into the neo-liberal and post-feminist rationalities conceptualising people as entrepreneurs of their lives (Rose 1998: 33; Gill 2007).

Pravdina's books pay no attention to structural constraints within which 'free choices' are made and 'individual responsibility' taken. Actors are portrayed as untouched by power relations that position them in different structural locations depending on gender, class or ethnicity:

> Today every one of us has an opportunity to have education, become a high-class professional in any sphere of action, occupy a respectable (*dostoinoe*) position in society, be independent, achieve success and recognition, live carefree and not to deny oneself anything.
>
> (IM: 67)

The books explicitly discourage addressing societal and structural factors. The readers are advised to 'never encourage discussion about unpleasant issues.

Refuse all attempts to draw you into a discussion about inflation, expensive prices, corruption of the powers-that-be, housebreaking, and so on' (IM: 134). The articulation of social inequalities is silenced, and indeed there is no need for it, because if, for example, enrichment is merely a matter of choice and will, it means that poverty and unhappiness are one's own fault. This same logic also applies to gendered power relations. The fact that women are poorly represented in political institutions in Russia is explained in the books as simply a result of women's lack of interest in politics, and not, for example, of gender-based discrimination. By overlooking structural constraints, Pravdina's books legitimise and naturalise social hierarchies, and contribute to the symbolic construction of the new class structure. Social problems are psychologised and treated as individual 'failures' caused by an undeveloped 'self'.

In contrast to Pravdina's individualist stand, Malakhov positions human life into the context of nature (*priroda*) and religion. They provide the framework within which work on the self is carried out. Nature serves as a model according to which human life should be organised. Readers are encouraged to live in harmony with nature and to develop their selves in dialogue with the 'Higher Power'. Self-healing (*samoozdorovlenie*) is the key concept for Malakhov and he aims at helping people to cultivate healthy ways of life. The methods of self-healing consist of correct diet and breathing, physical exercise, cleansing of the body (e.g. by fasting), urine therapy, water and 'tempering' procedures (*vodnye i zakalivaiushchie protsedury*),[15] and working on one's character and consciousness. The last two in particular are reminiscent of the Soviet self-training tradition. Similar to Pravdina, societal constraints are largely omitted from Malakhov's self-healing project.

Malakhov's and Pravdina's books invite readers to devote themselves to long-term work on their selves. This intensive work on the self is also promoted in the Anglo-American self-help genre (see e.g. McGee 2005: 12) but it is an equally central feature of the Soviet individual self-training practice (Kharkhordin 1999). Strengthening of the will was a key element of self-training and its influence shows clearly in Malakhov's books, which constantly stress the crucial role of self-discipline and willpower in shaping one's body and health. Pravdina and Malakhov also share the belief in intimate interconnectedness between body and mind.[16] They portray consciousness (*soznanie*) as regulating and shaping the body. There is a firm belief in the power of thought: the body appears as malleable material that the mind can shape. The body will become healthier and younger if one actively imagines an ideal body (Malakhov) and praises one's body aloud (Pravdina). Because of the centrality of the physiological framework in Malakhov's books, he devotes considerably more attention than Pravdina to shaping the body through physical exercise.

The understanding of gender in Malakhov's and Pravdina's books draws on the belief in essential, 'natural' sexual difference. Both authors textually construct a bi-polar, complementary and heteronormative gender order by drawing on the Chinese philosophy of Yin and Yang, the Russian discourse on the 'female and male principle' (*zhenskoe/muzhkoe nachalo*), and by writing in singular forms ('a man', 'a woman'), portraying women and men as representatives of a 'breed' (cf. Tainio 2001: 138–9).

> Men and women are created as absolutely different and no modern ploys (*ukhishchreniia*) can make us forget our natural destiny (*prednaznachenie*). A man has initially been assigned the personification of Yang – an energy of creation, creativity, constant movement and striving forward. A woman reserves and maintains in herself the energy of Yin, and together they embody and create harmony in the world.
>
> (IM: 9)

> A woman is essentially considerably closer to Nature. She lives according to its rhythms...A woman is more emotional than a man, her intuition is more developed. In contrast to a man, who has more developed logical thinking, a woman perceives the world by intuition and emotions. A woman is more predisposed to empathy and to feel the most delicate spiritual concerns (*perezhivaniia*); she has refined emotional organs.
>
> (ZO: 5–6)

Make way for the woman – get rid of the mother

I now move on to analyse in more detail how Pravdina and Malakhov signify gender and sexuality in their books. I begin by examining Pravdina's gender imagery. A central feature of her books is envisaging the 'new Russian woman and man'. Here, the Soviet gender ideals implicitly function as the 'other' against which the new ideals are constructed. The ideal subject outlined in the books is culturally coded as masculine, characterised by autonomy, self-reliance and independence. Women are encouraged to incorporate this model of subjectivity. Thus, women are positioned as the primary audience in need of help and advice, as those who particularly have to work on their selves.

In Pravdina's texts, the culturally strong equation of womanhood with motherhood is questioned and women's economic and emotional independence is called for. As she states, 'an ideal woman has to be first and foremost self-reliant, independent, and successful in the area she herself has chosen' (IM: 64). Women are advised to prioritise self-realisation and career and to give up the traditional model of femininity characterised by self-sacrifice and martyrdom. Hence, the books question the long Russian cultural–historical tradition of representing self-sacrifice as a key feature of femininity (Riabov 2001; Rosenholm 1999). Pravdina declares: 'Forget about a saviour on a white horse!...You, and only you, can help yourself' (IM: 62).

The books encourage emotional detachment and pathologise women's dependency on men by medicalising it. Women's economic dependency is interpreted as leading to emotional dependency, which 'is called neurotic dependency (*nevroticheskaia zavisimost'*) in the medical terminology' (IM: 72). Pravdina warns that dependency is 'an abnormal and unnatural phenomenon. ...For every man a woman dependent on him is a real ordeal' (IM: 71–2). The books portray dependency as an individual 'choice' and 'incapacity', not influenced by gendered power relations, such as endemic socio-economic inequalities between women and men. Although Pravdina's message of women's independence and self-realisation could be empowering, overlooking the material basis of gender relations and the pathologisation of women's emotional investments makes it stigmatising.

The call for emotional detachment has also been a crucial tenet of much of the Anglo-American relationship self-help (Hazleden 2004). As Arlie Russell Hochschild (1994: 14) has remarked, we may very well have global warming, but the intimate sphere has increasingly experienced a cultural cooling: 'The heroic acts a self can perform…are to detach, to leave and to depend and need less. The emotion work that matters is control of the feelings of fear, vulnerability and the desire to be comforted. The ideal self doesn't need much, and what it does need it can get for itself'.

However, Pravdina's books constantly balance between individualism and emotional detachment, on the one hand, and positioning the heterosexual relationship as the essential fundament of women's lives, on the other. Women are portrayed as 'the weaker sex' that needs protection from men, but at the same time they are warned about taking up the position of a powerless victim. Although women's independence is called for, the author warns women about becoming too independent ('it's not healthy', IP: 82) and idealises heterosexual relationship as an ultimate source of happiness. In this way, individualism is destabilised and portrayed partly as a gendered disposition.

Women and men are encouraged in the books to show emotions in different ways. Men are advised to share their concerns and feelings with women ('your girlfriends highly appreciate your openness and ability to express your anxieties', CK: 52), whereas women are flatly forbidden to share their anxieties with and seek comfort from their partners:

> My dear women, I ask and beg you never tell a man about your problems…! Men are built so that they expect pleasant impressions from relationships with women; they want the joys of love. They don't need your complaints and problems! If you have chosen a man to be your psychotherapist, you have made a mistake. Men love successful, self-confident women.
>
> (IP: 28)

I suggest that by encouraging women to support and comfort men, women's 'maternal' caring functions are, paradoxically, called into play. Women are assigned an omnipotent subject position: they can and should solve not only their own problems, but also the problems of their partners.

Pravdina's books negotiate gender contracts in contemporary Russia by contemplating women's and men's domestic and professional identities. In the Soviet Union the hegemonic gender contract was that of a working mother, but the contracts have become more diversified during the last decade (Rotkirch and

Temkina 2007). The gender contract Pravdina's books offer as ideal is reminiscent of what Rotkirch and Temkina (ibid.) call a gender contract of a career-oriented, professional woman. The domestic domain is still considered to belong to women, but it is increasingly externalised to paid (female) employees. It is not suggested that domestic work should be equally divided between the spouses. Both women and men are encouraged to realise their interests in the public sphere, and women to alleviate their double burden by relying on other women's labour in the domestic sphere. This brings class into the picture, as this type of gender contract assumes a certain level of income. Pravdina illustrates this gender contract with a moral tale about Tat'iana, who was a committed wife, mother and homemaker. She did everything herself at home, was deeply unhappy and her husband did not show her any respect. As a solution she decided to hire a nanny and a housekeeper and returned to her professional employment. Consequently, Pravdina approvingly notes, her husband developed a renewed respect for her (IP: 38–9).

Pravdina's books question the 'traditional' feminine identity by prioritising women's career and relationship with the spouse over motherhood. In other words, women's main framework is a heterosexual relationship, not the family. Pravdina advises that 'a real man knows that a woman is not a servant or even the mother of his children. She is above all a Woman' (CK: 59). Women are warned about becoming 'universal nanny-washerwomen-cooks' (IP: 40):

> If marriage, family and children permanently occupy the first position in your list of priorities, it means you are still governed by the old stereotype of a "woman's lot" (*zhenskaia dolia*). ... To be the homemaker (*khranitel'nitsa domashnogo ochaga*) and to procreate is secondary.
>
> (IM: 76)

As this individualist message about women's independence and career-orientation could be 'misinterpreted' as feminist, Pravdina explicitly disassociates herself from this line of thought:

> Unlike militant feminists, who accuse men of all deadly sins, I dare state that without men our world wouldn't be so unique and wonderful. ... I don't by any means invite you to join the ranks of feminists, who lead a pitiless fight against men about a place in the sun and who declare they don't need men for anything.
>
> (IM: 8, 80)

The representations of masculinity in Pravdina's texts are familiar from both the Soviet gender ideology and bourgeois nuclear family ideology. Men are associated with the public sphere and portrayed as having no caring obligations or rights in the private domain. The books do not encourage men to be more involved in the family; the only role articulated for them at home is that of a breadwinner, a cultural ideal that has been strongly promoted in post-Soviet Russia (Rotkirch 2000; Ashwin 2006). Men are portrayed as the main providers in the household, whereas women bring a supplementary livelihood through their professional engagement. Economic success appears as a key characteristic of the 'new man' and the criterion on the basis of which women choose partners. Pravdina repeatedly presents women as active agents making choices in relationships, whereas men appear as objects, having a rather instrumental role. Although Pravdina wishes to downplay motherhood, she nevertheless occasionally smuggles it back in the descriptions of ideal relationships:

> A real man regards with calm the fact that a woman is interested in his income ... because he knows that his money is part of him. And if a woman wants to know how successful he is, she is interested in money. ... Don't forget, my dear women, that a woman first and foremost evaluates a man as a potential father of her children who will maintain and protect them. ... Our [ideal] man understands very well that it's in a woman's nature to strive to secure a decent life for herself and her children.
>
> (IM: 50)

The masculine identity continues, as in the Soviet Union, to be strongly defined through work. Pravdina, however, is careful to draw a distinction between work today and during the Soviet era: 'Remember that time when work for the benefit of society was regarded as the citizen's highest achievement, selfless (*beskorystnyi*) and most exhausting [work], in the name of the idea. We know where that ideology took us' (IM: 15). Whereas in the Soviet era work was to be performed for the common good, nowadays work is supposed to make one successful and wealthy. The books openly celebrate consumerism and materialism as key dimensions of the identity of the 'new woman and man'. In this way they dismantle the Soviet cultural virtue of modesty (*skromnost'*). Interestingly, the emphasis on individual responsibility and wealth is not linked with social justice and the collective good in any way. For example, the books do not encourage philanthropy or help to those less well-off in society.

The image of the 'new ideal Russian man' sketched in the books is characterised as constantly striving to achieve success (this is described as being 'in his genes'); luxury (*roskosh'*) is a norm of life for him and he does not hesitate to spend money on himself and his significant others. He is strong, decisive and respectable; he has a sense of direction in life and leadership qualities. Women are portrayed in the books as yet another consumption item for successful men and as symbols of their success: 'A beautiful, elegant and self-confident woman can offer a man unique happiness and it is because of this that a new man strives to have such a woman by his side' (IM: 46). Attractive appearance is interpreted as an obligation and pivotal feminine capital. Pravdina recommends that women should 'constantly take care of [their] appearance' and advises that 'you always have to be beautiful and attractive!' (IM: 128).

These images of a 'new Russian man and woman' are, of course, far from the daily realities of many Russians. For example, widespread poverty, violence against women, and the massive problem of alcoholism that plagues especially the male population are not discussed in the texts. Pravdina offers her readers a narrative of the fairytale world 'out there', which arguably serves the function of helping to entertain, inspire or escape life 'here and now', similarly to many women's and lifestyle magazines.

Towards matriarchy

Malakhov positions the self firmly in the framework of nature and family. This association is produced, firstly, by invoking women's child-bearing capacity: 'After all, future life is born and develops in a woman! And this mission requires specific vital reserves that Mother Nature generously bestows upon a woman' (ZO: 5). Unlike Pravdina, Malakhov defines womanhood in the framework of motherhood and often refers to women by the term 'woman-mother' (*zhenshchina-mat'*). Women are described as having a great mission in raising 'a new generation of people with high moral principles' (ZO: 66). In this sense, Malakhov reproduces the culturally powerful Russian discursive formation of womanhood *as* motherhood. Second, women's association with nature is also constructed by claiming that weather conditions, such as 'magnetic storms' and changes in the air pressure and temperature, influence women's well-being, whereas this issue is not discussed in relation to men.

Malakhov idealises women as 'the basic model of a human being' (ZO: 6), upon which the male model is built. This leads Malakhov to suggest that the planet originally lived in a state of matriarchy. This natural and harmonious order was later superseded by a patriarchal order, which is characterised as aggressive and destructive. With this mythical origin story Malakhov envisages a new social order: a return to matriarchy.

> The time is coming when … kinship will again depend on the maternal line, and the wise female principle (*zhenskoe nachalo*) overcomes unnecessary male aggressiveness. Self-knowledge (*samosoznanie*) about the woman's role and importance in the life of society unavoidably increases and gathers strength. And when this comes to pass in full, the world will become much softer, more understanding and better.
>
> (ZO: 6)

Women's maternal mission in the world is presented as bringing about a 'new humane society that facilitates people's spiritual development' (ZO: 66). Malakhov assigns women the subject position of a saviour of the planet. In this way he circulates what the Russian philosopher Oleg Riabov (2001) has called 'the mythical Russian woman discourse', which has been embedded in Russian historical, philosophical and aesthetic discourses for centuries. This discourse includes the idea of female Messianism – women saving Russia – and portrays women as mothers, inherently morally superior, peace-loving, self-sacrificing and having a civilising mission in the world. As Malakhov argues, 'male leadership has clearly shown its aggressiveness and untenability: we have now a man's world: cruel, hostile, ruthless and insensitive. But Planet Earth needs a world with empathy, love, tolerance and understanding' (ZO: 66).

Malakhov discusses extensively the impact of emotions on health and well-being. He encourages positive thinking, as a reasonable amount of positive emotions strengthens the organism, whereas negative emotions (or too many emotions) weaken or, in the worst case, destroy the organism. Emotion management is portrayed as distinctively gendered: unlike 'rational' and 'logical' men, women are constantly haunted by emotions, implying that they need more help in managing them:

> A woman's consciousness is characterised by very high emotionality and tendency to worry. All this makes women's organism vulnerable, susceptible to psychosomatic diseases.
>
> (ZZh: 69)

Interestingly, although the health guide for women includes a long chapter on mental health, this issue is not discussed in the health guide for men. Malakhov advises women to approach everything in life 'philosophically, rationally, sensibly and logically' (ZZh: 79) – i.e. to adopt the culturally masculinely marked model of subjectivity. The ideal self emerging in Malakhov's texts is a person that is able to control his desires, does not react to external impulses and is characterised by vigilant self-monitoring, suppression of emotions and self-discipline – not unlike the ideal *Homo Sovieticus* (cf. Kharkhordin 1999: 241).

In contrast to Pravdina's consumerist messages, Malakhov's books advocate a simple, modest and natural way of life. He emphasises the importance of spiritual development instead of pursuing wealth. In this way, he embraces the cultural virtue of modesty familiar from the Soviet value system. He condemns egoism and a lifestyle that only aims at 'chasing material well-being' and pursuing 'commercial interests' (ZM: 97). He interprets these as leading to a self-inflicted syndrome of chronic fatigue (*sindrom khronicheskoi ustalosti*). This syndrome is portrayed as a partly gendered phenomenon. According to Malakhov, women 20–50 years old who have achieved much in life are particularly susceptible to this syndrome. In this way he presents women's ambition as pathological and does not contemplate the syndrome, for example, in relation to gender division of labour in Russian society.

Unlike Pravdina, Malakhov discusses gendered power relations, including violence against women, and occasionally articulates gender relations with the equality discourse (*ravnopravie*). He portrays women as victims of aggressive male oppression in society. He laments that women are not viewed as 'equal and faithful life partners', but are rather treated as 'an instrument through which men satisfy their instincts' (ZZh: 69). He advises women to be cautious with men who do not view them as 'an equal personality' (ZZh: 69) and urges them to leave violent relationships.

In Malakhov's books women are assigned a greater responsibility for their health than men. Men are encouraged to work on their health and consciousness, but this work is for their own good, not explicitly connected with any collective goal. The health guide for men offers a strong self-help message on its cover: 'A person's health and well-being depends on himself. Thanks to the correct organisation of life he can himself manage all diseases'. By contrast, women's health is discussed in relation to family, society and the future of Russia. Women are obliged to take care of their health not only for themselves, but very importantly, because as mothers it is their duty towards the family and society: 'Health is essential for all, but for women it is essential in two ways. A sick woman is a catastrophe for the whole family, and of course, for herself' (ZZh: 6). Malakhov further states that 'to a large extent the health of our society depends on a woman's health' (ZO: 2). Whereas Pravdina avoids a discussion of the collective good, in Malakhov's books this collective good emerges gendered: women are required to sacrifice themselves and work on their health for the benefit of the Russian society and nation. Thus, women's health appears as a collective and men's health as an individual concern.

Women's and men's health problems are also described in different terms. As was explained earlier, women's health is discussed in the framework of emotions and reproduction, whereas the health guide for men states right at the beginning that 'the majority of illnesses men encounter in their lives are self-inflicted' (ZM: 7). Men are portrayed as a risk group destroying their health; this is connected with the concern for men's extremely low life expectancy in contemporary Russia. The health guide for men discusses destructive ways of life (alcoholism, smoking, overeating) at length, whereas these play only a marginal role in the books devoted to women's health. Looking after appearance, in contrast, is interpreted as an important part of women's, but not men's, health. Malakhov's texts contain detailed advice to women on how to take care of their skin, hair and lips.

The strategies of writing and convincing readers are also gendered in the health guides. The book for men draws extensively on scientific knowledge (statistics, research results and so on) and includes information about 'general' diseases, such as heart and lung problems, that plague both men and women. Although the books for women also include references to scientific knowledge, it is noteworthy that religious discourse plays a much more central role in these books. In *Society's health in a woman's health*, in particular, medical and physiological frameworks give way to a highly religious and metaphysical understanding of conception, birth and motherhood. In line with reincarnation, Malakhov suggests that God is likely to give a morally pure and clean-living woman who regularly prays and attends church an exceptionally talented new soul (child). The man/father has practically no role in this constellation. A woman carrying this new life is described as a divine creature. Giving birth is the woman's holy duty and she is praised for her readiness to 'sacrifice herself' in order to give birth to a new life. In this framework, infertility emerges as a consequence of immoral life and bad karma collected in previous lives. If the child is restless or ill, it is explained to stem from the fact that the woman's soul and organism were not pure at the time of conception, and/or she has not led a morally pure and emotionally harmonious life during pregnancy. Thus, women are always to blame for any child-related problems.

The gender contract that Malakhov offers to his readers follows the pattern of working mother with a breadwinner husband:

> Usually the man carries the main responsibility for providing for the family, and he is ready to work self-sacrificingly for its prosperity. However, a young husband is often faced with the fact that he is assigned such obligations that he didn't have before and that, in his opinion, undervalue his dignity as a man (*muzhkoe dostoinstvo*). Now he is confronted with doing housework: helping to clean the house, cleaning away his dishes after a meal. He has to show interest in the professional interests of his working wife, promote an atmosphere of optimism, take the initiative in spending pleasant leisure time…For the majority of men this is difficult to understand. How can one avoid overstepping the line after which one turns into a henpecked husband (*byt' u zheny pod kabulkom*), or into a family tyrant?
>
> (ZM: 125–6)

Men as fathers occupy a marginal role in discussions concerning birth, child-care and upbringing; they are mentioned only in passing, if at all. The gender division of labour in the domestic sphere is not questioned: men are portrayed as only 'helping' their wives at home. Indeed, housework and family life are interpreted in the quote above as somehow 'demeaning' for many men.

Sexuality: Pleasure and obligation

Both Pravdina and Malakhov portray heterosexuality as an important dimension of gender relations, health and happiness. They discuss sexuality and intimate relationships openly, thus departing from the Soviet-era conception of sexuality as a taboo issue. The main framework for discussing sexuality in Pravdina's books is pleasure, whereas for Malakhov sexuality belongs only to marriage and its primary function is procreation; pleasure is secondary. When writing about sexuality and family life, Malakhov usually uses the terms 'husband' and 'wife' instead of 'man' and 'woman'.

Pravdina encourages her readers to get rid of guilt concerning sexuality. Because of the puritan attitude officially taken towards sexuality in the Soviet society, she spends considerable time persuading her readers that there is nothing 'dirty' about sex. However, this potentially liberating message turns into pathologisation of 'sexually inhibited persons'. Pravdina cites the American self-help author Louise Hay, and writes that 'even infectious diseases, including HIV, more often afflict those people who have feelings of guilt and unworthiness' (IP: 66). Thus, medical conditions are psychologised and explained by the individual's underdeveloped mental structure. The books also display a highly instrumental view on sexuality. Pravdina advises that sex should be made use of in enrichment: during sex one should think of money and say aloud one's wishes, for example, 'I will buy a new flat'. One should also hang a picture of one's dreams (car, apartment) on the wall and stare at the picture during sex, in order to make this dream come true.

Both authors naturalise sexuality by arguing that women and men as 'breeds' have different sexual needs and behaviour patterns. The representations of sexuality in their books display stereotypes similar to those found in Western advice literature (see, for example, Yesilova 2001; Helén 1997) and in sexuality education lectures in St. Petersburg examined by Rivkin-Fish (1999).[17] Sexuality is portrayed as an essential element of male subjectivity; it is a self-evident 'natural force'. Female sexuality is described as emotional and romantic. Consequently, male sexuality is presented as a simple and straightforward biological/physiological phenomenon, whereas female sexuality is understood as complex and psychological. Paradoxically, here men come to be associated with nature more strongly than women (cf. Yesilova 2001).

For Malakhov, sexuality is an important component of health. As he argues, 'one should always remember that normal sexual activity is one of the physiological functions of a healthy organism' (ZZh: 147; ZM: 127). Both authors construct sex as an obligation for women. Pravdina advises women to make an effort to please their partners sexually in order to prevent infidelity and dissolution of the relationship. Malakhov, for his part, medicalises sexuality by suggesting that without an active sex life, women's hormonal balance suffers and the organism ages, causing various old-age diseases. Sex emerges as a duty for women who have to take care of their health for the sake of society. There emerges an equation between healthy sexuality and a healthy self (cf. Rivkin-Fish 1999: 808).

Sexual reluctance is discussed only in relation to women. Malakhov explains that reluctance often stems from the motherly and domestic responsibilities that burden women and have a negative effect on their sexuality. Women 'forget about taking care of themselves', they are 'exhausted by everyday life' and they are 'not desirable in the eyes of their husbands in the same way as before' (ZZh: 150). He cautions that in such a situation a husband may seek a mistress – and the marriage is in danger of dissolving. Instead of advising readers to solve the problem, for example, through more egalitarian division of labour at home so that women would not be so exhausted, Malakhov encourages women to make time for sex, even if it means devoting less time to paid work and taking care of the household. In this way, he obliges women to sacrifice for the sake of the family. Women, not men, are encouraged to change their behaviour.

The descriptions of sexuality are internally contradictory in the books. On the one hand, Pravdina emphasises that women can be sexually active, but on the other hand, she also metaphorically presents women as objects of men's sexual desire: 'It [woman's body] is reminiscent of a delicate musical instrument, which expresses itself in full only in the hands of a professional musician' (CK: 106). Malakhov's books are a combination of open and detailed advice concerning sex, on the one hand, and sexual conservatism, such as the emphasis on women's moral prudery and marriage as the only appropriate context for sexuality, on the other.[18] Malakhov portrays men as active sexual subjects, whereas women appear as passive objects of male sexual desire; female sexuality is something that the male-subject has to delicately 'awaken'. Because Malakhov finds women's mental and emotional structure fragile, he interprets that women are easily traumatised in intimate relationships and may become 'sexual invalids' (ZO: 73). Interestingly, the only context in which women are assigned a position of an active sexual subject in Malakhov's books is in 'therapeutic sex', in which sexual energy is used to heal illnesses. Thus, women may take the position of an active agent only when they seek to cure their husbands.

Conclusion

As this chapter has elucidated, Pravdina and Malakhov offer partly different interpretations about self, gender and sexuality, and these interpretations also both reproduce and break away from the Soviet ideals and norms. Pravdina's texts are located in the Anglo-American New Age and post-feminist self-help discourses, which introduce a model of self that is rooted in individualism, consumerism, sexual liberation and the rhetoric of free choice and responsibility. Malakhov, in contrast, draws on Orthodox Christianity, Eastern philosophies and the Soviet self-training and physical culture tradition, and describes the ideal self as an able-bodied mother or father who is a stoical master of his/her emotions and desires and lives in harmony with nature. Pravdina's books have a rather light-hearted and entertaining tone and they focus on self-fashioning as a project of self-pleasure and material success. Malakhov's texts, in contrast, employ an educative tone and connect the 'healthy' and happy self with the good of the planet and the Russian nation, in particular in the case of women. Both Pravdina's and Malakhov's books are silent about the regulatory power they exercise: they overlook the idea that the readers are complexly enmeshed in the workings of power, being governed through the persuasive normative messages of self-help technology.

Similarly to the Soviet gender ideology, Pravdina and Malakhov rely on an essentialist understanding of sexual difference, and position heterosexuality as an unquestioned norm. They also define masculine identity through work and regard the domestic sphere as a 'woman's realm', although Pravdina encourages women to outsource domestic work to paid employees. Malakhov reiterates the culturally dominant association of womanhood with motherhood, whereas Pravdina emphasises women's self-realisation and career, and questions motherhood as women's primary mission. However, she does relativise this individualist stand by invoking a heterosexual relationship as an essential fundament of women's happiness. Both authors also conceive of sexuality as a key element of happiness and health.

The books glue together an amalgam of ingredients stemming from multiple discursive sources, carrying with them different understandings of gender, sexuality and subjectivity. For example, in Pravdina's texts post-feminist ideas bring forth the celebration of women's independence and self-fulfilment, whereas the influence of Chinese philosophy on Yin and Yang tends to emphasise the complementarity and harmony of the genders. In Malakhov's case, Soviet equality discourse intermingles with religious ideas of sacred motherhood, and with the Russian century-long discursive formation of women as saviours of the Russian nation. By mixing the 'old, new and borrowed', the books analysed here provide their readers, on the one hand, with a sense of familiarity and continuity, and, on the other hand, introduce new conceptual frameworks for re-thinking gender relations and sexuality in a rapidly changing society.

Although self-help authors tend to advertise their books as liberating, empowering and as helping people to achieve happiness and a good life, scholarly analyses of self-help literature have tended to be informed by a certain 'epistemology of suspicion' (Illouz 2008: 4). Self-help techniques have been criticised for promoting an individualist world view and an ethos of self-reliance, for encouraging people to internalise inequalities, and for thus deflecting a collective protest against systemic and structural inequalities (for a succinct summary of this criticism, see Illouz 2008) . Undoubtedly, self-help technologies exercise regulatory power by normalising certain modes of acting and thinking, as the analysis in this chapter shows, but the effects of these technologies merit further investigation. I suggest that in order to better grasp the functions and meanings of self-help and to move beyond the binary models of liberation/oppression, it would be necessary to study both production and reception of self-help. Interpellation is a complex and unpredictable process and it is not necessarily always 'successful': one may not recognise oneself as the target of interpellation, or one may resist inhabiting the subject-positions on offer in a particular discourse. An interesting topic for further research would be to examine this analytical space between representations and subjectivity. How do readers of self-help literature negotiate and interpret the models of sexuality and gender that this literature offers? How do they react to interpellations of self-help technologies?

Notes

1 Many thanks to Virve Peteri, Galina Miazhevich, the participants of the 'Spaces of Democracy' seminar and the study group of Russian and Eastern European studies at the University of Helsinki for their helpful comments on the earlier versions of this paper. I also wish to thank Kordelin Foundation and the Academy of Finland for their financial support of this project.

2 I use self-help literature as an umbrella term to refer to the multifaceted, commercial field of advice books that encourage one to work on their selves. In Russian this genre is not called 'self-help', which would literally translate as *samo-pomoshch*', but it is often classified in bookstores and publishing houses as (popular) psychology (*popularnaia psikhologiia*) and folk/non-traditional medicine (*narodnaia/netraditsionnaia meditsina*).

3 Self-help literature is also immensely popular in Western societies, and the past two decades, in particular, have witnessed a dramatic growth in self-help publishing (Illouz 2008).

4 'Psy' refers to a host of psycho-sciences and disciplines, such as psychology, psychiatry and their cognates, and the ways of thinking and acting that they have brought into existence. 'Psy' has played a key role in the ways self and subjectivity are currently understood and conceptualised in the West (Rose 1998: 2).

5 See Catriona Kelly's (2001) seminal study of Russian advice literature, which covers an impressive time span from the eighteenth century to 1991.

6 This Soviet tradition of individual work on the self can find, paradoxically, common ground with the Western self-management techniques that similarly emphasise incessant work on and monitoring the self.

7 Compared to private medical and psychotherapeutic services, self-help literature offers an accessible source of support as the books are generally quite affordable, ranging from 50 to 200 roubles.
8 Feng shui is an ancient Chinese practice of arrangement of space to achieve harmony.
9 Pravdina has published over 20 and Malakhov over 40 books; see their websites for more information: www.genesha.ru (Malakhov) and www.npravdina.ru (Pravdina).
10 Pravdina, however, tends to address women more than men in her books.
11 Although New Age spirituality is difficult to define unequivocally, it is nevertheless possible to identify certain principles that unite its different streams. Characteristic of New Age spirituality is the belief that human beings are essentially gods in themselves; that they undergo successive reincarnations as part of an evolutionary process; that the individual has to take responsibility for his/her life and that one is responsible for creating his/her own reality. In addition, New Age spirituality has a deep-seated conviction of the power of positive thinking in shaping one's destiny, and promotes personal growth and development of a new, higher consciousness (York 2001; Heelas 1996).
12 This alternative or hybrid spirituality seems to be a wider phenomenon in contemporary Russia; see, for example, Turunen's (2005: 199–200) study on young people's religiosity in Russia.
13 Rosalind Gill (2007) defines post-feminism as a sensibility characterised, among other things, by a celebration of femininity, consumerism, emphasis on natural sexual difference and the rhetoric of choice, autonomy and sexual freedom. According to her, post-feminism has become a pervasive element of Western media culture and it is closely connected with neo-liberal rationality.
14 However, it is worth noting that Malakhov's activities in self-healing are also a commercial business.
15 These water and tempering procedures refer to abundant use of water; for example, taking cold showers and baths (Kelly 2001: 208), and were part and parcel of the Soviet physical culture. The underlying idea is that this water treatment strengthens the organism and mind. This idea is also embedded in the Christian ethos of a 'healthy mind in a healthy body'. The discourse of tempering (*zakalivanie*) refers to tempering of both material and persons; cf. Nikolai Ostrovsky's classical socialist realist novel 'How the steel was tempered' (*Kak zakalialas' stal'* 1936).
16 This interconnectedness was already central for pre-revolutionary Russian thinkers and it was also endorsed by Marxist-Leninist thought (Riordan 1978). It manifested itself in the Soviet Union, among other things, in the physical culture (*fizkul'tura*), which played a key role in creating the ideal Soviet person with 'an all-round personality' (ibid.; Attwood 1990). Physical activity was seen as an essential part of character training and development of a healthy mental structure.
17 Malakhov's advice in fact is largely consistent with the bestselling marriage and sexuality manuals published in the West before the Second World War (see Helén 1997).
18 His texts occasionally sound rather outdated: for example, he presumes that husband and wife do not have sexual experiences before marriage. However, Russian boys experience their first intercourse on average at the age of 16 and girls at the age of 18 (Rotkirch 2007: 31).

References

Argumenty i Fakty 20 May 2002.

Ashwin, S. (2006) 'The post-Soviet gender order: imperatives and implications', in Ashwin, S. (ed.) *Adapting to Russia's New Labour Market. Gender and Employment Behaviour*, London and New York: Routledge: 32–56.

Attwood, L. (1990) '*The new Soviet man and woman. Sex-role socialization in the USSR*', Bloomington, IN: Indiana University Press.

Etkind, A. (1997) *'Eros of the impossible. The history of psychoanalysis in Russia'*, Boulder, CO: Westview Press.

Foucault, M. (1988) 'Technologies of the Self', in Martin, L.H. *et al.*, *Technologies of the Self: A seminar with Michel Foucault*, London: Tavistock: 16–49.

Foucault, M. (1998) '*Seksuaalisuuden historia* [*History of Sexuality*]', Helsinki: Gaudeamus.

Gill, R. (2007) 'Postfeminist media culture: Elements of a sensibility', *European Journal of Cultural Studies* 10(2): 147–66.

Gladarev, B. and Tsinman, Zh. (2009) 'Dom, shkola, vrachi i muzhei: potrebitel'skie praktiki srednego klassa', in Zdravomyslova, E., Rotkirch, A. and Temkina, A. (eds) *Novyi byt v soveremennoi Rossii: gendernye issledovaniia povsednevnosti*, St. Petersburg: Izdatel'stvo Evropeiskaia universiteta v Sankt-Peterburge: 189–221.

Hazleden, R. (2004) 'The pathology of love in contemporary relationship manuals', *The Sociological Review* 52(2): 201–17.

Heelas, P. (1996) '*The New Age Movement. The Celebration of the Self and the Sacralization of Modernity*', Oxford: Blackwell publishers.

Helén, I. (1997) '*Äidin elämän politiikka: naissukupuolisuus, valta ja itsesuhde Suomessa 1880-luvulta 1960-luvulle*', Helsinki: Gaudeamus.

Hochschild, A.R. (1994) 'The Commercial Spirit of Intimate Life and the Abduction of Feminism: Signs from Women's Advice Books', *Theory, Culture & Society* 11: 1–24.

Illouz, E. (2008) '*Saving the modern soul. Therapy, emotions, and the culture of self-help*', Berkeley, CA: University of California Press.

Kelly, C. (2001) '*Refining Russia: Advice Literature, Polite Culture, and Gender from Catherine to Yeltsin*', Oxford: Oxford University Press.

Kharkhordin, O. (1999) '*The Collective and the Individual in Russia. A Study of Practices*', Berkeley, CA: University of California Press.

de Lauretis, T. (1987) '*Technologies of Gender: Essays on Theory, Film, and Fiction*', Bloomington: Indiana University Press.

McGee, M. (2005) '*Self-help, Inc.: Makeover Culture in American Life*', Oxford: Oxford University Press.

Petukhov, V. (2005) 'Political Participation and Civic Self-Organization in Russia', *Russian Politics and Law* 43(3): 6–24.

Riabov, O. (2001) '*Matushka-Rus'. Opyt gendernogo analiza poiskov natsional'noi identichnosti Rossii v otetchestvennoi i zapadnoi istoriosofii*', Moscow: Ladomir.

Riordan, J. (1978) '*Sport in Soviet Society*', Cambridge: Cambridge University Press.

Rivkin-Fish, M. (1999) 'Sexuality Education in Russia: Defining Pleasure and Danger for a Fledging Democratic Society', *Social Science and Medicine* 49: 801–14.

Rivkin-Fish, M. (2005) '*Women's Health in Post-Soviet Russia. The Politics of Intervention*', Bloomington, IN: Indiana University Press.

Rose, N. (1998) '*Inventing Our Selves. Psychology, Power and Personhood*', Cambridge: Cambridge University Press.

Rosenholm, A. (1999) '*Gendering Awakening. Femininity and the Russian Woman Question of the 1860s*', Helsinki: Kikimora Publications.

Rotkirch, A. (2000) '*The Man Question. Loves and Lives in Late 20th Century Russia*', Helsinki: University of Helsinki.

Rotkirch, A. (2007) 'Seksi Venäjällä: Vapautumista ja vanhoillisuutta', in Korhonen, E. (ed.) *Venäläiset perheet ja seksuaalisuus murroksessa*, Helsinki: Väestöliitto: 26–45.

Rotkirch, A. and Temkina, A. (2007) 'Sovetskie gendernye kontrakty i ikh transformatsiia v sovremennoi Rossii', in E. Zdravomyslova and A. Temkina (eds) *Rossiiskii gendernyi poriadok: sotsiologicheskii podkhod*, St. Petersburg: EUSP: 169–200.

Shlapentokh, V. (2006) 'Trust in public institutions in Russia: The lowest in the world', *Communist and Post-Communist Studies* 39: 153–74.

Tainio, L. (2001) '*Puhuvan naisen paikka*', Helsinki: SKS.

Trud 24 February 1996.

Turunen, M. (2005) '*Faith in the Heart of Russia*', Helsinki: Kikimora.

Woodstock, L. (2005) 'Vying Constructions of Reality: Religion, Science, and "Positive Thinking" in Self-help Literature', *Journal of Media and Religion* 4(3): 155–78.

Yesilova, K. (2001) 'Sukupuolittunut seksuaalikasvatus', *Sosiologia* 38(3): 192–204.

York, M. (2001) 'New Age Commodification and Appropriation of Spirituality', *Journal of Contemporary Religion* 16(3): 361–72.

Part 3

Media as the arbiters of style

8 'Family – that's an opera'

Creativity and family representations in Russian women's magazine *Krest'ianka*

Saara Ratilainen

> If your husband is a plastic surgeon, it is possible to become a beauty and never get old…These thoughts did not even occur to Ekaterina's mind before, because her head was occupied with other things. If your husband is a surgeon and a very good one, you are supposed to help him.
>
> (*Krest'ianka* 10, 2001: 10).

The above paragraph begins a feature called 'Wife for Pygmalion' in the October 2001 issue of the Russian women's magazine *Krest'ianka* (henceforth K). This four-page illustrated article presents a story of a contemporary Russian family consisting of the father, the mother and their daughter. At the same time it is a representation of family dynamics and a lifestyle in which 'everything is subordinate to work'. The father is portrayed as the head of the family, a perfectionist in his work and so enthusiastic about enhancing his mastery of plastic surgery that he deserves to be called Pygmalion. According to the article, he focuses on nothing but his work and this even led him to marry his favourite nurse. He considers himself as a mole living in his 'burrow of surgery', which is probably why he needs the wife to be his 'loyal soldier' capable of keeping things organised both at the practice and home. Meanwhile, their young daughter has to sit at home after school with a dog, because her parents work long hours at the practice and 'there is no grandmother to look after her' (K 10, 2001: 12–13).

If the original Pygmalion myth deals with transforming man's ideals of feminine perfection into living beauty (with a master touch and the blessing of the gods),[1] in the modernised version of this old myth, perfection in a female life companion is attained by matching her professional skills and ambitions to those of her husband. Of course, the notion that striving for the perfect appearance is every woman's (and man's) duty is also present in this article through the very theme of plastic surgery. Nevertheless, according to this story feminine beauty plays a secondary role in constituting successful family relations. What counts most here is the professional success of the family – especially the husband. The contemporary Russian Pygmalion is the main hero of this feature and his ability to re-build, correct and perfect human bodies is emblematic; it makes him resemble God the creator. Yet he does not demand that physical corrections be made to his wife.

Instead, he wanted to make another surgeon – his professional likeness – out of her. Ultimately, this dream was never realised. The wife, Ekaterina, explains that it is not realistic to have two surgeons in one household due to the overwhelming demands of the profession.

The circulation of this well-known myth in a women's magazine raises an interesting interpretation of the contemporary Russian family. It serves as a perfect example of a portrayal of the family as a productive unit (in many senses), and in doing so it encapsulates the main issues that I will discuss in this chapter. The 'Wife for Pygmalion' story suggests that not only the members of the family need to be re-created, moulded and educated in order to become successful citizens, but also that the whole family unit needs to be organised to align with greater goals, which are often of a professional nature.

The aim of this chapter is to identify potential motivations for this interpretation of the family unit. I will do this by looking at representations of work and creativity as introduced in the framework of marriage and family life. As in the above-mentioned example, many other *Krest'ianka* stories concerning families also entail a story of professional success that emphasises serious devotion and distinguished individual skills as a pathway to both familial happiness and a socially privileged lifestyle. In other words, this women's magazine seems to repeatedly portray professionalism and creative activity as part of good family dynamics. In addition, the manifestations about families of professionals, careerists and creators are often accompanied by the idea that the proper functioning of family life is based on a gender-specific comprehension of the concept of work, even if both parents are highly educated professionals. Therefore, I claim that the figure of a male creator serves as one of the most important organising motives in the attempt to marginalise feminine creativity aside from creativity connected to reproduction. I also claim that professional women and successful career women are accepted and even glorified, but female creativity as *individual property* and a *natural gift* remains in *Krest'ianka*'s representations of families if not completely denied, at least marginalised by means of several discursive and textual methods. The materials analysed in this article consist of features published in *Krest'ianka* under the rubric 'The Family Stories' (*Semeinye istorii*). Each installation of this feature presents an extensive interview of a famous or otherwise interesting married couple. 'The Family Story' is told both in words and images, as family portraits and other pictures depicting the family life of interviewees (both those photographed especially for the feature and those taken from private family albums) accompany the text. This segment has been published systematically in the magazine since 2000, and it appears in almost every issue as the first feature.

The description of Pygmalion as a father figure and, supposedly, also as a metaphor of the new and successful Russia fearlessly rebuilding itself and its citizens, corresponds with the ideas that can be found in several sociological studies about the new gender identities and the public reconfiguration of gender relations of post-Soviet Russia. The recent trajectories in Eastern Europe and Russia have resulted, according to several sociologists, in the emergence of post-Communist 'neo-traditional societies' (Watson 1993: 481) and a 'patriarchal renaissance'

(Gapova 2005; Zdravomyslova 2003: 5). These analyses refer, on the one hand, to women's diminishing role in the public sphere and a decline in women's occupation of high-profile posts. Explanations for this development are found in the Soviet tradition of 'preserving and promoting' patriarchy in public institutions and the absence of gender sensitivity in labour policy (Watson 1993: 472). On the other hand, the corrosion of social security offered by the state has increased the role of private, unpaid care work. The family unit is also often seen as the ground for discussions about the division of labour. For example, Anna Temkina and Anna Rotkirch suggest that changes in the societal system of post-Soviet Russia have resulted in the emergence of gender contracts, i.e. models of sexual division between productive and reproductive work, which are based on the marginalisation of women's role in paid work (Temkina and Rotkirch 2007).

Krest'ianka and the post-soviet media market

I have chosen here to analyse stories from *Krest'ianka* because this publication poses an interesting question about the way a traditional *Soviet* women's magazine has re-invented itself as a *post-Soviet* women's publication. *Krest'ianka* started publishing as early as 1922. It was known as one of the two official women's magazines of the Communist Party aimed at mass readership. In Soviet times, the titles of mass women's magazines expressed a strict and clear division of the reading audience; *Rabotnitsa* was published for factory workers whereas *Krest'ianka* was aimed at women working on communal farms (*kolkhozy*) (Attwood 1999: 25–6).[2] Contemporary *Krest'ianka* uses its Soviet history as a means of identification and differentiation. For instance, in every issue *Krest'ianka* dedicates a special section to the reproduction of old covers and articles. The latest redesign of *Krest'ianka*'s cover art makes the connection to the past even more visible. In September 2008 the magazine started a series of cover pictures imitating the style of Soviet magazine covers and posters from past decades. In search of either a more authentic expression or a more confusing reading experience, the magazine's editors have chosen to place the old logo of the Soviet state publishing house Pravda along with a small image of Lenin's head under the magazine's title with the slogan: 'In publication since 1922' (instead of 'Workers of the world, unite!').

Because of the challenges caused by the new post-Soviet economy and an ever fragmenting popular magazine market, *Krest'ianka* has had to create an image that appeals directly to readers and advertisers. By developing a modernised image and making itself a brand, *Krest'ianka* has survived in the market and continues to publish under the same title as before, despite the fact that compared with several competitors of Western origins that have appeared on the market in Russian editions (e.g. *Vogue*, *Cosmopolitan*, *Elle* and *Gala*) the title *Krest'ianka* sounds old-fashioned and definitely distanced from the original meaning of the word 'peasant woman'. Thus, the title *Krest'ianka* doesn't really try to address the real peasant woman as the current ideal reader, but rather evokes a feeling that this publication, unlike its many contemporaries, is produced in the spirit of the 'good old days' and emphasises the idea that some continuity can be found even when everything around seems to be changing.[3]

The contemporary *Krest'ianka* is addressed to urban middle- or upper middle-class women. With a circulation of only 151,000 copies, it reaches a rather small and specialised audience (Prosmi 2009). Based on the concept of Western women's consumer magazines, the contemporary *Krest'ianka* has become one of many products that can be considered as representatives of the developing post-Soviet consumer culture. Contemporary *Krest'ianka* is currently owned by one of the largest Russian media enterprises, Rodionov Publishing House, which also publishes other glossies aimed at both men and women (such as *Domovoi*, *XXL* and *FHM*). Of all these publications, *Krest'ianka* is the only one based on a Russian format.

In terms of the development of consumer culture, one of the post-Soviet glossy women's magazine's tasks can be regarded as educational, as Djurja Bartlett (2006) notes in her article on the first seven years of the Russian edition of *Vogue*. Bartlett presents the launching of the Russian *Vogue* in 1998 as a kind of dream of Western fashion that came true after long decades of stifling conditions for style and femininity in the Socialist system. She emphasises the role of the nouveau riche as the most reliable group to respond to the magazine's call for spreading new practices of style and fashion in post-Soviet Russia. According to Bartlett, the newly rich appeared at the time of the rise of the Russian market economy – people with plenty of money but short on taste and, most importantly, fond of purchasing expensive clothing with Western designer labels.[4] Besides targeting the richest of the rich in order to educate them in tasteful luxury, fashion magazines (and women's magazines in general) also showcase consumer goods in a broader sense. Even if the reader could not afford to purchase the actual product or have the kind of lifestyle the magazine stands for, the reader can buy the magazine and enjoy looking at the images and reading the stories.

The process of rebuilding the Soviet model of femininity, also found on the pages of *Krest'ianka*, has led to representations of women as free and cultivated shoppers and consumers.[5] Leaning heavily towards the imagery in post-Soviet luxury, *Krest'ianka* still regards itself as a forum for every woman, especially for the Russian or even *Slavic* woman. To this definition one could add that *Krest'ianka* is intended for adult readers rather than teenagers or young adult women, for whom the Russian women's magazine market offers several magazines.[6] Currently the most popular of these and of all women's magazines in general, is the Russian edition of *Cosmopolitan*, with a circulation of 1,050,000 (*Cosmopolitan* 2009).

Women's magazines as shared fantasies

Jennifer Scanlon writes that mass-oriented women's magazines provide an 'emotional formula', where 'fostering anxiety' is balanced by the 'offering of positive messages', and this encourages readers to repeatedly return to the magazine (Scanlon 1995: 5). Ellen McCracken connects the seeking of balance between 'anxiety' and 'satisfaction' with consumer culture. She states that advertisers have the most influential role in the creation of messages in contemporary women's consumer magazines (McCracken 1993). She also states that the appeal of contemporary women's consumer magazines is based on an endless cycle of consumption and pleasure, which guarantees continuous or recurrent purchasing of these publications by the audience (McCracken 1993). Besides advertising the newest trends and products, mass media produce ideological tools that the audience can adopt and consume in their daily lives. In so doing, women's magazines (and mass media in general) prompt their readers to acquire certain values and lifestyles characteristic of a particular time and society.

I agree with Maija Töyry when she writes that women's magazine contents are generally based on a certain amount of 'untrustworthiness', i.e. regardless of the fact that articles are often based on interviews with real people, they display a selective and revised version of what the interviewees really tell the journalist. Of course, this can to some extent be applied to any kind of journalism (see Fairclough 1995: 18, 48), but I would still argue that women's magazines (and popular lifestyle magazines in general) are among the most eager to maintain their agenda, which in this case could be a combination of the magazine's construction of its ideal reader and maintaining the air of 'women's magazine talk'. Töyry argues that features about relationships published in women's magazines are first and foremost interpretations of human relationships packaged by the producers of the particular publication and they 'don't convey the everyday life [...] to the readers with the accuracy of a documentary but as shaped interpretations aligned with the magazine's own purposes and values' (Töyry 2005: 37).

Women's magazines' messages can be seen as fantasies supporting the social order of consumerist society in the same sense that romantic fiction is seen as reinforcing capitalistic society and its patriarchal rule in Janice Radway's study *Reading the Romance: Women, Patriarchy and Popular Literature* (1991). According to Radway, reading romantic fiction connects the pleasures of consumption and imagination. She argues that pleasure attained by reading romantic stories (and also viewing advertisements or reading glossies) is vicarious by its very nature and entails 'a clash between two value systems' inherent in the market economy: 'One system serves to sustain a consumer-oriented economy, while the other, developed by an economy designed to accumulate and to concentrate capital, tacitly labels consumption for pure pleasure both wasteful and dangerous' (Radway 1991: 116). In *Krest'ianka*'s romanticised stories about families, the locus for producing the practices of a fulfilling lifestyle (both in terms of finances and social status) and preserving the social order needed for the continuity of this lifestyle is the home. Sometimes the magazine shows quite clearly how the process of collective fantasising takes place. A good example of how the act of collective daydreaming is presented as being based on certain consumptive practices and taste can be found in the dialogue between the interviewer and the interviewee in one of *Krest'ianka*'s family stories. Here, the journalist is talking with the famous detective writer Tat'iana Ustinova about her work and family. The interview takes place in the writer's house. When they are talking about the ideal home, the dialogue creates a fantasy peppered with nostalgia about (new) Russian manor life, simultaneously challenging the reader's imagination and welcoming her to join the fantasy.

JOURNALIST: I think that the very best things in Russian culture were born in the mansions among aristocrats where life close to nature was interconnected with books and a grand piano.

USTINOVA: Yes, yes, books, music… […] a plate of strawberries, and even better wild strawberries, sunlight on the terrace walls, a child swinging in a hammock, birches, barking from a doghouse. You just cannot do without all this.

(*K* 10, 2005: 14)

By repeating the journalist's last words, Ustinova attaches herself to the fantasy world common to both speakers. After this she enriches the picture by adding more details. A perfect idyll is created in just two lines, and the way it is created invites the reader to add her own details to the picture too. Accordingly, I approach my materials as representatives of 'shared fantasies'. Even though the main characters in *Krest'ianka*'s family stories are always real people and usually well-known to the reading public, I would still say that the symbolic order of *Krest'ianka*'s stories belongs to the realm of celebrity gossip or even fairytale – they represent the everyday or mundane as a fantasy world that is also present in other forms of popular culture and mass media.

Similarly, the concept of family in 'The Family Stories' is discussed in the framework of a story. In fact, by introducing a new family story in almost every issue, *Krest'ianka* creates its own style of docudrama: a feature that is based on real events from the lives and marriages of real people, but written in a prosaic style with an emphasis on the fairytale likeness of everyday life. Each story is often built around certain key components that are circulated from issue to issue and by which the notion of family attains the meaning of 'a family with a history worth telling'. Therefore, the journal has developed a template for the *family story* that is used to legitimise heterosexual marriage as a natural rule. Against this background the concept of family can be seen as cultural fiction and a 'social artifact' that is 'produced and reproduced' (Skeggs 2004) within a certain kind of semiotic framework. The underlying idea of these texts is that the family constitutes the 'natural' and 'organic' basis on which the life of a person is (or should be) built.

As in the case of the plastic surgeon and his wife Ekaterina, the majority of the 'Family Stories' are depictions of collegial marriages or marriages where both parties at least work in the same professional field. Altogether, the heroes of these stories constitute a group that can be called the intellectual or creative elite of Russia and so the stories present a lifestyle of rich, cultivated and well-educated people. The most common professions represented in the stories are actors, dancers, singers and other performers, journalists and writers. Therefore, the family stories are based on the two-fold meaning of the Russian word '*sem'ia*' (the family), encompassing human relations based on both kinship and the brotherhood of ideas. One of the definitions that the Russian dictionary gives for the word family is 'a group of people connected by common activity, interest or friendship'.[7] In this sense the stories not only deal with couples whose professions are closely connected to each other, but they also portray 'creative unions' (*tvorcheskii soiuz*), which is how one of the features describes the togetherness of the famous folk singer Nadezhda Kadyshevaia and the composer Aleksandr Kostiuk. Their 'Family Story' begins with a paragraph that introduces many of the principal ideas also found in other articles concerning men, women and marriage.

> The creative and human union of Nadezhda Kadyshevaia and Aleksandr Kostiuk is evidence of the fact that men and women really were created as couples, and you can comprehend the plenitude of life only if you were lucky to meet your other half.
>
> (K 9, 2005: 12)

In my view, the key phrases in the above quotation representing *Krest'ianka*'s attitude towards marriage are 'if you were lucky' and 'your other half'. These phrases are also markers of fatalism, which influences the family stories in general. On one hand, the ideology of fatalism offers a magical and other-worldly explanation for the attraction between two people. On the other hand, the fatalistic approach helps the reader to become absorbed into the text and understand some of the other more problematic culturally and socially bound messages (including the gender-specific division of work and, especially, gender-specific perceptions of creativity) as if they were natural and 'meant to be' like that.[8] Other 'Family Stories' also introduce external and other-worldly agents bringing people together. These can be, for example, God, fate or just 'obscure forces'. Another crucial technique for creating the core of a family in family stories is to present the spouses as halves of the same whole, i.e. 'two of a kind'. In this way, the couple is seen as both compensating for and consisting of each other. In fact, this is the most crucial idea connecting the fatalistic worldview and the concept of creative unions when introducing marriages and family life.

The poetry contract

The division of work between men and women, husbands and wives is one of the most prevalent themes in the 'Family Stories'. In this section I will look more closely at how the division is portrayed and where the discursive boundaries dividing masculine and feminine spheres of work are drawn on the semiotic matrix of *Krest'ianka*'s texts. More accurately, I will pinpoint the kinds of differences the stories demonstrate between feminine and masculine professionalism and how this gender difference is discussed using the framework of creativity. In my view, *Krest'ianka*'s 'Family Stories' provide an interesting case because they discuss the 'reality' of the lives of the interviewees and 'ideal reality' – i.e. family values and gender identities – with mixed messages. In this framework, the notion of work can be understood as consisting of three different conceptual layers, and every layer may involve differing ideas about the division of work between the masculine and feminine spheres. First, work can be seen as professionalism and a career. Second, in most of these stories work equals devotion; the career dictates the life path of a person and as a result work and private life cannot be separated. Third, work and career are in most cases also represented as a privilege that is not 'given' to everybody. It is seen as something natural, intrinsic and essential to the identity of a person.

According to Temkina and Rotkirch (2007: 196), the gender contract consists of 'rules, rights and responsibilities defining the gender-based division of work in the spheres of production and reproduction'. I agree with Yvonne Hirdman's critique of the term contract when analysing the gender-biased division of work in the society. She states that the term 'contract' is to be used when lacking a better term, but keeping in mind that in addition to a contract concluded by two equal partners, the gender contract should also be considered as a culturally inherited and coercive bond dictating the social roles of women and men (Hirdman 1990: 78).

In *Krest'ianka*, the delegation of work between the spouses is often discussed and articulated specifically as a mutual agreement, certainly entailing the characteristics of a contract. Although the contract does not necessarily refer directly to the questions of 'who is to be the main breadwinner of the family' and 'who should take care of the housework', it inevitably derives from these distinctions. More specifically, the question that is raised and on which the contract is to be concluded, should be formulated as 'to whom and on what basis is to be given the privilege of defining one's career and becoming devoted to it'. In addition, the contract is negotiated and justified in terms of creation. That is why I consider the negotiations concerning the distribution of creative work, career and devotion represented in my materials to be a question of the *poetry contract.*[9] I'm borrowing the term from an illuminating line published in the 'Family Story' entitled 'Unhealthy Advice for Domestic Use' (December 2000). In this story, the father writes books for children and the mother works as a journalist. In one of her quotations where the mother is speaking about the details of the everyday life of two writers with children, she characterises their profession-driven family life, interestingly enough, in terms of the relationship between the mother, soup and poetry.

> Our poor children are repeatedly forced to listen to and evaluate our work (*tvorchestvo*). Grisha [the father] reads them his upcoming books and I the next issue of the journal. Along with the duties of a wife, mother and stepmother, I am the head editor of two children's magazines *Ieralash* and *Spokoinoi nochi malysh*. Luckily enough, I don't write poems. In my opinion, it is very important for a woman not to write poems and always make the soup.
>
> (K 12, 2000: 6)

When analysing this statement, one could broaden the meaning of soup to represent nursing and housework in general and poetry to symbolise all of the work that belongs to the realm of high culture, the arts and creation. With this statement, the speaker does more than present the fundamentals of the division of labour that supposedly function in this particular family. The idea of the line drawn between soup and poetry serves as a discursive tool constituting the shared fantasy about the post-Soviet patriarchal family and here this mother's statement reaffirms the ideology also present in *Krest'ianka*'s other 'Family Stories'. This quotation is interesting because the speaker not only says that there are different expectations of what men and women should do when living as a family, but she also makes it clear what women are not supposed to do. Also, here the question of work division is not dealt with in economic terms, but in terms of the distribution of emotional work and devotion. In other words, in the semantic framework of maintaining the family, 'poetry' and 'soup' are seen as two opposing paradigms. Poetry stands for the sphere, into which women should not trespass by devoting their time and emotions. This means that inside the home men can lock themselves in the world of art, whereas women should create the daily life. Thus, the poetry contract articulates the threshold between masculine and feminine emotional spaces and spheres of devotion.

Poetry also functions as an interesting motive articulating the locus of the mother's self-expression in another family story. Here, it defines the spaces of creativity and devotion in a different way, but still entails the idea of a separation between feminine and masculine duties. In this story, the woman writes poems, but only for a certain purpose and in certain circumstances that do not deal with work or supporting the family. A hockey player's wife explains her relationship to poetry in the following words:

> If I'm feeling sad and lonely these days, I write a poem, read it to him [the husband] and start to feel fine again. To be able to live, I need to know that I'm being loved and that I love. That's all.
>
> (K 5, 2000: 10)

The story is entitled 'Tret'iak's Triangle'. The word 'triangle' refers to the fact that the life of a famous Soviet hockey player Vladislav Tret'iak and his wife Tat'iana consists of a three-fold union of 'him, her and hockey' (ibid.). This marriage is not a 'creative union' in the same sense as the cases of the above-mentioned writer and journalist or singer and composer. However, the third side of the triangle here dictates the conditions of the whole family in the same way as the creative/artistic profession in others: it demands full devotion on the part of all family members. 'Sport was everything' says the wife Tat'iana when reflecting upon the early years of their marriage (ibid.). The wife's role as an emotional worker is emphasised in this story. Consequently, poetry in this sport-based context represents Tat'iana's love and devotion and, in contrast to hockey, it is represented as a secondary and feminine activity. Tat'iana's poems are also a vessel of her self-expression. Poetry writing here is not meant to be a public, life-giving power of the family – that role is given to hockey. In contrast, poetry is represented as a means for Tat'iana to support herself in difficult moments when nobody else is around. On the other hand, both Tat'iana's voice and her reading aloud her own poems play a crucial role for the whole family because providing consolation is the main duty assumed by Tat'iana's voice. Vladislav also refers to this when describing the hardships of being a hockey star: 'And here is the wife, the main person who is always supporting you and saying that you are better than the others' (ibid.).

By comparing the way both of the above examples deal with poetry as an expression of family dynamics, one can come to the conclusion that the creativity of a woman as a family member (and, especially, as the mother) is connected to ideas about the differing arenas and objects of the activities of the spouses. Also, the family as a social institution sets different conditions for creative activity depending on gender identity. According to *Krest'ianka*'s texts, female creativity is more anchored to the private sphere. In the context of concluding poetry contracts, concepts of individuality, naturalness and prestige are intertwined in a very peculiar manner. By presenting the stories of people working in public and creative professions, *Krest'ianka* emphasises the significant role of individualism assumed for the whole society. In other words, according to the 'Family Stories', society's value depends, at least partly, on the individual, his or her skills and natural aptitudes. A family is an arena on which female and male individuality can be evaluated and *Krest'ianka* seems to use discussions on creativity to define individuality first and foremost as a male characteristic. The fact that the most of the mothers and wives presented in the family stories also work in the most respected professions, becomes re-evaluated by displaying the family dynamics in a way that is based on the co-operation of male *creator* and a female *helper/dilettante/performer*.

The 'Family Stories' represent a symbolic rather than a social order, based on the masculine privilege to combine professionalism, creative activity and devotion. The family, and especially motherhood, defines female identity by limiting it, with all its creative characters, to the private sphere. What, then, is the value of the female individual in these family representations? Carol Pateman deals with the question of women and individuality in the framework of political history when discussing the social contract theory in her book *The Sexual Contract* (1988). She argues that the social contract theory is based on a fiction of individual freedom. Margaret Whitford sums up Pateman's idea: 'Peopled by individuals who freely enter into contractual arrangements with each other, it conceals, beneath the civil contractual order, a patriarchal sexual contract which gives men access to women' (Whitford 1991: 174). Historically, civil society is a patriarchal construct and in this construct the individual is a male. Women are excluded from the 'individuals party of the contract' (ibid.). *Krest'ianka*'s stories on families do not represent a social order where women are bound only to the private sphere, but there is a sense that women are indeed represented as objects under the symbolic patriarchal rule.

In this symbolic arrangement the boundaries of feminine creative work can also be represented in a more subtle way by pointing out that, if not the entire meaning of female creativity, at least the ultimate culmination of it lies in the sphere of nurture and housekeeping. A careful reading can reveal textual devices, such as word play and semantic shifts, connected to this theme and used for a multilayered discussion of the preferred spaces for female creativity. For example, in the article called 'Scientists' house' (*Dom uchenykh*), the word culture functions as a central concept around which the life of the family of two scientists is organised. The whole family of mother, father and two sons is devoted to the sciences (physics, medicine, mathematics) in their professional lives and, additionally they are fascinated by all types of high culture in their leisure activities. The article includes a long passage in which the spouses describe the wonders of Classical English literature and the pleasures of learning sophisticated English language by reading Shakespeare. In particular, the mother Elvira is represented as a person whose interests are in classical literature. She cannot, for example, understand why her husband reads contemporary literature such as Viktor Pelevin's books for they are written in 'non-normative language' (K 11, 2001: 18). At the end of this passage, Elvira's conversation suddenly shifts from the themes of literature and language (i.e. high culture) to the making of sour cream (*kefir*). The semantic shift to the domestic sphere as an object of a mother's ultimate fascination and the culminating point of her creativity is made with the help of the word culture. Unexpectedly, she starts to describe how she has been *culturing* bacteria for homemade sour cream already for seven years.

Another important point in this semantic shift is that the transfer from the sphere of high cultures to the activity of culturing sour cream happens at the same time as the concept of family enters the picture. Just before getting into the topic of sour cream, Elvira explains: 'when I get excited about something it usually involves the whole family, like English literature now' (ibid.). The fascination of the mother – her interest in culture and the sciences – involves the family, and the culmination of this activity is in nurturing (i.e. culturing sour cream and feeding the family with healthy food). But when it comes to making sour cream, the mother alone is responsible for culturing, and only the end product involves the whole family, as the father Valerii explains: 'I, generally speaking, can't stand sour cream, but in the matters of nutrition Elia is so solicitous and wise. We trust in her absolutely' (ibid.). The borderline of feminine creativity, which is here described in terms of wisdom and intellect, is drawn again between 'soup' and 'poetry' as the father excludes himself from the domestic sphere. Also, when Elvira and Valerii are discussing their different tastes in literature, they are, most likely, discussing the boundaries of a 'normative' and 'non-normative' understanding of language and, eventually, different levels of intellectual activity. Valerii explains his interest in Pelevin's books to his wife (and the readers) in the following way: 'Games of intellect. I love those. And you avoid non-normative vocabulary, as if you were living in a crystal castle' (ibid.). The locus of the father's *fascination* combined with *intellectual activity* (which could also be regarded as the formula of creativity) is in the world of post-modern literature, whereas the same combination of fascination and intellect in the mother's case is located in sour cream.

Family as the stat(u)e of pygmalion

Art historian Victor I. Stoichita (2008: 5) writes that 'the history of the Cypriot sculptor who falls in love with his work, which the gods [...] decide to bring to life, is the first great story about simulacrum in Western culture'. Probably the most crucial point in this myth, according to Stoichita, is that (unlike, for example, in the Narcissus myth) the object of love (the statue) 'is not imitating anything' – it is purely a product of a creative mind. This is the key to understanding the romantic idea of an artist as the vessel of God and also as the creator, so emblematic to the representations of the father figure in my materials. I argue that *Krest'ianka*'s stories about elite families naturalise the poetry contract existing between the spouses by using a semantic pattern, that Stoichita calls the 'Pygmalionian relationship' (2008: 182), according to which intra-familial relationships should be organised. In this section, I will scrutinise how *Krest'ianka*'s stories turn the modern family into an artefact created and operated by the father-creator and his professional ambitions. Following Stoichita's ideas about the meaning of Pygmalion's statue as simulacrum, I claim that the career of the mother (in both senses – the professional career of the mother and her career as the mother) in these stories is represented as a simulation of the father's ambitions. The father's vocation for his career functions as both the vanishing point and the centre of eternal return (see Deleuze 1990: 264) of the mother.

A simulacrum is an image without any precise model. Gilles Deleuze (1990: 258) writes that 'The simulacrum is built upon a disparity or upon a difference. It internalizes dissimilarity. This is why we can no longer define it in relation to a model imposed on the copies, a model of the Same from which the copies' resemblance derives'.[10] In this sense, a simulacrum is an image saturated with alterity. For example, Ekaterina, the wife of the surgeon, Pygmalion from the first example is represented as the multilayered 'other' of her husband. She is mentioned as 'the loyal solider' in his work command, a nurse standing by the master surgeon in the operating room and a reminder of the husband's unfulfilled desire to live with one of his own, i.e. another plastic surgeon. In both her profession and her role as a wife she is always defined by and through her husband, and most importantly as a non-resembling image of his 'model' (surgery), created by pursuit rather than imitation. Consequently, Ekaterina's image represented in the story remains fluid; it has no centre or model comparable to the way that her husband's image is fixed to his 'burrow of surgery'.

The father/plastic surgeon and mother/nurse are perhaps the most illuminating examples of family dynamics based on a Pygmalionian relationship, but they are by no means the only ones that can be found in *Krest'ianka*'s Family Stories. Other rather simplistic examples of this are stories where the husband (remarkably older than the wife) is represented as an artist who picks up and teaches his wife-to-be after noticing potential material waiting in her to flourish, after the husband has moulded the material with a masters' touch and been driven by his visions. These visions encompass both the professional and private roles of his feminine other. For example, in a story published in February 2004 and entitled

'Artistic Patriarchy' (*Khudozhestvennyi domostroi*), the young wife of the artist Evgenii Evgenievich Lansere (who is a sculptor and a member of a famous family of artists) needs to be educated as a mother and a wife (to fit into a family with long-standing traditions) and re-educated professionally (transformed from being an economist to an art historian). In this example, both the husband's age and his background in a dynasty of famous people signify the dissimilarity and non-resemblance between the wife and the model according to which she is to be moulded. This whole setting is wrapped in a sense of fatalism when the wife Alla pronounces: 'I know why Zhenia (the husband) did not get married for such a long time; he knew that he would meet a girl and create (*vospityvaet*) a wife out of her' (K 2, 2004: 8).

Again, when the husband represents a fixed image, sanctioned by the ancestors and his art, the wife is represented as physical material that is 'pliable' and 'responsive', as Susan Gubar describes the female life idealised in Pygmalion's statue. Gubar sees the importance of the statue as a symbol of a male artist's other (creation–companion) originating from the denial. She states that by carving a statue, Pygmalion 'has evaded the humiliation [...] of acknowledging that it is *he* who is really created out of and from the *female* body' (1985: 292, italics original). A similar kind of denial of any feminine life-creating power is also present in my materials. In several stories, even the meaning of the mother as the origin of reproduction is diminished by binding together creating a family, maintaining a career and having a calling to recreate the whole society. And, finally, all this becomes embodied in the character of the father. In these stories, not only the woman by the side of the father figure, but also the whole family can be understood as a simulacrum, a nucleus or potential for the 'new society' and a pathway to the creation of new Russia. Through close reading of the last examples, I will show how *Krest'ianka*'s 'Family Stories' present the father as a creator of the 'new' society that can be equated with the future of Russia, and how the blessing for this project is presented as being 'given' from above.

Folk singer Nadezhda Kandynskaia declares that it is impossible to have two leaders in the family: 'I was brought up that way, the man is the head of the family' (K 9, 2005: 16). The 'head of the family' motif gives a moral explanation to the idea that the ability to create and establish not only cultural artefacts but also societal institutes lies in men's hands only. Upon closer reading, Nadezhda Kandynskaia's and Aleksandr Kostiuk's story represents a narrative of man's morals as the resource and origins of all creation. In terms of reproduction, the man's 'decision' is told to be the origins of both marriage and childbirth. Aleksandr interprets the creation of marriages as a product of feminine emotions and masculine decision: 'I think that first women fall in love and then the man decides whether she is to be his woman or not' (ibid.). The same pattern works when he describes the issue concerning their first child: 'It was I who made the strong-willed decision: either you give birth or we'll get a divorce' (ibid.). That's how Aleksandr's iron will works as a creative power when establishing the family and breeding. The same rule also exists in their professional life. The husband composes the songs performed by the famous spousal duo *Zolotoe Koltso* and, finally,

Aleksandr reconstructs an old film theatre in Moscow to be a *National Theatre of Folk Music 'Zolotoe Koltso'* where they and other 'Russian national ensembles, who at the moment are popular only in the West, are given the opportunity to reach fans in the homeland' (ibid.: 17). In this way, Aleksandr's 'strong-willed' decisions, 'magnificent plans' and 'connection with the cosmos and clouds' (that is how he describes his composing) are represented as the original source and driving force of both their family life and professional careers. In addition, creating culture and even bringing Russians their own culture from the West (i.e. making the contemporary culture of his homeland more Russian) seems to lie in the hands of Aleksandr.

Another story, entitled 'In front of God and the people' from February 2005 draws upon the creation myth and introduces the orthodox priest Father Sergii and his family. This story uses language emblematic to folktales and refers to the Russian countryside as the cradle and protector of spiritual 'origins', which here means mystical knowledge and archaic religious forms. At the same time, the article represents a recreation story of the post-Soviet church and religious education. 'Once upon a time', both of the spouses were philologists 'loving each other and the science of language' until the father finds his 'path' in religious life (K 2, 2005: 10). After his metamorphosis from scholar to priest and becoming renamed as Father Sergii, he reconstructs an old church out of abandoned and savaged ruins and starts a monastery school. If the father's calling from God is emphasised in this story, so is the sacrifice that the mother had to make for the church. She gave up her career as a philologist and started to work as an elementary school teacher in her husband's monastery school. In this way, the couple personalises the shift from the Soviet ideology of egalitarian marriages to the post-Soviet renaissance of patriarchy. The wife explains that the change in her profession was *automatic*, ineluctable: 'When the husband becomes a 'batiushka', his wife becomes automatically a 'matushka'. I had to reject the worldly life' (ibid.: 12–13). Interestingly, the husband explains that becoming a 'matushka' and denying the 'outside world' meant to his wife that she must give up almost all her potential for self-expression and for being a professional, an artist and a woman: 'She could have written a dissertation in linguistics, could have developed herself more in the outside world as a poet, as a distinguished, educated, beautiful woman' (ibid.: 13).

It seems that the future of Russia had to be built by marginalising mothers' professional skills and creative talent. A story from January 2004 entitled 'Singing lessons' portrays a picture of family dynamics organised around 'the voice'. The picture is clear in one aspect; the one who has the voice is the future of the family and perhaps also of a more glorious Russia. The voice also maintains the family more concretely and is responsible for its success, because the father of this story is a famous opera singer Vladimir Red'kin and leading vocalist in the *Bol'shoi Theatre* opera. Needless to say, the glorification of the voice as the key motive in this story comes from the father's profession; the family's story is wrapped around the multilayered meaning of his 'beautiful baritone'. In this story, the simulacra of 'the voice' are duplicated in both the mother and the daughter of the family. They are signified as the positive and negative other of the father and their difference is marked by the presence or absence of the voice.

The daughter has inherited the voice and in this way she can be seen as a positive picture of the future, like the *National Theatre of Folk Music* and Orthodox school in the above-mentioned examples, created with the father and originating in his connection with transcendence (God and the 'connection with cosmos'). That is why it is also important for the story's message that the father himself has not inherited the voice from anyone. The father-creator needs to be represented as a direct link to powers beyond ordinary genetics. The story repeatedly points out that the voice of the opera-singing father is a 'gift from above', 'gift from God', 'rare gift' and 'as if it was given from nowhere and for no particular reason' (*slovno niotkuda i ni za chto*). The mother, for her part, represents the negation, a simulacrum, of the original (i.e. the father), because in this story the mother is marked by the absence of a singing voice. In the expression used to describe the mother's condition of 'voicelessness', it can be read that she is indeed seen to lack the essential blessing of God because she 'is not given' ('*ne dano*') a beautiful voice. Whereas the voices of the daughter and the father are moving spectators in public performances (the *Bol'shoi Theatre* and school concerts), the mother's voice remains in the void or even totally muted. The daughter recounts that when she hears her mother singing in a car, the father responds that 'not once in my lifetime have I heard your mother sing' (K 1, 2004: 8).

Absence of voice is also the culmination point of the mother's failed career. In the interview the mother says that her 'path' towards the arts was preordained, but her point of departure is represented as more secular in character than her husband's; she was born in a family of intellectuals and art scholars. Her upbringing included private tutors in music, the English language and the arts. She studied choreography for ten years, but, again, her dream of becoming a ballerina 'was not given to come true' (*ne dano bylo sbyt'sia*) (ibid.). Instead of dancing, she decided to study in the Russian Academy of Theatre and became a critic. At the time of the interview she worked as a press officer in the *Bol'shoi Theatre*, the same institution where her husband is a celebrated star. Even she herself implicates failure when describing her educational trajectories: 'Since I was not allowed (again, *ne dano*) to become a professional dancer, I decided to write on ballet' (ibid.).

Conclusion

In this chapter, I have analysed representations of families published in recent issues of the women's magazine *Krest'ianka*. Because of its history as the official women's magazines in the Soviet Union, the contemporary *Krest'ianka* has rebranded itself in order to reflect changing trends in the media market and cope with the increasing number of Western-format-based rivals. The post-Soviet attitude towards history appears to have reached a point where certain Soviet brands, slogans and images are quite readily viewed with sentiment and nostalgia. *Krest'ianka*, inevitably, wants to be one of these brands and it strives to create new traditions.

The Pygmalion-like father figure so emphasised in my materials could stand for these 'new-old' traditions proposed by *Krest'ianka* magazine in the hope for a more stabile future. The family can be seen as a microcosm existing within the larger state. In *Krest'ianka*'s articles, the story of a family can in most cases be paralleled with the story of the father's professional success. In so doing, the family story becomes *his*tory – the story of the father-creator. Close reading of the texts reveals that in many cases the 'Family Stories' are based on the heteroglossia of two different interpretations of careers and success when represented in the framework of the family – those being the leading and often mystified history of the father and silenced personal history or failed professional history of the mother. When depicted in this way, the image of the mother becomes a simulacrum, a product that ultimately originates from the work of the father. The image of the mother is repetitively marked by dissimilarity to the father and his professional ambitions. The families are represented as belonging to the class of privileged first and foremost because of the status and cultural capital achieved by the parents' hard work. In addition, the stories suggest that the mother's hard work includes devotion to the well-being of the family under the masculine moral rule.

The primary purpose of my close-reading was to reveal the methods of naturalising the masculine rule in both the family and professional life. This was done in most cases by emphasising the exceptionality of the father, portraying him as a natural talent and/or making semantic connections between him and the unseen world of transcendence. I have also shown that my research materials articulate a certain kind of agreement – a contract that exists between feminine and masculine work. Because the agreement does not frankly deal with the question of who is the main breadwinner, i.e. it does not discuss the division of work in economic terms, but in terms of emotional attachment and devotion – I call this agreement 'the poetry contract'. When looking through the lens of the poetry contract and seeing a profession's vocational character as a privilege, the 'Family Story' can also be seen as a narrative that cements representations of creativity as the male's natural character. When trying to preserve the traditional gender roles of the patriarchal family, creativity and creation serve as the main sphere for articulating the gendered division of work. Arts and creativity seem to mark the boundaries of feminine and masculine spheres.

In my interpretation, the neo-traditional symbolic order created by *Krest'ianka* magazine's 'Family Stories' has particular meaning for establishing the image of the post-Soviet patriarchal family and legitimising its symbolic use. Revealing the repetitive textual patterns and conceptualising the underlying ideologies of what are often at first glance diverse yet – simultaneously – culturally myopic media materials demands close reading and elaborative analysis. In further studies it would be interesting to see whether my arguments that the 'poetry contract' and 'Pygmalionian relationship' organise the messages of family representations could be applied to other types of contemporary Russian women's magazines, or even more generally, to other texts produced by contemporary post-Soviet popular culture, or whether they remain as special characterisations made by a specific publication counting on its readers' sense of history repeating itself.

Notes

1 According to the myth, 'Sick with the vices with which the female sex has been so richly endowed', a sculptor Pygmalion was living wifeless. He carved a female figure out of ivory so fine that he fell in love with his own creation. After seeing the old man's devotion to this breathless creature, Venus gives it life (Ovid 2004: 394–6).

2 For more information about the history of *Rabotnitsa* and *Krest'ianka* magazines, see Tolstikova 2004 and Dashkova 2001.

3 This chapter does not try to track down the demographic features of contemporary readership of *Krest'ianka*; although this would be interesting in view of the success factors and future perspectives of the magazine, it would need further research. However, it is important to note that although the circulation of the magazine has dropped drastically from the Soviet days, *Krest'ianka* has managed to keep its circulation numbers on an average level for today's magazine market, and of all the glossies and monthlies owned by the Rodionov Publishing House its circulation is the largest. According to the publisher's website, *Krest'ianka* magazine is more widely read in the Ural region, Siberia and Southern Russia than in the economic centres of Moscow and St. Petersburg (Publishing House Rodionov 2009).

4 On the style of newly rich, see also Vainshtein 1996: 71.

5 See my previous article on style issues in *Krest'ianka* magazine (Ratilainen 2008).

6 Magazines for teenage girls started publishing in Russia in the mid-1990s. These days girls can choose from several monthlies by both domestic and foreign publishers. The most popular are *Cool Girl* (Publishing House Burda), *Seventeen* (Hearst Magazines), and *Devich'i slezy* (Izdatel'skii dom Medamir). Circulation of these magazines varies from 150,000 to 200,000 (Litovskaia 2008: 272–3).

7 *Bol'shoi tolkovyi slovar' russkogo iazyka*: 1175.

8 The 'meant to be' discourse so widely used in my materials in the form of different metaphors can also be seen as one technique with the help of which the stories, according to Nancy Ries, 'fabricate a sense of shared experience and destiny' (Ries 1997: 46).

9 On Gender Contract theory, see Hirdman 1990; Rantalaiho 1994. Anna Temkina and Anna Rotkirch write on the gender contract in Russian society and state that post-Soviet development in the dominating gender contract, i.e. the model of division of labour between men and women in the society and different micro-societies (e.g. family) has resulted in the disintegration and fragmentation of the dominant Soviet gender system and its central figure of 'working mother' (Temkina and Rotkirch 2007).

10 When discussing simulacrum, Deleuze refers to Plato's motivation to distinguish images into two categories; *copies* and *simulacra*. Copies like icons are understood through well-founded resemblance with the original model, simulacra for their part are built upon dissimilarity and distortion (Deleuze 1990: 256).

References

Attwood L. (1999) *Creating the New Soviet Woman: Women's Magazines as Engineers of Female Identity 1922–53*, London: Macmillan.

Bartlett D. (2006) 'In Russia, At Last and Forever: The First Seven Years of Russian Vogue', *Fashion Theory* 10 (1/2): 175–204.

Bol'shoi tolkovyi slovar' russkogo iazyka (2008). St. Petersburg: Nornit.

Cosmopolitan (online), Available: www.cosmo.ru/about/magazine/Cosmo_Mediakit_2009.pdf (Accessed 25 Jan 2009).

Dashkova T. (2001) '"Rabotnitsu – v massy": Politika sotsial'nogo modelirovaniia v sovetskikh zhenskikh zhurnalakh 1930-kh godov', *Novoe literaturnoe obozrenie* 50: 184–92.

Deleuze G. (1990) *The Logic of Sense*, New York: Columbia University Press.

Fairclough N. (1995) *Media Discourse*, London and New York: Edward Arnold.

Gapova E. (2005) 'O gendere, natsii i klasse v postkommunizme', *Gendernye issledovaniia* 13: 101–18.

Gubar S. (1985) '"The Blank Page" and the Issues of Female Creativity', in E. Showalter (ed.) *The New Feminist Criticism: Essays on Women, Literature and Theory*, New York: Pantheon Books.

Hirdman Y. (1990) 'Genussystemet', *Demokrati och makt i Sverige*. Maktutredningens huvudraport 44, Göteborg: Graphic Systems.

Litovskaia M. (2008) 'Obraz dostoinogo budushchego v postsovetskikh izdaniiakh dlia devushek-podrostok', in M. Litovskaia, A. Rosenholm, I. Savkina, E. Trubina (eds) *Obraz dostoinoi zhizni v sovremennykh rossiiskikh SMI*, Ekaterinburg: Ural University Press.

McCracken E. (1993) *Decoding Women's Magazines: From Mademoiselle to Ms*. Houndmills and Hampshire: Macmillan.

Ovid (2004) *Metamorphoses*, London: Penguin Books.

Pateman C. (1988) *The Sexual Contract*, California: Stanford University Press.

Prosmi (online), Available www.prosmi.ru/catalog/27 (Accessed 25 Jan 2009).

Publishing House Rodionov (online), Available www.profil.orc.ru/content/?idp=code_65 (accessed 25 Jan 2009).

Radway J. (1991) *Reading the Romance: Women, Patriarchy and Popular Literature*, London and New York: Verso.

Rantalaiho L. (1994) 'Sukupuolisopimus ja Suomen malli', in A. Anttonen, L. Henriksson, R. Nätkin (eds) *Naisten hyvinvointivaltio*, Tampere: Vastapaino.

Ratilainen S. (2008) 'Den nya ryska skönheten: damtidningen Krest'yanka's "Tio stilfrågor"', *Nordisk Østforum* 3–4: 313–35.

Ries N. (1997) *Russian Talk: Culture and Conversation during Perestroika*, Ithaca and New York: Cornell University Press.

Scanlon J. (1995) *Inarticulate Longings: The Ladies' Home Journal, Gender and the Promises of Consumer Culture*, New York: Routledge.

Skeggs B. (2004) 'Context and Background: Pierre Bourdieu's Analysis of Class, Gender and Sexuality', in L. Adkins, B. Skeggs (eds) *Feminism after Bourdieu*, Oxford: Blackwell Publishing.

Stoichita V. (2008) *The Pygmalion Effect: From Ovid to Hitchcock*, Chicago and London: Chicago University Press.

Tolstikova N. (2004) 'Rabotnitsa: The Paradoxical Success of a Soviet Women's Magazine', *Journalism History* 30, 3: 131–40.

Temkina A. and Rotkirch A. (2007) 'Sovetskie gendernye kontrakty i ikh transformatsiia v sovremennoi Rossii', *Rossiiskii Gendernyi poriadok, sotsiologicheskii podkhod*. St. Petersburg: European University in St. Petersburg Press.

Töyry M. (2005) *Varhaiset naistenlehdet ja naisten elämän ristiriidat: Neuvotteluja lukijasopimuksesta*, Viestinnän julkaisuja 10, Helsinki: Gummerus.

Vainshtein O. (1996) 'Female Fashion, Soviet Style: Bodies of Ideology', in H. Goscilo, B. Holmgren (eds) *Russia Women Culture*, Bloomington: Indiana University Press.

Watson P. (1993) 'Eastern Europe's Silent Revolution: Gender', *Sociology* 27 (3): 471–87.

Whitford M. (1991) *Luce Irigaray Philosophy in the Feminine*, New York: Routledge.

Zdravomyslova O. (2003) *Sem'ia i obshchestvo: gendernoe izmerenie rossiiskoi transformatsii*, Moscow: URSS.

9 Modern Russian entertainment TV

'Live well now – ask me how!'

Natalia Mikhailova

'In November 2001, a new period in modern Russian entertainment TV history began.' This is how a TV review referred to the broadcasting of the reality show *The Last Hero*. *The Last Hero* was the Russian version of *Survivor*, a very well-known show, extremely popular in Europe and the USA. *The Last Hero* was broadcast from 2001–6 on the state-owned First Channel. However, the Russian version lasted for only six seasons. It was not the first Western[1] TV programme broadcast under licence in Russia,[2] but it was the first reality TV programme of this genre.[3] The advertising slogan promised the audience: 'It's not a game! It is real life'. The first reception was ambiguous. The programme had the highest rating among all audience categories throughout its first season. On the other hand, TV critics viewed the show quite negatively. The main point of disagreement was that this show directed its viewers toward 'the wrong values'.[4] In numerous interviews, however, producers of the Russian version actively promoted quite different ideas about the show. 'Our show is not about how to eliminate one's rivals but rather about the difficulties in making the right choice...The main thing for the winner is not to get three million rubles but to preserve self-respect, dignity' (Bodrov 2002b). 'We wanted more or less decent people (*dostoinye liudi*) in the finals' (Bodrov 2002a).

I conjecture that in contrast to the original Western reality show, the Russian version has gone beyond entertaining spectators or portraying some kind of real life of ordinary people in unusual circumstances. The intention of the broadcasters (producers as well) was to present to the audience a certain lifestyle model to achieve success (in the 'real' game and in perspective in real life). In this chapter, TV is treated as a medium that produces images of reality, representations of society as well as of the 'others' and transmits social norms and values (Bell 1998; Comstock 1975). As a technology and a medium, TV defines modes of thinking and feeling and proposes ways of communicating on different levels. It is necessary to take into consideration that modern Russian TV is the most influential form of mass media to promote guidelines for future social and cultural transformations in post-Soviet society. Thus, Russian entertainment TV develops according to the requirements of a modern consumer society and chooses and creates living, moral and other standards for the TV consumer audience.

I suggest that in the Russian version of the reality show *Survivor* there are significant transformations. The first is that the main premise for the game is 'to win with and live in dignity'. Even if we suggest that the promotion of a certain lifestyle through a reality show is hidden beneath the ethical jargon, the question arises as to why the discussion of a game show is conducted in moral terms of 'dignity', not in terms of 'getting a prize'. I think that this ethical constituent of the general idea of the reality show may be denoted as one of the main features of its 'glocalization' on the concept level for the Russian audience. The term 'glocalization' was coined by R. Robertson to reflect the changes occurring when a TV programme moves into a new local market (Robertson 1995; Chang 2000). The basic elements of the show are constant due to licence requirements. At the same time, once a programme becomes popular, its 'inner content' (plot and characters, for example) tend to be adapted in order to accommodate some cultural expectation of a national audience. Thus, only the technology of communication is 'global' but the content, functions, and aims are 'locally marked' and 'culturally bounded' (Kato 1975). Western scholars noted the Russian desire to consider all phenomena first and foremost from a position of morality. According to Anna Wierzbicka, 'the most important points of Russian language-specific picture of the world are to love morality, to see human life in absolute terms of morality' (Wierzbicka 1996: 34).

The Russian adjective *dostoinyi* ('decent') is used very frequently in statements made by the producers of the Russian version of the show, and this word seems to be central in the definition of the specifics of its general idea. In order to understand why the use of this word in the media discourse of the 2000s is 'unexpected', I would like to make a brief digression into the semantics of this adjective. The *Concise Academic Explanatory Dictionary of the Russian Language* (*MAS*) explains the adjective *dostoinyi* as 'fair, rightful, worthy of' (*MAS* 1999: 438). So there is a very strong connection between goodness, decency and morality, and truthfulness in the Russian language. In the same way, official rhetoric reflects this meaning. Soviet ideology considered not wealth but high morality as part and parcel of a decent life. To live a 'good life' meant 'to live for others', 'to choose moral strategies of behaviour to achieve success'.[5] At the same time, linguistic analysis of the usage of these words in printed media texts of the 1990s makes it clear that there are essential differences between its meaning in the written and spoken language. For example, a 'good, decent life' means not only a 'highly moral' but rather a 'well-to-do life', even a 'bourgeois life'.[6]

Thus, since the early 2000s, the concept of *dostoinyi* (worthy/decent people, decent life, etc.) has been connected, on the one hand, with the old-fashioned Russian and Soviet norms of behaviour and, on the other hand, with the bourgeois idea of (personal) prosperity as the foundation of the 'good life'. The attempt to glocalise the Western show about individualistic values via their combination with traditional Russian or Soviet rhetoric was of fundamental importance for understanding this television message. By analysing this concept in the TV programme we will understand what kinds of content and meaning the 'good life' acquires, and how a Russian entertainment programme constructs and offers models of the good life/well-being. This chapter addresses two main problems: first, how the concept *dostoinyi* is represented in the Russian version of the reality show *Survivor*, and, second, how the model 'to live in dignity' (*zhit' dostoino)* is constructed and presented via the behavioural practices of the characters in this media text.

The solution to these specific research problems will help us to define general tendencies in the development of modern entertainment TV in Russia. We will also study the specificity of this process from the point of view of how Soviet practices and concepts (such as *dostoinaia zhizn'*) collide with Western lifestyles, and what is the outcome of this new trend. Consequently, the question is: 'What kind of ideology of everyday life as a "good life" is being transmitted via entertainment programmes in the 2000s?'. On the other hand, the presence of educational content in entertainment programmes also points out the peculiarity of modern entertainment on Russian TV.

Russian TV of the 2000s as entertainment TV

Cultural studies consider the cinema as one of the most informative audio-visual cultural–historical sources. It has been assumed that the cinema is a snapshot of its time, and that it preserves the behavioural norms accepted by society and suggests for discussion, acceptance or rejection new norms and ideals. Lenin's well-known slogan, 'The cinema is the most important art for the Soviet State', reflected not only the position of the state but also the attitude of the audience. The cinema used to be one of the most-favoured entertainments of mass audiences during the Soviet era. However, the cinema of post-Soviet Russia has been, little by little, losing ground to TV. To some extent this is due to problems inside the Russian cinematographic community: declining production quality, generational differences, as well as financial problems of movie theatres and film production in the market society. As a result, TV became the main source of information and entertainment in the 2000s. In terms of 'centre–periphery' of the cultural semiosphere (Lotman 2001: 254, 257–60), this means that TV as a part of the semiosphere moves from the fringe to the centre of culture.[7] While moving from the fringe to the centre, TV culture and media texts are transformed to blend with the inner semiotics of Russian culture (Lotman 2001: 262).

Another tendency concerns the correlations among different TV genres. The sociological polls by Gallup Media demonstrate that the real rating of news programmes is lower than that of entertainment programmes, such as TV series, talk shows or comedies. The thesis that 'entertainment constitutes the largest category of TV content almost everywhere in the world' (Cooper-Chen, 2005: 3) depicts a common tendency in global TV network development. Western media scholars state that 'entertainment offerings obtrusively dominate media content' since the late 1980s (Zillmann and Vorderer 2000: 8). On Russian TV, the entertainment epoch began a decade later. However, since the beginning of the 2000s, entertainment programmes have formed a significant part of the TV content of Russian TV as well (Gudkov and Dubin 2001).

The most popular entertainment genres on Russian TV are the internationally licensed TV reality and game shows. During the past 20 years, the game show has replaced older, traditional TV genres. Television game shows and popular sports commentaries now get top ratings and are the most profitable. So, the TV game show is one of the main genres of mass culture. The game has two purposes: as emotional relaxation and as a source of information about the world. Traditionally, the latter purpose has been suitable only for children. Modern TV presents this method of world cognition for adult audience as well.

This is consistent with another typical feature of Soviet mass culture – Soviet ideology employed entertainment genres in cinema and on TV. While discussing the entertaining nature of Soviet mass culture, scholars stress the ambivalent role of entertainment in politics with shifting the border between the political and the non-political (Kotkin 2001). 'Popular genres' (comedies, for example, or pop songs) were actively used to translate certain ideological values, combining entertainment with direct propaganda. It is clear that post-Soviet TV is also a product of the transformation of the system of Soviet TV. Therefore, it is interesting to investigate whether the modern entertainment genres of Russian TV are free of this ideological constituent and, if so, what kind of ideology of everyday life is being transmitted via entertainment.

As the main material for the analysis, I have chosen *The Last Hero* (2001) and *The Heart of Africa* (2006), the first and sixth seasons of the Russian version of the show *Survivor*. The diachronic analysis will help to detect changes in dynamics in models of *dostoinaia zhizn'* over the period 2001–6. In the context of the reality game show, we will see that modern Russian entertainment TV presents a game as a method of world cognition and as a way to cultivate life principles for adult audiences.

Moral education/moralising and influence via entertainment

Comstock wrote, 'Television and human behaviour is a topic for which there is neither a single methodological paradigm nor a primary discipline. It is a campground for many methods, and for many disciplinary tribes' (Comstock *et al.* 1978: 11). As there are a number of methodological approaches to analysing the relation 'mass media–audience', I shall compare briefly some theoretical frameworks to see which one is best suited to describe what is taking place: the dependence model, the psychological model, the social constructivist model and/or a semiotic model.

The dependence model of mass media (Ball-Rokeach and DeFleur 1976) makes it possible to explain the success of media influence at the macro level, i.e. on the social level. The extent of the individual's dependence on mass media and the intensity of media influence are closely connected with the level of (non-)stability in society and with the social importance of mass media as a source of information. The extent of dependence of the individual on media information is proportional to the degree of non-stability, i.e. it increases during critical periods in the life of society. Hence, during crises, the cognitive, affective, behavioural influence of the media system on the audience is stronger. For almost all strata of Russian society, the late 1990s and the early 2000s were one such critical period. In the opinion polls conducted by FOM (Public Opinion Foundation) in 1998, 88 per cent of respondents agreed that informational, socio-political TV programmes influence the moods and behaviour of people (Zadorin, Burova and S'utkina 1999). The reality show *The Last Hero* was one of the top-rated programmes of 2001–2. It is quite likely that the novelty of the material was not the only reason for its success. It is evident that certain ideas and concepts of behaviour presented in the show were needed and/or discussed in Russian society in 2001.

In contrast, the psychological model of media effects (Comstock *et al.* 1978) explains the power of the media to create an 'epidemic' of certain behaviour based on those representations in the media.[8] Television's fictional portrayals 'cultivate' the congruent beliefs of viewers (Comstock *et al.* 1978: 15). The individual perceives the type of behaviour broadcast by TV and can adopt it. Thus, TV acts as a mediator between social norms and ideals, both present and future (those that are emerging), and an individual (Robinson 1972; Belson 1967; Gerbner 1970). Whether the new behavioural strategies replace the old ones depends on their psychological importance for the individual, the degree of (his or her) 'agitation' and motivation. According to this communicative model, the intensity of media influence is directly connected to the degree of realism in promoting a certain behavioural model. The more realistic the presentation, the stronger the psychological impact on the viewer and the more probable its influence on the viewer's future behaviour. From this point of view, the reality show is a programme whose aim is to achieve maximum realism in the events on the screen. It is the kind of TV format that is the most likely to influence the audience on a micro-level.

According to the theory of social constructivism, I link such social constructs as morality and gender with the particular (national) culture and society. These concepts are apprehended as natural, but, at the same time, they remain conventional artefacts within a concrete society or culture (Searle 1996). Consequently, the collapse or transformation of society provokes a transformation within the system of social constructs. Conversely, the cultural continuum has to ensure the unity of the permanently reconstructed reality with the previous value system.

From my point of view, however, the most productive methodological approaches for studying the relationship between TV and the audience are semiotic approaches. To understand the extent of the influence of the mass media (and television) message on the audience means to understand what is its impact on the audience, both through the programmes it likes and dislikes (Eco 2003). It implies that a TV programme is analysed as a text with some intention of the sender (producers), with an objective structure of the message (TV programme), and the reception of the recipients (addressee, viewers). Thus, a TV programme to a wide extent can be regarded as a system of signs. A system of signs is defined (by Saussure) as a combination of a sound and an image (signifier) and a concept or understanding (signified). Thus, a media text as a semiotic entity is organised as an audio-visual 'relatively solid symbolic combination that appears to be somewhat clearly defined … as a communicative artifact, in other words, human-produced instrument of communication' (Lehtonen 2000: 72–3). The textual analysis in the case of a media text (a TV programme) means a special way of reading, de-coding or defining a meaning, 'which is affected by the position of the reader in contexts and cultural practices in addition to the text itself' (Lehtonen 2000: 78; Dashkova 2007). At the same time, the ethical (ideological) constituent in the visual source (TV programme, cinema, etc.) can be reconstructed only by means of analysis of the style and expressiveness of the language of TV (Dashkova 2007).

According to Umberto Eco, 'codes and sub-codes are applied to the (TV) message in light of a general framework of cultural references, which constitutes the receiver's patrimony of knowledge: his ideological, ethical, religious standpoints, his psychological attitudes, his tastes, value systems, etc.' (Eco 2003: 13). Within a nation's culture, TV content is one of its most accessible sources to study the representation of diversity, the ethics of contestant behaviour, the construction of identity, etc. (Montemurro 2008). From this point of view, the TV reality show as an entertainment genre is both international and easily localised. According to the basic principles of the genre, a reality show should present to the audience the absolute reality, the real behaviour of the participants of the game in extreme situations. At the same time, according to the laws of mass culture, any character in the show should present a certain *habitus*, so that any recipient would easily recognise himself in them. Thus, a 'close reading' of this media text makes it possible to draw some conclusions about the behavioural norms, which are relevant in this or in some other society. On the other hand, by the 'reality of mass media' we mean the double sense of reality: something that really happens, and the constructed, artificial reality (Luhmann 2005). P. Romanov studies certain norms presented in the cinema and shows how the same duality of the reality is constructed: 'Creating the characters of the film, the director selects certain facts of the reality, wraps them into his representations, putting them into shape with cinematographic and social stereotypes' (Romanov 2002). Such 'duplication of reality' can be also found in the entertainment programmes aiming at 'real life on the TV screen'. By turning the events of modern life into a show, TV moulds them using special television means: close-ups, setting sequences of shots, background music, etc. Thus, media reality is constructed, but this construction is influenced from outside.

The history of the reality show *Survivor* on the Russian TV screen demonstrates that we are dealing with a special reality when certain models of behaviour are not only presented but rather constructed (by special TV techniques, music and sound effects, and the image of participants in the game) and arranged into a certain paradigm that may be more or less attractive for the audience.

I begin my 'reading' of the reality show with a short description of the cultural context of modern Russian entertainment TV in the last decade. I have mentioned above the changes in semantics of the word 'good' (*dostoinyi*) in the context of transformation in Russian society. While reading media text, I attempt to depict what understanding of the 'good life' (*dostoinaia zhizn'*) in its behaviourist aspects ('good, proper, decent behaviour to become a winner' (*dostoinoe povedenie*)) was promoted by the senders via the concept of 'hero'. In so doing, I analyse the gender representation in the show from the point of 'worthy *dostoinyi* man/woman'. The revival image of hero as an iconological sub-code I consider to be the main issue, which occurs in the definition of the Russian version of the Western reality show in 2001.

The concept of Hero in the context of the Good Life

As mentioned above, the concept of the 'good life' (*dostoinaia zhizn'*) is closely connected with so-called good/proper/ethical behaviour. The question is what kind of behaviour strategy is presented in the reality show as the most successful for a man and for a woman?

Media scholars, even Western scholars, have just begun to relate the ideas about the multidimensional nature of culture to media content and consumer behaviour. It seems natural to study TV in order to understand the 'knowledge, beliefs, perceptions, attitudes, values, and patterns that people learn by growing up in a given society' (Moran 1998).

Speaking about Russian TV throughout the 1990s and 2000s is extremely interesting because we are speaking about two different societies, two different models of lifestyle. 'Old' Soviet behavioural norms were relevant for middle-aged and elderly generations of Russians. At the same time, new trends, ideas and pictures of Western models of lifestyles appeared with Western magazines, soap operas and TV programmes. Adherence of the new Russia to the Western values of democracy and freedom was declared at the official level. Privately, while watching soap operas on TV, people saw more than different interiors. They also saw different relations inside the family and in society. The TV critics of that time were adamantly negative towards the new trends. They branded the new entertainment TV programmes as propaganda of the 'different', foreign values, such as attaining leadership or eliminating competitors. However, the Russian version of *Survivor* was totally different from other entertainment shows of that time. This was clearly stated by the producers of the Russian show. The theme of the Russian *Survivor* was closely connected to the concept of the heroic, hero and heroine. This was the first and fundamental feature of the first Russian version of the show.

In the Soviet period, the concept of heroism was central to the official ideology, as seen in the slogan '*V zhizni vsegda est' mesto podvigu*' ('It is always possible to do a heroic deed'). 'Heroism of everyday work' was the cornerstone of the ideology of late Soviet society. On the other hand, the underground culture was in its own way also exploiting this concept ('the unknown hero', the so-called non-heroic hero such as one finds in the character in Vysotskii's songs).

It was quite logical that during the *perestroika* period in Russian cultural space (and in the cinema in particular), rejection of the heroic theme should have occurred. The 1990s became the 'time without any hero'. Or, alternatively, criminals were offered as anti-heroes (in films such as 'Brother', 'Boomer' and 'Anti-killer'). In any case, in the late 1990s the concept of 'Hero' for the Russian TV audience had been clearly labelled as a basis or a sign of the Soviet behavioural model. The first Russian reality show in 2001 initiated the rehabilitation of this well-known Soviet behavioural concept. Thus, the concept of Hero becomes the central issue for different levels of this media text.

During the first season of *The Last Hero*, the most important thing was to be not 'just' the winner but also 'the real man', the Hero. The attention of the audience was concentrated not on victory as such but rather on 'fair play'. The first host of the game, S. Bodrov, said in an interview: 'The main thing (in the game) is not to survive but to remain a human. Thus, the Russian mentality has blown up the American model, its tasks, forms, and objectives' (Bodrov 2002a).

This is clear from the very beginning. The title of the Russian version was not *Survivor* but *The Last Hero*. From a linguistic point of view, the direct translation of the title *Survivor* was quite possible, as *Vyzhivshii*, for example. However, this direct translation was impossible as a title for a reality about 'how to remain a human', about 'fair play', because of the polysemy and the negative connotations of the Russian equivalent of the English verb 'to survive' – *vyzhivat'*: 'to stay alive by hook or by crook', 'to go mad' or 'to drive somebody out of somewhere'.[9] For the Russian linguistic picture of the world, 'to survive' may be easier than simply 'to live'. Thus, producers rejected such a negatively connotative title and chose the new heroic connotations for the reality show.

Who is the host?

The heroic theme for the show was continued in the image and the role of the host. This was a character with a strong patriarchal and heroic image of masculinity, chosen by Russian producers (and the audience) as the host for the Russian adaptation of the international reality show in 2001. I think that in this case we can see how one of the concepts of popular culture is used. J. Cawelti defined it as 'the performance-persona principle'. He wrote that 'a popular performance is not just a way of presenting a particular work to an audience, but an act by a persona which relates both to a larger social context and to previous acts by the same persona' (Cawelti 2004: 70).

Before the show began, the producers organised an Internet poll to choose the host. The winner, and as a result the first host, was Sergey Bodrov, a movie actor and a TV journalist, a cult figure of the 1990s.[10] It seems that any study of post-Soviet masculinity mentions S. Bodrov starring as Danila in A. Balabanov's 'Brother' (1997) and 'Brother-2' (2000) (e.g. Romanov 2002; Volkov 2005). Everybody repeated after him: 'Do you think that power is in money? No, brother, power is in fairness…'. According to Romanov, Danila presents the image of 'classical masculinity' in the context of post-modern society (Romanov 2002). (He is free; he was at war; he was a soldier; and the brotherhood is more important for him than other relationships.) We know nothing of where he comes from, but we know he is '*svoi*' – 'one of us, a friend'. But the main word for his role is 'the brother'. Being a brother, blood-based brotherhood is the final archaic layer that unites people in post-modern society, when everything is null and void, and there is nothing between people, neither ideology, nor social bounds, nor even national self-identification. 'You are my brother', says Danila, and this explains everything, even his willingness to kill for the sake of the family. I see a return to the rather traditional normative gender model of Soviet hegemonic masculinity. One of the most important features of this cultural and anthropological type is comradeship. Heroism is defined as a distinctive feature of 'father' in the late Soviet period. There had been Soviet cult images of the father, the defender of his country, his land and women. The character of 'brother' had the same functions on the private, family level. So it is logical that in the post-Soviet, post-modern world, this feature has passed from 'father' to somebody who is closer to the audience, to his 'brother'. 'The brother' is a man, so serving his country is his duty. His life is the life of the soldier, the leader. This service is worthy of reward and he becomes a hero. Thus, there is no country, no father; it is the brother who takes the role of the wise defender of the family. As Zdravomyslova and Temkina wrote, the revival of patriarchal types of masculinity becomes a way to overcome the crisis of masculinity in post-Soviet Russia (Zdravomyslova and Temkina 2002). The most important constituent of the movie character, 'being a brother', was used in the character of the host, as well.

'Being a brother' and the heroic essence of the host were understood and accepted by the audience. The comments on the Internet forum of the show make this obvious. The audience interpreted Bodrov's being a host as an extension of his movie image – the young 'national hero'. He was 'a host and a friend to participants': 'a good guy and he was fair', 'hard and well-wishing' and again – 'a brother'.[11] He was 'inside the game'. And at the same time, he was 'above the game'. He was a fair judge. He helped the participants to show their best sides: 'We just wanted to think about life and to provoke 16 people to do something they'll later be proud of...We were interested in common things, which are dignity, justice' (Bodrov 2002a). Thus, the host became 'the hero of the game', who met the requirements of the Soviet concept of masculinity and heroism. This behavioural model was presented in media text as a social code, which was easily decoded by the audience in 2001 (Chandler 2002: 149).

The subsequent history of the Russian version of *Survivor* demonstrates that the heroic concept of the host has been lost.[12] The producers picked out actors with the same image: a masculine strong hero, a knight and a cowboy (popular actors D. Pevtsov and A. Domogarov). But their role in the show became more neutral. They were 'just the announcers to start the next competition'. The general position of the audience, their attitude to the host, became calmer and less heroic. The audience no longer considered the host as a model. Typical comments were: 'I just like him', he is 'charming', 'handsome' and 'a good actor'. To sum up, the following comment makes clear whether the audience needed a 'hero' in the role of the host in 2006: 'As for Pevtsov and Domogarov, they are such nice fellows that they can just do nothing at all, let's just look at them on the TV screen!'. As a result, the producers' strategy changed in the last season, 2005–6. We see an average European host, the handsome and charming actor Domogarov. The female part of the audience discusses his suitable or unsuitable white shirt, or if 'this stupid beard' suits or does not suit him. These problems are discussed more often than his actual participation or non-participation in the game (the main theme of discussions when Bodrov was host). He is a classical 'man from the glamour magazine's cover'. He is famous and charming, and he is able to make a decision. (The rules of the game demand this from him, and he puts out a fire when somebody leaves the game. And finally he says: 'You must go out!') His clothes are not trendy but good quality and expensive. Thus, the host represents the so-called narcissistic type of masculinity, a type of modern Russian male identity. S. Oushakine writes: 'There is the transformation from the concept of "male heroism" toward the more ordinary – and accordingly – less martial idea of masculinity' (Ushakin 2002).

Thus, the comparative analysis of the images of the hosts in 2001 and 2006 demonstrates that heroic characteristics have been replaced by more neutral or even glossy ones. 'Good, proper man' means not a hero but 'just a handsome man'. At the same time, the name of the show was also changed. The last version (2005–6) was called *The Heart of Africa*. The main goal (as announced by the producers) was 'to learn to understand each other'.[13] The very word 'hero' has disappeared from the title of the show. The moralistic aspect of the game, 'to be a hero', has also disappeared. The role of the host as a model for those who want to become a hero has also disappeared.

Revising gender representation

In the ordinary mentality, gender representations become apparent as gender stereotypes. By means of gender identity and social institutions, gender stereotypes have an influence on producing certain hierarchical relations in a concrete society. In different periods inside different age groups belonging to different social strata, different gender stereotypes may be articulated. Ways of (re-)producing a gender system in a visual culture were analysed using the material of the mass cinema (Usmanova 2001; Oleinikova 2007). It seems that TV programmes do not only reflect the gender stereotypes prevailing in a society, but rather present certain gender behaviour as more (or less) attractive to the audience. And from this point of view the analysis of the Russian version of the reality show *Survivor* may help to understand what types of gender representation or what gender stereotypes were more relevant for Russian society between 2001 and 2006. Another question is which models of gender representation were presented as the models for success or (in the context of the game show) for victory. If, as was mentioned above, the strategy of the Russian show was to promote 'decent victory', the question would be 'who were a "proper"/ decent (*dostoinyi)* man and a "proper"/decent (*dostoinaia)* woman'? Does having a winner in *The Last Hero* mean 'the real hero' or simply 'the best'?

There were six winners in the Russian version of *Survivor*: two women and four men. The image of the first winner (Sergei Odintsov) is the best answer to the question, 'Who was the real man for Russia in 2001?'. The first winner of *The Last Hero* was an ex-soldier, a 'real defender of the Fatherland'. He was the charismatic leader from the very beginning. He tried to be honest during the game and in dealings with other participants. He even saved his friend from drowning during the competition. From the perspective of the created reality in the TV programme, I conjecture that to some extent this real man (Sergei) created his image of 'honest hero' because he 'knew' from his cultural background how the hero had to act in extreme situations. The analysis of the Internet discussion around the game proves that, in general, the audience accepted him as the winner and as the real hero of the day. As was commented, 'Who would be the real winner if not he?'. This was a fairly widespread opinion, in spite of the fact that during the game another player (Ivan) won more often than Sergei. But Ivan presented quite a different image: he was a student, a smart guy. As one of the players (Natalia) said, 'My heart belongs to Ivan, but I give my vote to Sergei. He deserves to be a decent hero'. After the show, the virtual image as 'the real Hero' had an influence on the real life of the real man. Sergei became a deputy of the city council just because of his positive image from the heroic show. His activities in public life were not successful nor were his business projects.

Comparing this male representation with other conclusions in the studies about 'man in contemporary Russian media', I suggest that the winner in *The Last Hero* may be regarded as a representative of masculine identity in 2001. This was based on the ideal Soviet model of the *real* man (*nastoiashchii muzhchina*), the so-called hegemonic Soviet masculinity (Zdravomyslova and Temkina 2001). R. Kay, in her analysis of the 'ways in which men have been represented in popular media discourses and ... how these media images were reflected and responded to in men's experiences of and comments on life in post-Soviet Russia', also puts post-Soviet man between heroes and villains (Kay 2006: 19). She notes that there are a significant number of articles describing the 'good man' in the beginning of the 2000s. According to her research, the 'good man' in contemporary Russian magazines is active both in private and in public; he is constantly striving to achieve more. His physical strength indicates not only good health, but also moral health. He is a charismatic leader with survival, team building, and social skills (Kay 2006: 40). It is obvious that this is exactly a portrait of our hero – the winner in *The Last Hero* of 2001. According to Kay, such representations of men 'frequently express views and convictions which strongly support traditional attitudes towards gender and relations… men as patriarchal figures, in both their private and public lives' (Kay 2006: 40).

Comparative analysis of the first (*The Last Hero*, 2001) and the last (*The Heart of Africa*, 2006) seasons of the Russian version of *Survivor* makes it clear that the show digressed from the promotion of the heroic component in the image of the winner as well as in the image of the host. In general, it lost its strong heroic background. The winner of *The Heart of Africa* works in a nightclub as a dancer. He is strong and smart; he is a classic 'hero-lover' straight out of romance novels. He named himself 'Conan', and his appearance (his created scenic image) imitated that of Tarzan. Thus, if in romance novels the hero is 'huge', is a 'mountain of muscles' and, of necessity 'a bit of a savage' (Ulybina 2004: 542), the winner of *The Heart of Africa* was the visual embodiment of such a hero.

Thus, I conclude that the 2001 Russian *Survivor* presented a traditional patriarchal type of Soviet masculinity as the most positive model to achieve success and to live with dignity. In 2006, another behavioural sub-code was used to glocalise the international show for the Russian audience. Not a patriarchal hero but a glossy celebrity becomes the most proper person to be a winner.

Such de-heroisation of an entertainment show has something in common with the transformation of literary tastes of the Russian reading audience. The sociologist B. Dubin writes that since the middle of the 1990s the interests of the readers have moved from cruel action with supermen characters towards love stories or psychological novels with elements of adventure or detective stories. Most people are getting bored with the frustration and descriptions of violence and collapse.

They would like to get some rest from it and prefer at least imaginary stability, even if it is dull and even silly. Still, it is more predictable (Dubin 2004).

Does this mean that the epoch of heroes ended in 2006? In any case, a comparative analysis of media content shows us that in 2006 the producers gave up the attempts to offer the audience a 'heroic game'. The audience also did not object to watching a standard, entertaining programme.

Worthy woman in the (non-?)heroic reality show

The gender representation of women in *The Last Hero* and *The Heart of Africa* confirms the same tendency of the transformation of the entertainment programme into a less propagandistic and glossier show.

According to the rules, the participants in the show have to represent different age groups. It is obvious, however, that belonging to different age groups in post-Soviet Russia also means belonging to the different social epochs when their mentalities were formed. The youngest of the female players in *The Last Hero* is 23 years old; the oldest is 37. In other words, the players grew up and formed as individuals in the Soviet Union of the 1970s, in the Soviet Union of the 1980s (age from 31 to 34) and in the post-Soviet epoch. If we speak about female participants in terms of the gender contract and gender representation, it is obvious that they will reflect the transformation of the Soviet gender system toward that of the post-Soviet era. According to Temkina and Rotkirch, 'while the basic features of the Russian gender system today still remain quite unchanged, there has been a dramatic change in the dominant gender contracts' (Rotkirch and Temkina 2002). In general, new trends are described as a recombination of elements from the three main gender contracts of Soviet time: the legitimate contract 'working *mother*', the 'counter' contract and the 'shadow' contract. From these points of view, I analysed the presentations of the female players: what they shared about themselves before the game (previous social activities, their reasons for participating in the show, and the strategy they used in the game).[14] All eight presentations can be divided into three groups. In the following paragraphs, I analyse the female players.

The first female player is Nadezhda, 37. She owns a dental clinic, so we know that she is a hard-working and successful businesswoman. But during the introduction, her maternal life is stressed, as well. She is the only one in whose introductory video we see her family. Her husband and their son discuss the news that 'mother is taking part in the Game'. About her life strategy she says: 'I expect presents from Fate. It is better than buying them myself. My dreams and hopes are the same ones any ordinary woman dreams of'.[15] During the game, she did not want to be the leader. Her strategy was to be close to the potential leader (an ex-seaman). During the hidden struggle between the two male leaders, she made her choice and started to act accordingly. And her main shadow activity was aimed at making this potential leader the real one and to support him. She got the rivals not out of *her* way but out of *his* way. Intrigue was her main weapon. The other players called her 'the Grey Cardinal',[16] and of course she was not popular among other players or with the audience.

Thus, in terms of gender representation we may conclude that, according to her behaviour type, she falls within the framework of the traditional Soviet gender contract. This type is closely connected with the typical Soviet gender contract 'working *mother*'. The symbolic representation of women is connected mainly with being a mother. At the same time, Nadezhda's behaviour is correlated with the Soviet type of 'active woman' in her work-place (a local trade-union leader) and in her family (the head of the household), whereas the father was some kind of a 'second child' in the family. As a result, her official status of 'the work-oriented career woman' was not confirmed by her behaviour in the game. Moreover, her behaviour turned her official status into some kind of simulacrum. The audience may possibly conclude that this type of life strategy is not the key to success.

The second female group can be called 'super-emotional woman' (Elena, 34, an actress, Irina, 31, a musician, and Anna, 23, a teacher). They claimed that emotionality was the main feature of their characters: 'Actors are more emotional...I can't cook or pick mushrooms'; 'I was not created to cook, clean an apartment, or wash clothes'; 'I can do anything for the sake of love'. So they presented the image of a 'really quintessential woman', a romantic image of a loving, more highly aesthetically organised martyr. The emotional component is paramount when describing this behaviour model. They did not pretend to be a leader or even some kind of 'bright person'. They were afraid to be without protection. One of them (Anna) explored the image of a young lady 'falling in love'. Her strategy in the first part of the game may be defined as 'waiting'. She did not co-operate with any 'leader' groups; she tried to avoid all conflicts. She only loved and missed her boyfriend. After the merging of the tribes, her viewpoint was again *to be with him*. This love story ended with the wedding, as it had to in a fairytale.

For Temkina and Rotkirch, the image of a 'romantic young lady' was one of the types of the Soviet 'shadow gender contract' and the main female hero in late Soviet society as well. According to the researchers, 'in the 90s the shadow gender contract has become more articulated and serves as the main basis for new kinds of behaviour' (Rotkirch and Temkina 2002). It was this model of behaviour that was introduced to the Russian female audience in the numerous soap operas and love stories that were extremely popular in the late 1990s. The same is also suggested in *The Last Hero*.

The behaviour model *to love and to be loved* as an inevitable attribute of a *decent life* is as attractive as *a decent life via a successful career*. The latter was chosen by four female participants (aged 23–31). They are independent, self-made women. The main words for their lifestyle are: 'I do it myself.' About themselves they say: 'Difficulties on the island don't scare me, I am used to it'; 'I make my life myself'; 'Independence is the main value for me'. These young women are not married, and, as one of them says, she 'has a plan to get married in spring but hasn't yet decided who will be the husband'. They promote a very strong, even aggressive, style of behaviour in the game. In the context of a reality show, this strategy was presented as successful. One of these women, Inna (a self-made woman, actress and successful model in real life), was in the leader group up to the end of the game.

This life strategy is very close to the first-mentioned model ('the working mother'), but really only to the 'working' part. I think that in this case we are dealing with the new type of gender representation: not 'a *working* mother' but 'a career woman'. This type of female behaviour was not common at the end of the 1990s (Rotkirch and Temkina 2002). Traditionally, in the Russian mentality, this type of female behaviour is assimilated as Western. At the beginning of the 2000s, it was widely presented in women's magazines (Chernova 2008). In *The Last Hero*, this kind of gender representation was announced as the most productive for the winning strategy. Five years later, in *The Heart of Africa*, this strategy became the only one. The choice of players was made along the same lines. Different age groups and different educational and social levels were represented. However, the eight female participants of the game cannot be divided into any groups. They all represent one group – 'the career woman'. Their life motto is: 'The main aim of my life is to achieve success, to strive for the impossible'. Interestingly, all the women's stories are very similar. They all stressed that the father was the leader in their families. All the stories present a very patriarchal type of family. We see a strong accent placed on the role of 'family' and 'father' in their biographies. This is the new line in the show in comparison with the first season. However, the principles of bringing up girls were not patriarchal at all but quite modern. For example, one young lady said that she made her life according to her father's words: 'Don't be afraid and take risks, and you will be the winner'. All of them played with boys in their childhood. Now their best friends are male ('It is easier to communicate with men'). Now all these women are successful in social life. They have very 'unfeminine' professions (from journalist to police officer). Each of them is a potential leader in the game. The whole show consists of a sequence of episodes in their struggle for the leadership. They do not 'help' *him* to become the leader. They (women) take *him* in their close circle as a helper for their own victory.

In general, we may conclude that during the last season of the game (*The Heart of Africa* in 2006) all the female players acted within the bounds of one and the same type of modern Russian gender contract. It is the 'career woman' as a sub-contract for '*working* mother'. Exactly this type of woman (the career woman) was presented as the hegemonic, the most successful and worthy one. But at the same time the youngest of all the 'career women' came second in the game. Her emotionality (maybe because of her young age) softened her 'self-made' behaviour model into a more patriarchal behaviour model for 'a girl from a good family, father's daughter who can do anything to achieve a good life'. Thus, in 2006 the show promoted the new Western lifestyle for a successful woman. But at the same time, there was an attempt to combine it with the reconstructed, patriarchal behaviour model.

Conclusion

Modern Russian TV is still mass media, which enjoys a fairly high degree of audience confidence. Its influence in forming a certain approach to life for the TV audience is accepted by producers, TV critics and by the TV audience as well. The same moralistic, educational and pedagogical role can be found in entertainment

TV. This is also understood and realised both by producers and consumers of TV productions.

The active adaptation of Russian entertainment TV to Western TV formats began during the 1990s. On the one hand, this was a result of the globalisation of the TV system. On the other hand, it correlated with the common tendency to transform Russian society according to Western models of everyday life. The market economy demanded a new behaviour strategy to achieve success, new behavioural and consumption practices (Oushakine 2000). The understanding of what is *proper*, *good*, *wealthy* was revised.

The audience could see these new practices in various licensed game shows. Their appearance on TV not only reflected the state of affairs in society, but also their legitimisation as suitable for the contemporary understanding of a 'decent life'. These behavioural norms quite often conflicted with Soviet norms, which were more familiar to most of the audience. Hence, the glocalising of Western formats in 2001 consisted of the active use of old concepts like heroism and heroic behaviour as a feature of a *decent, good life* and the priority of moral wealth above material wealth. This tendency has been demonstrated in the example of promoting heroism in *The Last Hero-1*. The high rating of the show confirms that the audience perceived this manner of glocalization and this type of *good life* positively. Thus, entertainment TV at the beginning of the 2000s did not exactly create models of a decent life, but rather re-created them by exploiting the historical memory of the audience.

The later development of TV as a part of mass culture consisted of an increase in the number of licensed entertainment programmes. The demonstration of new behavioural practices dominant in the programmes focused on reflecting reality. The first and the last season of the Russian *Survivor* (*The Last Hero-1* and *The Heart of Africa*) illustrate that the paradigm of the gender stereotypes presented in the show has changed, advancing towards the Western model of a successful woman. In the context of a *good life*, the new Western behaviour practices were often presented in combination with the traditional Russian (or Soviet) concept of *good* behaviour. Moreover, new models of decent behaviour were often not used at all in the game show (new daily consumption practices, for example). However, it is obvious that the entertainment programme changed from the Russian heroic quest of the hero towards being 'just a show'. This Western style of show is most clearly visible in the latest version of the programme. The process of glocalisation (using global tendencies with a local twist) reached a peak in the first season of the programme and sank to the bottom in the last one. Nationally coloured Russian entertainment TV has capitulated to colourful programming for everyone. From this perspective, Russian entertainment TV becomes a part of global mass culture. The most important phenomena of global mass culture become clear to the Russian TV audience.

Does it mean that the strengthening of Westernisation in other areas of social life is expected? Or is true that modern Russia only entertains, as the whole world does, without trying to do more? To achieve the complete picture of the changes that took place and of those that are on the horizon, it would be necessary to compare our conclusions with behaviour models presented as *good* or *decent* in other mass media (from glossy magazines and TV soap operas, serials, news and documentary programmes). It would also be necessary to analyse the existing statistical data (the numbers of businesswomen, the most popular ways of investing money, etc.). One more research issue would involve comparison of the main trends in the transformation of entertainment TV with the official rhetoric. The return to patriotic, pan-Slavonic, and uniting metaphors in the political discourse has intensified in recent years. It is possible that the future activities of entertainment TV in teaching the audience a new lifestyle could clarify the picture. Or was it accidental that the prize of the Russian TV Academy of 2007 for 'Entertainment programme: Way of life' was won by a Russian version of a Western cooking show?

Notes

1 I use the adjective 'Western' as the general adjective for European and US TV programmes. In the Russian language the term 'Western' has a deeper connotation than just geographical.
2 The first one was the Russian version of 'Wheel of Fortune' ('Pole Chudes'), which started in 1991 and is still broadcast on First Channel every week.
3 The term 'reality TV' is used in media studies as an umbrella term for a wide range of programmes. The main features of these programmes are to portray ordinary people in unscripted situations in ordinary or (versus) exotic locations (Sparks 2007).
4 For example, 'Play GULAD'; 'There are instructing films to aggression'; 'Don't forget to switch off your TV!'; 'The Fear Factor – the fear factory'; 'Russian TV creates the single uncultured space', etc. (according to the Integrum database service).
5 See, for example, The Moral Code of the Builder of Communism.
6 Concerning changes in the semantics of the word '*dostoinyi*' see Vepreva and Kupina 2008; Kruglova 2008.
7 Concerning the end of the epoch of 'literaturocentrism' in Russian culture see Berg 2000.
8 I use this term in its sociological meaning, as the social behaviour specifically directed at other people. The social behaviour of an individual becomes apparent through his social actions in the community and is evaluated in accordance with social norms and regulated by informal social control (Berger and Luckmann 1967; Searle 1996).
9 Concise Academy Explanatory Dictionary of the Russian Language (1999), v.1: 256.
10 Now, because of the circumstances of his death under a glacier in Dagestan in 2002 while shooting his last movie, he has become a figure of truly mythic proportions.
11 All comments are taken from the official site of the show www.1tv.ru.
12 This assertion is relevant only for this particular programme. Heroic rhetoric is not gone; it is very actively promoted in such TV genres as police and crime shows.
13 From the official site of the show.
14 See the visual presentation on the official website of the show *The Last Hero*.
15 Official website of the show *The Last Hero-1*.
16 Well-known idiom in Russia: someone who is a Grey Cardinal exerts power behind the scenes without drawing attention to himself or herself.

References

Ball-Rokeach, S. and DeFleur, M.L. (1976) 'A dependency model of mass media effects', *Communication Research* 3: 3–21.

Bell, W. (1998) 'Making People Responsible: the Possible, the Probable, and the Preferable', *The American Behavioural Scientist*, 42(3): 323–39.

Belson, W.A. (1967) *The Impact of Television*, Hamden: Archon Books.

Berg, M. (2000) *Literaturokratiia: problema pereraspredeleniia i prisvoeniia vlasti*, Moskva: NLO.

Berger, P.L. and Luckmann, T. (1967) *The Social Construction of Reality: a treatise in the sociology of knowledge*, Garden City, NY: Anchor Books.

Bodrov, S. (2002a) 'Igra v zhizn', *Rossiiskaia Gazeta*, 2 September.

Bodrov, S. (2002b) 'Id'et igra narodnaia', *Kinoart*. Online. Available www.kinoart.ru/file/people/02-5-1/ (accessed 20 June 2009).

Cawelti, J. (2004) *Adventure, Mystery, and Romance: essays*, Madison, WI: University of Wisconsin Press.

Chandler, D. (2002) *Semiotic: the basics*, New York: Routledge.

Chang, Y. (2000) Pathway to 'glocalization': star-TV in Asia, 1991–1995, *International Communication Bulletin* 35:14–21.

Chernova, Zh. (2008) *Media reprezentatsii pola: rossiiskie varianty*. Online. Available www.ecsocman.edu.ru/db/msg/149606.html (accessed 20 June 2009).

Comstock, G. (1975). *Television and human behavior: The key studies.* Santa Monica, CA: Rand Corporation.

Comstock, G., Chaffee, S., Katzman, N., McCombs, M. and Roberts, D. (1978) *Television and human behaviour*, New York: Columbia University Press.

Concise Academy Explanatory Dictionary of the Russian Language (MAS) (1999) RAN, Institut lingvisticheskih issledovanii, Moskva, v. 1.

Cooper-Chen, A. (2005) *Global Entertainment Media: content, audiences, issues*, London and New York: Routledge.

Dashkova, T. (2007) 'Ideologiia i kinoprezentaciia (liubov' i byt v sovetskih kinofil'makh 30-50-h godov)', in E. Iarskaia-Smirnova, P. Romanov, V. Krutkina (eds) *Vizual'naia antropologiia: novye vzgl'ady na sotsial'nuiu real'nost'*, Saratov: 205–23.

Dubin, B. (2004) 'Chitatel' v obshchestve zritelei', *Znam'a*, 5. Online. Available http://magazines.russ.ru/znamia/2004/5/dub9.html (accessed 20 June 2009).

Eco, U. (2003) 'Towards a semiotic inquiry into the television message', in T. Miller (ed.) *Television: critical concepts in media and cultural studies*, London and New York: Routledge, v. II: 3–19.

Gerbner, G. (1970) 'Cultural indicators: the case of violence in television drama', *Annals of the American Academy of Political and Social Science*, Mar. 1970; 388: 69–81.

Gudkov, L. and Dubin, B. (2001) 'Obshchestvo telezritelei: massy i massovye kommunikacii v Rossii konca 90-kh godov', *Monitoring obshchestvennogo mneniia: ekonomicheskie i sotsial'nye peremeny*, 2(52): 31–45. Online. Available www.ecsocman.edu.ru/db/msg/295922.html (accessed 20 June 2009).

Kato, H. (1975) 'Essays in comparative popular culture', *Papers of East-West Communication Institute*, 13:35.

Kay, R. (2006) *Men in contemporary Russia: the fallen heroes of post-Soviet change?* Aldershot: Ashgate.

Kotkin, S. (2001) *Armageddon Averted: the Soviet collapse, 1970–2000*, Oxford: Oxford University Press.

Kruglova, T.A. (2008) 'Kontsepty "trud" i "delo": konstruirovanie dostoinoi zhizni v sovetskii i postsovetskii periody', in Rosenholm A, Trubina E., Litovskaia M.; Savkina I. (eds) *Obraz dostoinoi zhizni v sovremennykh rossiiskikh SMI*, Ekaterinburg: Izdatel'stvo Ural'skogo universiteta.

Lehtonen, M. (2000) *Cultural analysis of texts*, London: Sage.

Lotman, Iu. (2001) *Semiosphere*. St. Petersburg: Iskusstvo.

Luhmann, N. (2005) *Real'nost' mass media*, Moskva.

Montemurro, B. (2008) 'Toward sociology of reality television', *Sociology Compass* 2(1): 84–106.
Moran, A. (1998) *Copycat TV: globalization program formats and cultural identity*, Luton: University of Luton Press.
Official website of the show *The Heart of Africa*. Online. Available www.geroev.net (accessed 20 November 2006).
Official website of the show *The Last Hero*. Online. Available www.1tv.ru/hero/?p_razdel_id=6216&p_topic_id=6219 (accessed 10 May 2006); www.1tv.ru/owa/win/ort5_static.static?p_page_id=428&p_show_id=439 (accessed 10 May 2006).
Oleinikova, I. (2007) 'Etnicheskie "chuzhie" v sovetskom kinematografe', in E. Iarskaia-Smirnova, P. Romanov, V. Krutkina (eds) *Vizual'naia Antropologiia: novye vzgl'iady na sotsial'nuiu real'nost'*, Saratov: 239–60.
Robertson, R. (1995) 'Glocalization: Time-Space and Homogeneity-Heterogeneity', in M. Featherstone, S. Lash and R. Robertson (eds). *Global Modernities*, Sage: 25–45.
Robinson, J.P. (1972) 'Television's impact on everyday life: Some cross-national evidence', in E.A. Rubinstein, G.A. Comstock, and J.P. Murray (eds) *Television and social behaviour*, Vol. 4, *Television in day-to-day life: Patterns of use*, Washington, DC: Government Printed office: 410–31.
Romanov, P. (2002) 'Po-bratski: muzhestvennost' v post-sovetskom kino', in S. Oushakin (ed.) *O muzhe(N)stvennosti*, Moskva, NLO, 609–29.
Rotkirch, A. and Temkina, A. (2002) 'Sovetskie gendernye kontrakty i ikh transformatsiia v sovremennoi Rossii', *Sotsiologicheskie issledovaniia*, 11: 4–15.
Searle, J.P. (1996) *The Construction of Social Reality*, London: Penguin.
Sparks, C. (2007) 'Reality TV: the Big Brother phenomenon', *International Socialism*, v. 114. Online. Available www.isj.org.uk/index.php4?id=314&issue=114 (accessed 10 November 2009).
Ulybina, E. (2004) 'Sub"ekt v prostranstve zhenskogo romana', in E. Saiko (ed.) *Prostranstva zhizni sub"ekta: edinstvo i mnogomernost' sub"ektoobrazuiushchei social'noi evoliuucii*, Moskva: Nauka, 538–55.
Ushakin, S. (2000) 'The quantity of style: imaginary consumption in the post-Soviet Russia', *Theory, Culture and Society* 17(5): 97–120.
Ushakin, S. (2002) 'Vidimost' muzhestvennosti', in S. Ushakin (ed.) *O muzhe(N)stvennosti*, Moskva, NLO: 479–503.
Usmanova, A. (2001) 'Gendernaia problematika v paradigme kul'turnykh issledovanii', in *Vvedenie v gendernye issledovaniia*, I, St. Petersburg: Aleteia.
Vepreva, I. and Kupina, N. (2008) 'Dostoinaia zhizn': izmenenie semantiki i formirovanie novoi identichnosti', in M. Litovskaia, A. Rozenholm, I. Savkina, E. Trubina (eds.) *Obraz dostoinoi zhizni v sovremennykh rossiiskikh SMI*, Ekaterinburg, Izdatel'stvo Ekaterinburgskogo universiteta: 35–45.
Volkov, V. (2005) 'Ot vymysla k real'nosti: "Brat-2" i "Bumer"', in *Neprikosnovennyi zapas*, 1(39).
Wierzbicka, A. (1996) *Iazyk. Kul'tura. Poznanie*. Moskva.
Zadorin, I., Burova, I. and S'utkina, A. (1999) 'SMI i massovoe politicheskoe soznanie: vzaimovliianie i vzaimozavisimost'. Online. Available www.library.cjes.ru/online/?a=con&b_id=207&c_id=1570 (accessed 20 June 2009).
Zillmann, D. and Vorderer, P. (eds) (2000) *Media Entertainment: the psychology of its appeal*, Mahwah, NJ: Lawrence Erlbaum Associates.
Zdravomyslova, E. and Temkina, A. (2002) 'Krizis maskulinnosti v pozdnesovetskom diskurse', in S. Oushakine (ed.) *O muzhe(N)stvennosti*, Moskva: NLO.

10 Russian glamour and its representations in post-Soviet mass media

Maria Litovskaia and Olga Shaburova

Introduction

On 17 January 2008, Russians for the first time selected the word and the anti-word of the year. Over 3,000 participants in an email poll by *Dar Slova* (*The Gift of Words*) made a list of the 50 most used words in 2007. The judges included specialists from the Centre for Russian Language Development under the auspices of the Association of Russian Language and Literature Teachers – novelists, poets, linguists, literary critics, ethnographers and philosophers. From the words nominated, these judges were to choose the one most characteristic of 2007. As a result of voting, the word 'glamour', which relatively recently appeared in the Russian language, won a landslide victory (35 points)[1].

The history of a new word entering a language and receiving definite meanings is at the same time the history of categorisation, i.e. the discovery and adoption of certain phenomena. How did the word 'glamour' appear in Russian speech and consciousness? What are its meanings and connotations? This is the first group of problems that inevitably arise when we encounter this phenomenon. The obvious answer is that this word was introduced to Russian society by the mass media. In the post-Soviet period, however, mass media bombarded consumers with hundreds of new words and expressions. What is 'glamour' considered to be in post-Soviet Russia? This is the second group of related questions, inevitably leading to a third. No less obvious is the fact that everything consumed is produced by somebody. What sort of activity do the producers of 'glamour' represent? What do 'glamour-producers' think of this activity? And what do 'glamour-consumers' think? How is 'glamour' supported and by whom? Can one consider the phenomena underlying this term to be a part of social and state cultural policy, embraced by the term 'ideology'?

Glamour: The history of this word in Russia

The word 'glamour' and its derivatives literally pervaded Russian speech. 'We need no glamour interviews!', angrily exclaims a TV news correspondent at the Moscow Fair of Millionaires. Every now and then the heroine of the popular TV series *My Fair Nanny* makes the comment 'What glamour – you'll go mad!'

('*Glamurnen'ko-ochumet'!*'). 'My muse is glamourous enough!', declares Daria Dontsova, the author of long-running detective novels, on the morning TV talk-show. The Glamourous Riffraff – this is the sobriquet of a 'resident' of a comic TV show *Comedy Club*. Jokes like 'Capitalism in Russia means high oil prices plus glamorisation of the country'[2] are widespread. But only ten years ago, very few people in Russia knew this word, which was used mainly in the fashion industry (marked by the luxurious style of Hollywood's Golden Age) and also as a professional expression in photojournalism, applied to the photograph of a model, where defects in appearance had been touched up using computer technologies (Pchelkina 2006).

The word 'glamour' belongs to the new lexical resources that have become current in Russian since the middle of the 1990s. Like many other post-Soviet loanwords, it came from English and at first was taken as a mere borrowing, marked by the use of Roman letters or placed in inverted commas (e.g. Heelless shoes are inappropriate in Hollywood 'glamour' style). The word itself had a neutral connotation (pretentious luxury in costume) and, when used for addressing the general public, it needed a special explanation like, the word 'glamour' means 'charm'.

Since the early 2000s, the word 'glamour' began to appear in its Cyrillic variant[3]. After that the word's frequency of use snowballed[4]. The word came into vogue and, as happened with many things in vogue, it spread in a number of successive waves. The non-evaluative definition of a certain stylistic trend in the fashion industry and media technologies was transferred to art: 'Glamour' – this is the word suited to characterise the pictures by Nikas Safronov. Gradually the word 'glamour' became widespread with a new meaning: 'The way of life of the rich, reflecting the consumer psychology of the post-industrial society and being popularized by glossies and trade books' (Vepreva and Kupina 2006: 104). For example, 'What is Oksana Robskii writing about? Glamour is her main topic'.

Little by little this word put down roots in the Russian language, creating a word-formative cluster: the adjective *glamurnyi* (glamorous) became frequent with many collocations including magazine, commentator, lifestyle, project, photograph, costume, evening-party, venture, etc.; adverbs *glamurno* and *po-glamurnomu* (glamorously); participles *priglamurennyi, oglamurennyi* (glamorised); word forms with attitudinal diminutive suffix '-en'k-' – *glamurnen'ko, glamurnen'kii* (little bit glamorous), etc. Linguists noted the emerging contradictions in the meaning of this word. Fashion magazines link the word 'glamour' to romantic charm, elegance and refinement, whereas in living speech 'glamour' is associated with a tinsel show covering a void; now this word is set in one sense-group with 'affected' and 'ostentatious' (Vepreva and Kupina 2006: 105). It is no mere chance that one synonym for 'glamour' is 'false gold'(*samovarnoe zoloto*); e.g. 'Foxtrot tunes, bossa nova and other "champagne splashes" sometimes carry a suggestion of false gold'.

In present-day mass media, the word 'glamour' has actually lost its neutral meaning. Usually it characterises phenomena with a contextually apparent, though at first glance concealed, negative connotation: 'A notebook may be decorated even with diamonds: if you want glamour – fork over tens of thousands euro'. More often still, things are reckoned as 'glamorous' with an obviously ironic characteristic. Here are a number of typical headlines: 'With Glamour through Life'; 'All Power – to Glamour'; 'Our Answer to Glamour'[5]; 'To Live and Die in Glamour' and 'Please Make It Glamourous for Me'. The same word is played up in poetic parodies, e.g. 'I love the glamour of your plans' (instead of 'I love the great bulk of your plans' by V. Maiakovskii) and 'On the high banks of glamour' (instead of 'On the high banks of the Amur' by B. Laskin). One can see growing incidences of the pejorative view of glamour: 'We want to make a magazine about real life, not the usual glamour'. This tendency is confirmed by the appearance of such words as *glamour'e*[6] (anti-glamour, hyper-glamour). Thus the word 'glamour' in Russian means at the same time: (1) showy luxurious style; (2) the lifestyle of rich media personalities; (3) media technology aimed at 'glossy foibles'; and (4) ostentatious magnificence and a show of prosperity. All of this leads to semantic fuzziness regarding the meaning of the word and creates prerequisites for its ever-growing use.

Glamour: Tendencies for the use of this word in modern Russian mass media

Let us consider, by looking at a number of characteristic examples, how the term 'glamour' functions in the Russian mass media. The first example concerns the popular culinary show *Cooking at Home*, shown for several years on Russian TV with the well-known film director Andron Mikhalkov-Konchalovskii as producer and his wife, actress Juliia Vysotskaia, as presenter. The shooting takes place in the kitchen of their country house, where before the eyes of TV viewers, Juliia cooks three new meals each time. The recipes are then published in popular TV guides all over the country; Vysotskaia has also published a number of recipe books. But, not infrequently, viewers and readers complain of her 'glamorous and unrealistic dishes', which are supposedly impossible to cook in ordinary Russian conditions[7].

Where does such irritation originate? Other culinary shows do not provoke such anger, though their meals are often much more expensive and difficult to make. The presenter has free-and-easy manners; her kitchen looks quite ordinary. She runs about, chats, licks her fingers, i.e. behaves like a simple housewife. Moreover, she continually advances the idea of a healthy life. She makes low-calorie meals, advocates ecologically pure products, comes out against junk food, etc. But the viewers know that she is from a large well-to-do family, which for decades has been spotlighted by the mass media. Such families, in the public's opinion, are notorious for living a glamorous life, i.e. luxurious, not accessible to ordinary people.

This opinion has been formed due to the peculiarity of the representation of wealth in a 'society in transition'. Whereas in Soviet society a rich man could be portrayed only in caricature, the post-Soviet world had to look for some practical experience to get people accustomed to the rich living next door. Thus, new methods, including visual ones, had to be found when speaking about wealth. Initially, the Russian mass media just imitated the methods of Western glossies and tabloids by depicting the luxurious lives of 'stars'. As a result, consumers associated wealth with paraded luxury; the absence of this luxury was interpreted as a kind of 'insincerity' and 'dishonesty', qualities that bring down the popularity of a media personality. Apparently, in order to smooth over this impression, Vysotskaia recently gave a series of interviews from which it becomes clear that she lives in a large mansion, her daughter goes to the most prestigious school, all members of her family have French citizenship, they spend their summers in Italy. etc. These interviews were accompanied by a series of obviously re-touched glamorous photos.

Wealth is inseparable from glamour; 'a clandestine millionaire'[8] is suspicious, so he cannot be a public figure – such is the opinion of the vast consumer audience.

The second example comes from *Psychologies* – a magazine oriented towards well-educated and well-to-do readers – were one can find the review of a new disc by rock-singer and songwriter Zemfira, immensely popular in Russia. The critic reproaches her as follows: 'The finished lyrics and heartfelt images in this case have been mainly sacrificed to the half-glamorous wordplay ('Take your Chanel, we're going home')[9]. Today, this woman of fashion, well-groomed and affectionately treated by the classes and masses, is far different from the sharp and impetuous singer Zemfira, who quite recently was ready to put up a fight at the concert against over officious security guards. Her new album *Thanks* shows respect for glamour and gloss. Will we see again that talented and aggressive girl, for whom love and music have been everything?' (Pevchev 2007: 62). This text obviously contrasts glamour with genuine talent. But if you glance through the same magazine, you see that glamour as a lifestyle – what Zemfira is criticised for – is in fact an integral part of *Psychologies*' publishing policy. Judging by its both overt and covert recommendations, the audience of this periodical consists of the people who enjoy all the niceties the present-day Russian consumer market can offer.

On the surface there is an evident contradiction: why does this magazine, inclined to glamour, object to this popular singer embracing glamour? At the same time, it is evident that, while rejecting the glamour aesthetics that level real art and bring it from the sphere of 'high art' down to mass culture[10], the critic here acknowledges that glamour is a marketable commodity and therefore its presence is justified in a money-making periodical. A consumer needs glamour, hence the journalists' personal dislike of glamour should not impede their professional attitude towards this phenomenon as a certain technique, effectively attracting the readers' attention – such is the line of modern glossy magazines.

The third example is Gennadii Iuzefavichius, the travel-writer and author of a glossy magazine, who is, according to some TV guides, 'the real creator of Russian glamour'. He exclaims in the show *The School for Scandal* when describing Myanmar: 'There are clouds under my feet – and no glamour at all!'. The women writers Dunia Smirnova and Tat'iana Tolstaia, presenting this show, nod their approval: 'It's very good, when something is without glamour'. Ksenia Sobchak, a TV presenter and fashion icon, confirms: 'The glamour in my life is just for the press. Actually, I live an ordinary life, do a lot of work, rejoice and worry, only I have more money [than many others do]'. Such statements are often made by people manufacturing glamorous products and propagating glamorous standards of living.

The Russian social lions, including those mentioned by the mass media as glamour icons, avoid defining themselves as glamorous persons. This fact can be explained both in superficially pragmatic and in more profound ways. The former is caused by the perception of glamour as a sign of *mauvais ton*, connected with the new Russians of the 1990s and their essentially anecdotal attributes like a 600-model Mercedes or black BMW, red jacket, a finger-thick golden chain around the neck, a huge country house in neo-Gothic or Soviet palace-of-culture styles, etc. There is a strong desire to dissociate oneself from this caricature using all kinds of the renunciation signs. (Mukhametshina and Chernenko 2007).

Aside from this, in accordance with traditional Russian views, the most important thing about a person is spirituality, i.e. something inward, something not for show. On the contrary, glamour aesthetics are based on demonstration. Everything devoid of spirit – *DUKH-less*[11] – according to the national outlook on life, is rejected as evidently defective. Therefore, the original English meaning 'charm' has not been realised in the Russian notion of glamour: it is just showy but does not touch the soul, does not really charm. The resistance to glamour may be also connected with the tradition of Russian intellectuals to resist any imposed ideology. Glamour aesthetics being widely popularised by mass media, glamour is perceived as a sort of ideologeme. The introduction of a new ideologeme into the system of traditional values provokes the resistance of those who consider themselves intellectuals, i.e. inwardly independent persons dealing with some spiritual work[12]. Those purporting to be intellectuals, irrespective of their financial standing, oppose the truly spiritual life to glamour as just showing-off.

Outline of the history of Russian glamour

The history of Russian glamour is rather short: it started 15 years ago. The accelerated (though still lagging) development of post-Soviet society causes the periods in the history of glamour to be marked out quite roughly, without distinct chronological boundaries between them. The term 'glamour' was variously assimilated by different social strata and cultural groups with greater or lesser rapidity and various versions of it appeared nearly simultaneously. Here, we outline five locally adopted versions.

In the first version glamour is seen as a kind of fairytale, shaping somebody else's wealthy and fantastically beautiful life. This initial vision of glamour was based on the common Soviet idea of capitalism as a society of commodity abundance. Thus, the glamour aesthetics were formed as a quality of the unreal world inhabited by beautiful and very rich people consuming unobtainable goods. This beautiful picture is taken as a fairytale alternative to the destroyed Soviet world and comfortless post-Soviet reality full of economic and political cataclysms. The message of this version of glamour is the one of a fairytale where *The Rich Cry as Well*[13] (while living in luxury). The models of this version are the Mexican and

Brazilian soap operas about local variants of Cinderella and the American TV series *Santa Barbara*.

In the second version glamour looks like a dream that theoretically could be realised in the post-Soviet world, though it is hardly likely. The newly formed network of Russian glossies describes the life of stars (actors, musicians, supermodels and sportsmen) and shows high fashion in clothes, technology and interior design. This approach ousts the traditional Soviet caricature descriptions of bourgeois life. Society becomes accustomed to seeing wealth as stylish beauty. Various forms of advertising goods develop rapidly. The new social segment appears, connected with the mass culture and represented as glamorous. The message of this version is 'What a life some people live! I wish I could do the same!', Its models can be found in the magazines *Elle*, *Cosmopolitan*, *Vogue* and *Officielle*.

The third version sees glamour as a spectacular luxury[14], which seems to be an attainable standard of living. The idea of Western lifestyle broadens and concretises. The West is seen as an impetus to development and as a provocation. The Western way of life shapes the new standard to be sought after. Glamour becomes the embodiment of the Western (consumerist) life one should study to live. At the same time, glamorous advertising starts to look more feasible and democratic. The glamorous realities are transferred to Russian soil, showing examples of unreal beauty adapted to the life of well-to-do post-Soviet people. New living standards and new life organisation are being practiced. Numerous publications for self-help appear, oriented towards more or less wealthy people. The message that is employed here is 'You deserve it!'. The models can be found in the magazines *Good Housekeeping*, *Your Garden*, *Gastronom*, *Somelier*, *How*, *Men's Health*, etc.

In the fourth, glamour is regarded as a media technique. Glamour is deconstructed and unmasked. The explanations of how media–glamour is made coincide with the examination and desymbolisation of the language of glamour mass media. Society divides into those capable of glamour deconstruction and those still charmed by glamour. 'Gurus' appear in the sphere of glamour production and representation. The message of this version is 'Glamourising means stupefying'. The models can be found in the magazines *Ogonek*, *Russian Newsweek*, *Esquire*, *Vse Iasno*, *Gala*, etc.

And, finally, in the fifth version glamour becomes an instrument of the new state ideology formation. The New Positive Idea is realised in the creation of Russia's image as a country with a beauty of its own – just as good as the Western one. Glamorisation embraces the official life (the manner of portraying statesmen, making a show of election campaigns, etc.) as well as Russian and, in particular, Soviet history. Consumers are presented with the latent low-key harmony of the recent past with its particular stylistics, so the promo make-up of the bygone Soviet epoch ousts (substitutes) memory, actualising positive elements of predictability, of keeping the directives received in the process of socialisation. For young consumers, the glamorised Soviet past has an exotic character that enables them to gain some lacking experience and gives the impression of joining in their country's history, of emotional ties between generations. The message is '*Davai,*

Rossiia! Davai-davai // Davai krasivo, davai-davai' (Come on, Russia! Come on Beautifully, come on!). The models can be found in the magazines *The Russian Reporter* (*Russkii Reporter*); TV news programmes (*The First Channel, Russia, Vesti* (*News*), *The Star*, etc.).

Glamour in the Urals: Looking for value models in local glossies

Glamour to date is a comprehensive and multifaceted concept, the basic idea of which can be expressed in the formula 'consumption is success'. The success of certain persons is evaluated on the consumer scale; the social spaces of post-Soviet society are also perceived through consumer semiotics. Consider the expression of these views in one Russian region, Sverdlovsk Oblast', and its centre, Ekaterinburg. The traditional image of this city is rapidly changing: for many decades Ekaterinburg (formerly Sverdlovsk) was known as the centre of an industrial region, a city of plants and factories, whereas today it is often called 'the consumer capital of the whole Ural-Siberian region'[15].

The spending philosophy and the strategy of success through consumption are revealed in the products of the vast Ekaterinburg media market[16]. When analysing this market, one can see that glossies are firmly in the lead, with glamour aesthetics being accumulated mainly in these publications. Here, we may mark out the demonstration of refined examples of consumer luxury, satisfying all modern European requirements and at the same time the examples of cultural mass-consumption with half-criminal overtones[17], corresponding to the vilest of tastes. As a result, the regional periodicals display at least several levels of glamorously shaped values. At one extreme, in a vulgar and inartistic manner, they create showy models of consumption, behaviour and the corresponding interpretation of success typical of the 'wild capitalism' period. Another extreme is marked by attempts to construct and represent another model of success, which can be realised in more civilised practices of consumption. Both positions may be illustrated by two periodicals representing the extremes of wild versus civilised glamorisation of capitalism.

The magazine *Vash dosug* (*Your Leisure*) is a weekly advertiser, which, according to Russian journalistic tradition, should remain neutral. But side by side with the typical appearance of sections such as 'Cinema', 'Theatre' and 'Children', there are sections like 'Saunas' and 'Relax' where sexual services are openly advertised. Initially these advertisements were published in the magazine itself; later they were transferred to its glossy supplement, being sold in sealed but transparent envelopes. At the same time the number of sexual services offered increased, and the symbolic message of this edition became clearly manifested.

In order to analyse the second trend in representations aimed at forming the new image of post-Soviet bourgeoisie, we looked through the magazine *Biznes i Zhizn'* (*Business and Life*). The principal genre of this edition is stories based on the lives of real people – businessmen who live and work in Ekaterinburg. The publishers consider the presentation of the values of the new Russian class (entrepreneurs, top managers, etc.) to be among the primary tasks of this periodical.

The editor Dmitrii Ivanov notes in his column that among the questions reporters address to those interviewed 'the totally prevailing question is 'What for?'... This question is aimed at ascertaining the values, i.e., the genuine things...' (*Biznes i Zhizn'*, February 2007: 2). The magazine's approach to its heroes is not a unified one. The histories of success, told by businessmen with the help of reporters, retain their individuality, and it is up to readers – fellow-townsmen with a clear view of the heroes' competence, influence, etc. – to draw general conclusions.

The choice of value priorities of the heroes in their stories varies depending on their age, personal experience and aims. Analysis of the magazine's materials reveals deep axiological contradictions, which demonstrate the problems of value model formation within the modern Russian administrative and business elite. Following tradition, a set of economic, political and social factors – the priority of private property, self-sufficiency, free self-realisation and the success based on it, and the lifestyle corresponding to a higher income level – allows us to call this model bourgeois or new-bourgeois, taking into account the pre-Soviet history of Russia. But as post-Soviet society still fails to define itself clearly, self-designations of this kind are practically absent in the magazine we analysed. The stories told by successful Ural businessmen reveal the paradox that does not allow them to identify themselves as bourgeois or capitalists. In our opinion, many of them – especially the older and middle-aged generations – personify the axiological concept 'successful capitalists with Soviet values'.

The periodical, raising a problem of values that could have formed the moral basis of businessmen's activities, has an obvious inclination for the analysis of really complex questions, including those connected with understanding the attitude of today's Russians towards wealth and wealthy people. In its stories about successful businessmen, *Biznes i Zhizn'* tries to create a positive image of the modern wealthy man as quite a normal person who has worked hard and ventured and whose financial success forms the basis of his further development as an individual. The images of people of action, shown through their monologues about the real complexities and contradictions of life, seem to be contrary to glamour aesthetics, because the prevalent discourse of glamour is based on the concealment of everything difficult and hard-earned.

The numerous advertisements play an important role in the magazine's context as a whole. On the one hand, the magazine shows active business as a matter of primary importance and views the social and philosophical aspects of the hidden motives of labour activity in the post-Soviet state. In this sense the periodical turns out to be 'a betrayer of glamour'. On the other hand, the editorial staff indiscriminately focuses its attention upon the consequences of labour: the welfare that forms the basis of full-scale consumption. The structure of this periodical is characteristic of itself. The section 'Business' is followed by 'Style-Hobbies', 'Style-Travelling' and 'Style-Private Life'. The workaholic heroes, interpreting the history of their success as first of all the history of business, may describe their working activity, obscure to the reading public, only in a general outline, whereas the results of this success – travels, hobbies, mansions, clothes, etc. – are much more demonstrative. So the readers' attention quite naturally shifts to the descriptions of the unattainable lifestyle of the rich, and the magazine has shown the specific character of this style formation via accounts of concrete people.

Thus, within the same geographical area one can observe the representation of various value models: those that are ready and those still in a stage of formation; the 'wild' and the more civilised ones, determining the life of the elite and of society as a whole. Primitive forms of advertising sexual services blend in with the well-practiced glamour format. The attempt to approach the consumption theme through the presentation of the diverse cultural experiences of mature self-made persons – discussing the philosophy of money and expenditures, the structure of demand, etc. – demonstrates a method new to the regional media market. In a glossy magazine, consequently, such attempts take a glamorous – though this time more advanced – shape. The differences in the priorities of the periodicals *Vash Dosug* and *Biznes i Zhizn'* allow us to describe not only the discrepancy between the existing and the newly acquired values of post-Soviet society, but also the inner discrepancy between the situation of an earnest search for new meanings and its glamorous wrapper foisted onto consumers[18].

Glamour as the reality of post-Soviet everyday life

The forms and practices of today's capitalist consumption in their media representations set behavioural patterns and lifestyles presupposing lustre and limelight as apparent signs of wealth. In the years since the emergence of the glamour industry, Western society has managed to create the cultural anti-glamour industry as well, thus forming the familiar 'glamour reserves' (consumer advertising, yellow press, etc.). As for post-Soviet society, initially it could counter the vigorous advertising of consumption only with the ideology of Soviet intellectuals (vigorously discredited by the same mass media) based on the superiority of spiritual life over the material one, the superiority of the inner world over the outside world.

The expansion of advertising as an unusual form of social visualisation for Soviet people, the proliferation of glossy publications, slick fiction and tinsel cinema together with other powerful social and economic factors – all proved efficient enough to produce rapid changes in the priorities of society: from the demonstration of inner life to its concealment and from the concealing of material well-being to its emphasised demonstration. When the pursuit of material well-being acquired legal forms in Russian society, it was the glamour production technique that exerted the greatest influence upon the unprepared audience due to the appreciable and distinct methods and forms of demonstrative consumption the glamour purveyed.

The bourgeois consumer values appeared more convincing and attractive than, say, the values of Western democracy or the incentives to comprehend money-related problems, social responsibility, civil society, etc. Besides, the adoption of previously unknown forms of consumption was a much more simple process. The initial surprise after the discovery of new consumer opportunities was replaced with a desire to seize these opportunities – whether it was learning by heart the names of haute couture firms, reading recipes for cooking lobster, or writing an article on country house renovation in the European style.

The problem was simplified by the fact that ostentatious luxury in its Russian variant does not require real financial prosperity. Even people on a low-income not only admire glamorous heroes, but actively try to imitate their lifestyle. When glossy magazines for the rich set the fashion, corresponding publications for the poor advise their readers on how to achieve similar results comparatively cheaply, creating illusions by imperceptibly substituting the visual image and at the same time teaching the readers some practices previously unknown to them – cooking gazpacho soup, practicing feng shui or just taking their children to a skating-rink in the shopping mall. The strategy of luxury simulation, brought forward by the mass media, proved to be optimal for the general public, anxious to join in prestigious consumption.

The techniques and strategies of glamour production came in handy when the formation of a new policy for developing the image of the country and state started (Zvereva 2008). The display of luxury and joyous prosperity embraced practically all social classes and domains in today's Russia, from semi-official circles through the high life and star-making industry down to the 'submerged tenth' (Penskaia 2006). Many periodicals – even business publications – develop in their contents not the theme 'how we earn' (much less 'how we work'), but the theme 'how we spend'. They tend to show everything – churches, factories, schools, farms, hospitals and hothouses – as beautiful places under the unclouded sky of success[19]. The national papers write about new glamorous military uniforms; the representation of social space objects in Russia is determined according to a glamour hierarchy. Thus, various clubs, restaurants, shopping centres and recreational complexes turn out to be of front-rank importance; the glamour parties are the main newsmakers for non-political and non-economic periodicals.

In post-Soviet society, glamour is produced both for the elite consumers and for the common people. In all cases it simultaneously works as a guide for new forms of consumption, keeps up with the latest fashions and cherishes the illusion of consumption as real happiness. The majority of glamorous images are produced by the mass media with journalists openly writing about how and why they do it, disclosing the technique of glamour and thereby acknowledging their economic and ideological dependence on sales requirements.

By now society has split into two groups: the majority goes on with the adoption of new consumption practices and the demonstration of consumption styles; the minority tries to analyse why glamour happened to be so infectious in post-Soviet Russia.

Glamour as it is interpreted by the post-Soviet media

The promotion of the glamorous lifestyle by the Western mass media (first of all by lifestyle magazines) is well-established and today taken for granted. In Russia, with its culture in transition – and therefore the new term, the phenomenon itself, and the mass media popularising it being yet relatively young – the history of the success of glamour has proven to be very illustrative and now is a point at issue in the Russian media and Internet.

The unfolding discussion of glamour by the intellectuals (*Kriticheskaia Massa* 2004; *Iskusstvo Kino* 2006; *Ogonek* 2008; Vishnevetskaia 2008, etc.) was quick to reveal two main trends in its comprehension, based on the fixation with the immense popularity of this word and the multivalent phenomenon in post-Soviet Russia.

The first trend is based on the severe criticism of glamour as a sign of spiritual degradation, which appears quite natural, given the historical Russian experience of contrapositions rich/poor and profound/superficial. Journalists constantly ridicule glamorous personalities, 'the disabled glamour-consumers' (Radulova 2008). Glamour becomes directly connected with the formulised mass culture exploiting people's dreams.

> This word embodies the apotheosis of 2007, the triumph of mass culture and its values, the ideal of Russian elite. The half-closed eyes, directed somewhere diagonally up, the half-opened mouth, and the clouds of mist and bliss all around. And the undisguised programming not only in advertisements, but also in the news and politic.
>
> (Tul'chinskii 2007)

The social criticism of glamour is based on the exposure of its ability to mask essential social contradictions. The visual discourse of glamour hides away the social history of success just as advertising hides away the social history of things. Jean Baudrillard, when exposing the advertising mechanism, gives a clue as to why glamour excludes any hints of death, illness, suffering and intermittent toil (Baudrillard 1995). When the new images of an individual's subjectivity become apparent only through the infinite demonstration of various consumption forms, the portrayal of a person and society undergoes a reduction leading to a substitution of outlooks. Critics deride glamour as quasi-religion confined to a simple formula. 'Wealth has taken the place of happiness, purchasing has supplanted action; sexual education instead of love, tests instead of self-knowledge, diets instead of wrestling with sin, fitness clubs instead of family, seasonal fashions instead of world view' (Smirnova 2004: 9).

The second trend in the comprehension of this phenomenon – and it is no less natural, given the historical experience of Russian populism – is based on the projection of glamour as a form of relaxation and escapism essential for people. Just like other popular phenomena, glamour is being justified because it deals with half-realised desires, including those engendered by Soviet consumer practices. Some glamour analysts in Russia explain its popularity as hyper-compensation for a deprived Soviet childhood. The Soviet society of deficiency, redistributive ethics, and corresponding values urged many Russians to link well-being directly with material sufficiency when 'one has everything he needs' (Gubin 2008; Ivanov 2008).

In addition, when following glamour images, people satisfy their need for play-acting, as these images are so distant from their real lives that they look like a sort of carnival. As the term 'glamour' includes the meaning 'tinsel show', the one who 'gets glamorised' ought to pose one's face in a peculiar manner, strike an attitude and display a contented look, i.e. for a moment live another, seemingly more successful, life. All this affords the satisfaction of a basic want: to feel like a person of importance (Chastitsyna 2006).

Populists are backed by glamour producers who note that glamour is historically based on a person's need to admire some models distant from his everyday life and associated in his society with notions of stylishness and elegance. A person needs to sweeten one's life, especially in modern society where aesthetics forms an important part of the capitalist economy. Thus, the star-producing industry in any sphere presupposes the creation of its glamorous images by the mass media (Iliin 2008).

It is assumed that, having a clue to the explanation of glamour technique[20], any consumer will be able to guess the meaning of the glamour message by oneself (Gurova 2009). Thus, it is pointless to feel sorry for those consumers who implicitly believe in glamour images; in due time they will grow wiser and understand everything themselves. It is also useless to condemn glamour-producers who just fill a kind of social order, calling up golden dreams and creating means of smoothing over contradictions, which is important, especially in a period of change.

Conclusion

The word 'glamour' has come into active usage among post-Soviet people, thereby symbolically legitimising the existence of the phenomena it designates in Russian society. Since it entered the Russian linguistic consciousness, 'glamour' has ceased to be just a superficial designation of some style and turned into a concept expressing a certain system of values. Glamour as a lifestyle, a technique and an orientation towards a show of prosperity is propagated both from below (by glossy periodicals seeking the optimisation and increase of sales) and from above (by the State structures, interested in coping with, or at least smoothing over social contradictions).

The totality of glamour and the concentration of the axiological quest in this concept (i.e. attempts to determine the structure and content of new values in today's Russian society) allows one to raise the problem of glamour as an ideology existing in post-Soviet society[21]. Ideology is first of all 'the system of convictions; it fuses together ideas and emotions, trying to turn them into social levers and transforming both ideas and people' (Bell 2002: 13). Ideology exercises the function of converting ideas into social actions. Among the aims of glamour messages are the changing of the value system, the transformation of *Homo Soveticus* (who has been brought up with the idea of the State caring about one's consumption and has been living in a situation of chronic consumer goods shortages) into a person whose main values are personal success and comfort, the latter being in turn ensured by high-status consumption.

The basis of the glamour-connected axiological system is the rigid model of success as consumption, the mobilising and omnipotent potential of money, and a hedonistic philosophy in the form of a consumer society under construction. In the glamour discourse, labour and production cease to exist, whereas the visual embodiment of an individual's success, expressed in a certain type and level of consumption, is put at the forefront. The idea of success and money is emotionally charged, and this emotional sublimation is steadily supported by the illustration of the glamorous lifestyle in advertising and in mass culture. Glamour proves to be to the benefit of state authorities, as it permits them to smooth over social contradictions through the hedonism of consumption. In the case of an economically polarised post-Soviet society, this is an urgent problem. Here, it makes little difference what in particular is being consumed: let it be just beautiful pictures of a comfortable life.

The basic consumer strategies of modern post-Soviet society determine the task of the application of glamour in actual practice: to reduce citizens to consumers, to conceal real social problems and contradictions, and to erode social (above all protesting) activity by means of consumption popularisation. The glamorous presentation of pre-Soviet and Soviet history turns this depiction into a marketable product, allowing the evasion of keen discussions of links between the past and the present, the problems of Russian history, etc. Here, glamorisation appears as the strategy of simulations and substitutions, creating a certain set of practices, slogans and symbols, which may act (and be interpreted) as disciplining, as therapeutic or as schooling people in the new rules of life.

Glamour as a sort of wrapper, in which one can pack anything at all, has become a habitual element of post-Soviet life. The mass media, being linked to the global streams of capitalism and using already proven techniques, actively creates a new consumer. By implementing glamour techniques, the new state order for creating a positive image of Russia can be achieved with professionalism and beauty. Understanding the possibilities of glamour ensures effective action. Understanding the limited nature of glamour allows its creators to distance themselves from non-responsive consumers and to feel that they are the new value-forming elite.

But the economic stratification and the traditionally low comfort level in Russia result in the fact that consumers' ideals set by glamour become unattainable for most people. On the one hand, it tempts consumers by its potential attainability; on the other hand, it raises suspicion of the absolute impossibility of attaining it. This internal contradiction has increased with glamour technique being used not only in advertising or portraying wealthy men's lifestyles, but also in describing Soviet and post-Soviet everyday life. The total simulation leads to supplementation of the glamour concept by a new semantic field with meanings false, and ostentatiously showy. The forms of glamorisation that are perceived as quite acceptable when depicting the fairytale life of the rich begin in the case of the post-Soviet image of life, to correlate with typical glossing over the truth, as it was called in Soviet times[22].

Today's Russian society, with its severe economic stratification and total non-concurrence of symbolic and economic statuses of different social groups, is saturated with various glamour messages. The glamorisation in the media sphere equalises different groups of consumers, offering them the same examples of unreal beauty. Glamour has become customary in advertising and is perceived as a requisite of a genre, though it is often ironically commented on. At the same time, glamour techniques used in depicting everyday life actualise the deconstruction mechanisms of the 1980s–90s: the denunciation of various ideological directives and the glossing connected with them.

Some people in Russian society accept glamour messages and more or less obediently become comfort-loving consumers. Others reject these messages based on revealing practices offered by Soviet and post-Soviet mass media, and their own experience when comparing glamorous pictures with reality. As a result, on the one hand, the task of a Soviet person's re-education by the use of glamour is being successfully carried out. The idealised examples of life and history are being more or less effectively foisted onto consumers. On the other hand, the attempts of State authorities to colour the truth meet with irritated rejection as one more State-sponsored fraud. In today's Russia this rejection remains the main form of popular discontent.

Notes

1 Second place was taken by the word 'nanotechnologies' (23 points) owing to the active mass media's promotion of state programmes for the country's technological progress; third place (15 points) was divided between the words 'blog' and 'blogger', which is connected with the popularity of the electronic Live Journal in Russia. Next came *raskrutka* (promotion) (11 points), *vybory* (election) (9) and 'gender', 'PR' and 'IMHO' (7 each). See Epstein 2008.

2 An allusion to the well-known utterance by V. I. Lenin: 'Communism means Soviet power plus the electrification of the country' (1920).

3 Today this word is written with Roman letters only in the names of magazines, 'Glamour' cigarettes, and on the facades of second-class beauty shops or boutiques. It is interesting to note that not the English but the French pronunciation of this word became established, which may be explained by the public's traditional association of the French with stylishness.

4 According to INTEGRUM data, during the year 2000 the national mass media used this word 300 times and in 2005 more than 8,000 times.

5 In these cases the well-known Soviet slogans are paraphrased: *With Song Through Life*; *All Power – to the Soviets*; *Our Answer to Kerzon*.

6 The use of the suffix and ending *-'e* forms a word with the meaning of abstract generalisation and hidden negative assessment.

7 In the Russian Internet there are a number of culinary sites created to challenge Vysotskaia, including the so called Anti-glamurnaia assotsiatsiia lyubitelei prostoi edy (*The Anti-Glamour Association of Simple Cuisine Lovers*) as well as *prosto_i_vkusno* (simple and tasty), *kitchen_nah*, etc.

8 The nickname of Aleksander Koreiko, a character in the novel *The Golden Calf* by I. Il'f and E. Petrov, who owned millions but lived the life of an ordinary clerk.

9 The word 'Chanel', here meaning a Chanel handbag, is consonant with the Russian *shinel'* – a soldier's greatcoat, which was originally mentioned in this line by B. Okudzhava in a Soviet-period song about the last day of the Second World War.

10 On the juxtaposing of high art and mass culture in the Russian critical tradition, see Dubin 2003; Kostina 2004.

11 The name of a book by Sergei Minaev, which has become a bestseller among young office workers, who are considered to be the main consumers of glamour.

12 Therefore, in Russian Internet comments on favourite periodicals, panic discussions arise from time to time on the problem of these publications 'getting glamorous'. See, for example, the discussion '*Esquire* smells of glamour!' at www.esquire-russia.ru/viewforum.php

13 The name of a popular Mexican series, shown on Russian TV in the first half of the 1990s.
14 The character of post-Soviet views on luxury deserves special study.
15 The municipal authorities, when speaking about their successes, designate the trends of city development not by the growth of housing but by the opening of new shopping and recreation centres. According to the article *The Centre of Consumer Attraction* in the pilot issue of magazine *Russkii Reporter*, 'Ekaterinburg is developing in the best traditions of a modern Western city, connecting the European part of Russia with its oil-producing Asian regions' (*Russkii Reporter* 2007, 1: 24). The city attracts capital from the whole of Siberia as it has many shopping malls and boutiques, the only Emporio Armani Cafe in Eastern Europe, the only Givenchy boutique in Russia, the largest Russian indoor water park, etc.
16 According to Kolesov (2006), there were 16 TV channels and about 300 local periodicals in Ekaterinburg in 2007. The most popular magazine in this city, according to TNS Gallup Media data, is the monthly *Cosmopolitan*, followed by *Glamour*, and *Karavan Istorii* (*The Caravan of Stories*). The leader among numerous radio stations was *Chanson* (being only the fifth in the national scale) and among TV channels was *TNT*. The top-selling local periodicals are the glossies Ia *pokupaiu* (*I Buy*), Stol'nik (*A Hundred*), *Vkus* (*The Taste*), *Banzai, Happy!*, *Le Somelie* and *Tatlin*. The editorial policy of all these publications includes an orientation towards advertising discourse, i.e. towards initial glamorisation of all realities that supply material for publication. It is only natural that these magazines are actively sponsored by advertisers, whereas the so-called independent publications, without regular grant aid from Western funds, survive for two years at best. These publications consistently pursue a policy of independence, in the 1990s from the imposed political stereotypes, in the 2000s from stereotypes of mass culture, the fashion industry and the consumer way of life. Publications of the third type stay afloat on state institution subsidies and moderate advertising support.
17 This is a backlash of the image of Ekaterinburg as the 'criminal capital' of Russia in the 1990s.
18 Vera Zvereva came to a similar conclusion when analysing post-Soviet TV of the 2000s (Zvereva 2006).
19 For example, the factory newspaper *Ural'skii Trubnik* (The Ural Pipe-Producer) has published the following paragraph about its new variant of symbolic stimulation for workers: 'The *New Style Leaders* photo gallery is the modern version of the traditional Board of Honor. But now the photos show not the typical workers in safety helmets and overalls, but elegantly dressed employees looking more like movie stars than like metallurgists. It's hard to recognize local workers in the glamorous jazzmen who seem to have been taken from the cover pictures of magazines"'(*Uralskii Trubnik*, April 4, 2008: 2).
20 Such clues are offered by the media as well, though not by popular glossy magazines but by those conducting sociological analysis; therefore not so many readers have an opportunity to get the key to the analysis of glamour.
21 The idea of a close connection between language and ideology has become commonplace in modern studies. 'The conditions for the production of ideology are the conditions for the production of language and can only be understood by reference to the structure of forms and social practices which systematically enter into the production of particular concepts and propositions in that language... we are not aware of these systematically generative interconnections because our awareness is organized through them' (Mepham 1972: 17). In the case of the word 'glamour' spreading through the Russian linguistic consciousness, the analyser has the unique opportunity to see with one's own eyes the process of these interconnections forming when the borrowed media-term determines the social practices, while the social practices, in turn, change the quality of a word.
22 The adoption of glamour technique and ideas in post-Soviet Russia was accompanied by the repeating public self-revelations of glamour-producers who at the same time explained that today's Russian society really needs glamour. Such a disorienting tactic cannot but cause feelings of defencelessness in the face of an all-powerful State and mass media toeing its line.

References

Baudrillard J. (1995) *Sistema veshei*, trans. by S. Zenkin. Moscow: Rudomino.

Bell, D. (2002) 'Vozobnovlenie istorii v novom stoletii. Predislovie k novomu izdaniiu knigi "Konets ideologii"', *Voprosy filosofii* 5: 13–25.

Chastitsina, A (2006) 'Diskurs glamura', *Bol'shoi gorod* 22(171): 2–5.

Dubin, B. (2003) 'Massovaia slovesnost', natsional'naia kul'tura i formirovanie literatury kak sotsial'nogo instituta', in T. Venediktova (ed.) *Popul'iarnaia literatura: Opyt kul'turnogo mifotvorchestva v Amerike i Rossii*, Moscow: Izdatel'stvo Moskovskogo universiteta: 9–17.

Epstein, M. (2008) 'Glamurnyi god pod znamenem politkorrektnosti. Vpervye v Rossii vybrany Slovo i Antislovo goda', *Nezavisimaia gazeta*, January 17:5.

Gurova, O. (2009) '"Gl'ianets": ideologiia mody v sovremennoi rossiiskoi kul'ture', in P. Romanov, E. Iarskaia-Smirnova (eds) *Visual'naia antropologiia: nastroika optiki*, Moscow: OOO 'Variant", CSGPS: 246–56.

Gubin, D. (2008) 'Kak moda stala ideologiei', *Ogonek* 12: 18–20.

Iliin, V. (2008) *Potreblenie kak diskurs*. SPb: Intersocis.

Ivanov, D. (2008) *Glam-kapitalizm. Obshaia teoriia glamura*. Sankt-Petersburg: Peterburgskoe vostokovedenie.

Iskusstvo kino (2006) Daniil Dondurei – Alena Doletskaia – Tat'iana Makkina, Krasota – eto strashanaia sila, *Iskusstvo kino*, 11. Available www.kinoart.ru/magazine/11-2006/ (accessed 29 September 2009).

Kolesov, D. (2006) 'Govorit: pokazyvaet', *Expert-Ural*, 36 (253). Available http://www.expert.ru/printissues/ural/2006/36/rynok_smi/ (accessed 15 March 2009).

Kostina, A. (2004) *Massovaia kul'tura kak fenomen postindustrial'nogo obshchestva*. M: URSS.

Kriticheskaia massa (2004) Tema 'Glamur i moda', *Kriticheskaia massa*, 4: 8–30.

Mepham, J. (1972) 'The Theory of Ideology in "Capital"', *Radical Philosophy* 157 (2): 12–19.

Mukhametshina, E. and Chernenko, E. (2007) 'Bogatye tozhe pr'achut', *Ruskii Newsweek* 152 (49): 34–7.

Ogonek (2008) Alkogoliki glamura:tema nomera, *Ogonek* 12: 4–48.

Pchelkina, E. (2006) 'Glamur - novaia ideologiia ili starye rany', Drugaya.ru. Online. Available www.drugaya.ru/content/doc 592 (accessed 24 June 2008).

Penskaia, E (2006) Vso slopaet glamur. *Russian magazine* 9 August.

Pevchev, A. (2007) 'Princessa rock-n-rolla', *Psychologies* 11: 62.

Radulova, N. (2008) 'Invalidy gl'iantsa', *Ogonek* 12. Available www.ogoniok.com/4988/3/ (accessed 24 September 2009).

Smirnova, A. (2004) 'Podsudimyi ne vsegda i ne vezde byl takim gadom…', *Kriticheskaia massa* 4: 9–12.

Tul'chinskii, G. (2007) Dar slova. Available http://elena-chernikova.narod.ru/slovo2007.html (accessed 24 June 2008).

Vepreva, I. and Kupina, N. (2006). 'Glamour', *Russkii iazyk za rubezhom* 4: 104–6.

Vishnevetskaia, J. (2008) 'Formula glamura', *Russkii reporter* 49: 44–7.

Zvereva, V. (2006) 'Poetika glamura', *Iskusstvo kino* 11. Available www.kinoart.ru/magazine/11-2006/now/vera1106 (accessed 24 June 2008).

Zvereva V. (2008) 'Glamur v sovremennoi rossiiskoi kul'ture', *Puti Rossii: Kul'tura, obshchestvo, chelovek*. Moscow: MVSHSEN: 128–38.

11 Between a good home and a good city

The privatisation of residential life in Russian lifestyle journalism

Elena Trubina

Introduction

Two old friends of mine, one the owner of a firm specialising in marketing research and the other a senator's assistant, recently bought a large plot of land in a prestigious lakeshore community. They have a kind of hut there and dream of building a large house on it, but at this time they have neither the money nor the ideas. My friend keeps saying, 'I'll soon have a couple of spare days. Please join me and we'll look through dozens of those magazines, start tearing them up, clipping and marking, and I am sure, once we come up with a nice exciting idea, everything else will follow naturally'. The next stage would be hiring professionals to put those ideas on paper and eventually realise them in brick and mortar.

As a rule, my friends work late, waiting for rush hour to be over before travelling to their new habitat. Traffic jams are such a part of our everyday life that one sees articles in magazines on how to meet interesting people while waiting in a traffic jam. The second, or suburban, home becomes for many people their major financial and emotional investment, but it is not so easy to reach when Moscow is continually on the verge of major infrastructural crises, as are so many other cities. The apartment my friends occupy in the city is in an old Soviet constructivist building. They have spent a great deal of money on endless improvements as their building, like many modernist buildings, has many structural defects. However, they are willing to do this because they simply like it there. Besides the fact that it is Soviet constructivist buildings that this city (Ekaterinburg) is famous for, the location is great – a quiet centre, part of a cluster of buildings that are conveniently secluded from the hustle and bustle of the adjacent main avenue. Both of my friends are involved in politics, but often they perceive the city they live and work in simply as an obstacle to cross on their way to their *dacha* or as something from which to protect themselves in the cosiness of their present and prospective homes.

With this vignette, I want to emphasise three premises on which this chapter is based. First, whenever one relies on lifestyle magazines, one has to take into consideration a complex dialectic of what is inside and what is outside one's house. One's negotiations with oneself and with home renovation experts are never about just a house or an apartment. Not only do home acquisition and renovations express improvements in living standards and increase in ownership, but also they are embedded in the wider network of social relationships and historic and national contexts that come together in the city. On the other hand, these magazines express the privatisation and individualisation of one's relationships with one's city as an inevitable and highly commendable process. Second, the values promoted in lifestyle magazines are the values of the upper urban middle-class, who embrace the cosmopolitan global lifestyle. Third, the lifestyle media's production of these values consists in democratising expert forms of knowledge along with promoting the paid services of experts. This chapter outlines the social and journalistic factors relevant to a recent outburst of lifestyle magazines in Russia, 'all about home' magazines in particular, while also raising questions about normative assumptions in consumption, urban and media studies.

It should be said from the outset that the dilemma of the normative and descriptive dimensions of an analysis of the present globalised reality has particular significance for post-socialist intellectuals like myself, insofar as the post-socialist studies following the 1990s radical changes continue to do a better job of providing thick descriptions of ongoing social changes than of positively re-imagining our (now increasingly common) reality. In fact, it is exactly because this reality has become globalised (as have ideas), it is getting more and more difficult to come up with positive imaginings. If all the great ideologies of the twentieth century (including socialism) possessed this inspirational power, globalism strikingly lacks it. As Ulrich Beck puts it:

> The new neo-liberal crusaders preach: 'You must become streamlined, downsize, flexibilize and get on Internet.' But that precisely does not produce a new feeling of belonging, solidarity, or identity. The opposite is true: the free market ideology undermines democratic politics and democratic identities.
>
> (Beck 2002: 40)

At the same time, although the universalistic ideas of the good life continue, in principle, to enrich human imagination, researchers need to pay more careful attention to the transformations that the normative notions themselves are currently undergoing. It is too often that, within the broad social discourse, 'normative' figures not as ideas one should pursue but as things and experiences one should have and 'ideal' refers to a home or a car. However, although a great deal of popular culture, including the lifestyle industry, rotates around the issues of good and bad, intellectuals, who are in principle capable of having an impact on people's normative ideas, seem to have withdrawn from promoting them . Put simply, it is the frames of reference and practical purposes of the 'new cultural entrepreneurs' (including those who are busy aesthetising current and especially past governmental policies in Russia) that are at work in many strata of society when it comes to matters of human worth and cultural taste.

This prompts us to take a reflective look at the key concerns of academic media research in general. What I have in mind is that just like most disciplines and the interdisciplinary fields of the human and social sciences, the study of mass media is marked by disagreements about concepts and methods, not least because its analysts have different research agendas and thus at times speak totally different languages. I mean not only the disagreements regarding the scale and validity of media analysis, although part of an ongoing discussion deals with exactly this issue:

> Cultural studies of media may also include inquiries into the consumption and uses of media. Because inquiry in these areas can appear deceptively straightforward until you try to do it properly, work in cultural studies of media can vary enormously in quality[...], research design can be complicated and the conduct of a good-quality investigation expensive and time consuming, often yielding disappointingly superficial findings.
>
> (Kuhn 2004: 1229)

I also mean that a significant part of media research is now paid for with private funds and has commercial purposes. The struggle to capture the viewers' or readers' attention leads many in the industry to follow an 'anything goes' strategy, from producing disgusting reality shows to investing in studies on how to keep the viewers' attention during multiple commercial breaks (Webster and Phalen 1997). Consequently, commercial audience studies aim at working out successful marketing strategies. However useful these might be as such, they leave unanswered many questions we should keep in mind as critically minded researchers. In other words, however efficiently the descriptions made within the framework of commercial research might serve the purposes of promoting the products of the research's sponsors, as a rule, the spectators figure in them predominantly as consumers whose preferences can be endlessly modified. 'Official' modes of media and scholarly knowledge thus overlap in their rendering of audiences as prone to absorbing nearly any impulse and reacting in a highly predictable manner. For this reason, we need an alternative 'truth regime', *pace* Foucault. Attention to the meaning-making practices of viewers and readers and to the realities of the media audience is important as an alternative to pragmatically oriented studies.

Unfortunately, when it comes to the normative assessment of the audiences' interests and preferences, there are just a few voices presently that express concern about people becoming increasingly indifferent towards matters of consequence to society as a whole (Dubin 2004). Values by virtue of their being not 'the property of an object or of a subject but, rather, the product of a dynamics of a system' (Smith 1988: 15), are increasingly determined by cultural economics, whereas those traditionally associated with public concern have been pushed to the margins. For instance, the city of Ekaterinburg has been promoted and even praised as a site of creativity (Boiarskaya 2007: 35) and an 'alternative cultural capital' (Zakharov 2004). In other words, it is hyped as a city of sophisticated cultural production and consumption. At the same time, the consumers of lifestyle media (e.g. the magazine *Cosmopolitan*, the TV channel *Domashnii* or cable TV), whether they read *Newsweek* or *Commersant* – judging from their content – have been busy making money and taking care of their private lives to the detriment of those few who are concerned with the public good. The two poles of the huge mass of people called the audiences of Russian media – those struggling to make ends meet and those with more demanding tastes – seem to be equally aloof regarding matters of public life and the public good.

Although many observations lead researchers to conclude that a significant part of contemporary audiences remains passive consumers who prefer high-quality entertainment to complicated political and social information, an 'ethnographic turn' in mass communication and audience research has led to a thorough investigation of the controversial meanings of the term 'audience'. Although the question of audience susceptibility to manipulation remains open, qualitative techniques in the study of audiences prove that it is more productive to concentrate on the meaning-making practices (Hagen and Wasko 2000; Ross and Nightingale 2003). Work of the cultural-studies theorists John Fiske (1987) and Stuart Hall (1980) was especially important in this context. They considered the ways power figures in the derivation of meaning. Fiske's notion of 'semiotic democracy', according to which the power to interpret rests in the hands of the audience, has led cultural theorists to search for traces of 'resistance' in the ways people consume goods and media products in particular. Stuart Hall introduced the concept of 'structured polysemy', according to which a text can possess many possible meanings while still keeping the dominant meanings assigned by its media producers. It allowed for a more critical look at the groups of consumers targeted by corporate powers and the dialectics of production and consumption in media. As the media ethnographer Elizabeth Bird puts it succinctly, 'While the active audience tradition has taught us that we, the audience, have a significant role in creating (the media's) effectivity, we cannot pretend that the power of corporate media producers can somehow be vaporized by the magic wand of audience creativity' (Bird 2003: 168).

I propose in this chapter to examine one important facet of the complex grid of relationships among audiences, new cultural intermediaries, globalisation and neo-liberal ideology, namely, home renovation and the ways it is being represented in the certain magazines. I argue that the real estate boom in globalised Russian cities is largely a neo-liberal phenomenon. Neo-liberalism relies on one of the fundamental achievements of Western civilisation in its highlighting of property and ownership as the foundation of subjective autonomy and certainty. In particular, a single family home or apartment figures as 'the symbolic token of having a stake in the social system' that, to many, 'represents the reaching of maturity and the achievement of success and potency' (Newman 1972: 51). The techniques of neo-liberalism, that is, everyday practices 'through which neoliberal spaces, states and subjects are being constituted in particular ways' (Larner 2003: 511) construct the owner's identity. So it goes without saying that it is for their own good and for that of their families that owners engage in the costly time- and energy-consuming processes of home building or renovation. Self-help schemes and neo-liberal 'responsibilisation' programmes go hand-in-hand. Such is the message of many lifestyle magazines. People are encouraged to shape their places so that they become a part of their living the good life. At the same time, the questions of choosing wallpaper, laminate floors, furniture, or light fixtures are seen as part of a lifestyle/self-expression discourse that draws numerous links between the ways people are engaged in a 'reflexive' self-improvement (Giddens 1991) and undertake informed renovation of their places.

Changing visions of good city

The juxtaposition of a good city and a good home in the title of this chapter aims at considering people's home-related desires and aspirations vis-à-vis normative ideas about the city. Aristotle's idea that a good city is where humans can flourish has been developed in the writing of Henry Lefebvre (about one's 'right to the city') (Lefebvre 1996), and in John Friedman's insistence on the need to materialise essential human rights in the good (accountable and responsive) city government and in the measures it undertakes towards fair housing allocation, health care, and meeting the diverse needs of its inhabitants (Friedman 2002: 110–11). Some researchers, while distancing themselves from the modernist utopian ideas of the 'good city', argue that society should retain its concern for urban justice, which can be amplified 'through practical efforts which might help to empower, materially and otherwise, sections of the urban community working or living in the most precarious of conditions' (Amin and Graham 1997: 423). Other researchers add that 'the political-economic and the discursive-ideological apparatuses that have infused everyday life over the past two decades re-shaped the urbanization process in decidedly new, but often deeply disturbing, directions' (Swyngedouw and Kaika 2003: 9).

However, this 'progressivist' approach to city government finds itself in competition with the increasingly popular neo-liberal assessments of cities and becomes intertwined with studies on urban globalisation. The expansion of the scope of analysis from national to global expresses itself in the change of criteria of evaluation of what comprises a good city. For one, 'the good city' is seen as the global city in which 'global citizenship becomes a genuine possibility' (Kemmis 1995: 147). There is an ongoing discussion about the global system of cities and their competitiveness as one of the main criteria by which they have been judged (Eade 1997; Sassen 2001, 2002; Turner 2000). Some researchers claim that only those cities are sufficiently 'good' that manage to attract enough people working in the 'creative' professions by virtue of developing a vibrant and diverse city life (Florida 2003). However, often cities are drawn as the magnet for investment without sufficiently taking into consideration what raising their level in the global competition costs in human terms. Moreover, 'if the cosmopolitan is to represent a normative vision of the future, the city is to be its empirical realization' (Keith 2005: 22). I argue that as one moves from the abstract concepts of the globalised good city to the more material analyses of it, space for the normative renderings of the ongoing tendencies has to be reserved.

'There are no limits.' One often reads this phrase on the pages of lifestyle magazines. It can be concretised by the billboards that one currently sees in the cities. A construction company advertises a new condominium complex built next to a public park with the slogan, 'Your home and your park'. In my view, this is a typical example of neo-liberal rhetoric. Neo-liberal policies have enabled businesses and governments to segment markets and thereby target high-yield, low-risk customers. In a sense, this exemplifies a broader tendency, namely, that 'while the normative principles of the past decades still possess a performative currency, beneath the surface they seem to have lost their emancipatory meaning or being transformed; in many instances they have become mere legitimating concepts for a new level of capitalist expansion' (Hartman and Honneth 2006: 41).

Aiming 'to extend market discipline, competition and commodification throughout all sectors of society' (Brenner and Teodore 2002: 3), neo-liberalism promotes privatisation as opposed to welfare provision. Privatisation often means the state shaking off once public responsibilities. As I argue elsewhere (Trubina 2006: 181–4), the peculiar uses of the words 'public' and 'private' in many parts of the world (including Soviet and post-Soviet Russia) further complicates matters. To many Russians, the meaning of 'privatisation' is different depending on whether one gained or lost something in the course of market reforms. When it comes to losses, in Russia, privatisation in the last two decades meant the loss of state housing, hospitals and sanatoriums, and public parks. This abandoning by the state of its public responsibilities often left people of modest means with no chance of receiving decent healthcare and other benefits. When it comes to acquisitions, many people were able to privatise their state-allocated apartments (although their quality remained, in many cases, truly questionable). In the 1990s, millions became the owners of the places they lived in by merely signing a few papers.

The popularity of lifestyle magazines among urban dwellers can be seen as part of a larger trend across cities. As the government relinquishes a significant part of its social policy and abandons social housing, city authorities are not able to provide those in need either with housing or with decent repair services or to deal efficiently with a crumbling infrastructure. They are too busy distributing juicy pieces of land among developers and themselves, operating as players on the real estate market. As a result, individual citizens are seen as self-seeking, responsible, economic agents, now expected to conduct their own apartment renovation management through hard work and self-education in order (in some cases) to be able to hire qualified workers and (in some cases) to conduct renovations themselves. Self-education is seen as needed for 'clever', 'informed' consumption that, in its turn, is seen as a realm for the actualisation of capacities for autonomous action. My argument is that the recent prevalence of do-it-yourself (DIY) and the home renovation industry (and of the magazines in which these are popularised) is a sign of neo-liberal times, when issues related to one's habitat are positioned as exclusively individual responsibility (rather than a governmental or social one). Reflecting a shift in the language of mass housing more generally, the lifestyle media tend to focus on the notion of homeowners as, first, responsibly managing their property and, second, possessing the means to engage professional help.

In the 1990s, Russia entered the global circuit of finance, information and image production (McCann 2004). Part of this process was a dramatic rise in the value of private domestic property. All major cities, but especially Moscow, became prime locations for real estate acquisition, conversion, large-scale building projects and related speculative activities. If, speaking about the integration of the real estate industry into global neo-liberal urbanism, Neil Smith cites high real estate prices in Mumbai, the prices in Moscow, St. Petersburg and other major cities in Russia are also a convincing proof of this trend. According to Smith, 'Gentrification as a global urban strategy plays a pivotal role in neoliberal urbanism in two ways. First, it fills the vacuum left by the abandonment of 20 century urban liberal policy. Second, it serves up the central and inner-city real estate markets as burgeoning sectors of productive capital investment' (Smith 2002: 446). This claim is equally true for Russia.

The global trend towards privatisation expresses itself in gated communities (Low 2008; McKenzie 2005), cities for the elite, 'private city' (Warner 1960; Goldberger 1996) and the 'splintering Metropolis' (Graham and Marvin 2001). Along with the gentrified neighbourhoods, new elite complexes, isolated from their surroundings by means of gates and surveillance, appear everywhere. Elite housing, gated communities and upmarket suburban cottage villages comprise a part of what Evan McKenzie defines as a 'global repertoire of modern proprietary developments that represent a new form of territorial organization and mode of governance invented and supported by neoliberal urban policies' (McKenzie 2005). Civic 'boosterism' enhances property values and results in the under-carpet struggle that, in its turn, leads to the construction of more new structures, often secondary in character. After the corporate developers come to this or that neighbourhood in numbers and a marketing campaign starts promoting the neighbourhood as elite or attractive, there follow the interior designers and workers whose services are skilfully advertised in the lifestyle magazines. Simultaneously, there is a corresponding expansion of development, construction, real estate and home re-development companies, not to mention the DIY industry, which in Russia has a long tradition. Previously, mass circulation lifestyle magazines addressed audiences who saw coping with various deficiencies as their main task. Advice that the magazines used to give to home owners usually assumed a so-called second life for things: pieces of old furniture and clothing put to new use. People waited for decades for a chance to move into a state-allocated apartment or, during the late stagnation years, to a co-operative apartment. Again, one's home decoration was a matter of skill, luck (whether or not one had the connections to get decent wallpaper) and resourcefulness. Today, many people spend considerable sums of money each year on repair materials in specialty stores throughout the country.

The rapid changes in the post-Soviet social fabric over the last 20 years have brought with them a new public vocabulary and discourse for understanding and appropriating these developments. The upmarket suburban home and the expensive automobile are the most popular embodiments of consumer-oriented life as a lifestyle option. They exemplify one's status and thus increasingly figure in all kinds of media, including TV commercials. In many of them, ownership is represented as the most telling expression of masculinity. 'A real man is the man with principles; he is the one who has an expensive car and who built his own *dacha*', says a recent beer commercial. As home improvement is surely something that concerns everyone, you see 'these magazines' my friend referred to nearly everywhere, from student dormitories to the local equivalents of Home Depot.

Many big cities became part of the global culture of consumption (Sklair 2001) and this had a profound impact on the individuals' experience. What Ulrich Beck calls 'internal globalization' or 'cosmopolitanization' (Beck 2002: 17) has found its various expressions in the symbolic economies of cities, beginning with the names of stores and ending with people's value shifts and identities. Triumphalist overtones of globalisation have been rapidly but neatly intertwined with the imperial pomp and nationalist sentiments so characteristic of the current politics of the Russian government. Anthony King, addressing the link between the prominence of high rises and globalisation, speaks of the popularity of tall buildings in today's political imagination, in which they are closely connected to power and economic growth. The tradition of the Stalinist residential skyscrapers remains popular among the architects who capitalise on Soviet nostalgia. This continuity is especially evident in the recently built *Triumf Palas* (Kovalenko 2006: Q 3). King notes, though, that 'a "global" meaning of high-rise tower, a public housing project, at any particular site in the world, will be de-coded and re-coded, invested with a myriad of different interpretation' (King 2004: 42). Similarly, the messages of the globalised, lifestyle media industry undergo this decoding when perceived by diverse local audiences.

Lifestyle media as part of the globalisation of the media

Globalisation produces various 'emotional climates' that lead to the appearance of different individual attitudes towards globalisation, ranging from conformist and defensive to privatist and autonomous (Lemert and Elliot 2006). The interdependence of social positioning and subjective attitudes towards globalisation and its stylistic demands is continuously negotiated by the lifestyle media, which itself is a global industry. 'Visions of financial transfers and investments all over the world' that, according to Frederic Jameson, express the workings of globalisation as a 'communicational concept' (Jameson 1998: 55–6) make pertinent an ongoing reflection on the complex relationships between culture and the economy. Jameson's understanding of globalisation as predominantly a communicational phenomena allows taking into consideration the merging of not only the global media and the global urban environment but also their local 'translations'. The relationships among space, architectural styles, and the social dynamic characteristics for specific urban locations are, in their turn, represented in homes. In a similar vein, Ahier and Moore speak about globalisation as a concept that penetrates everyday talk through mass media and becomes 'common currency…the touchstone for collective understandings of "the way things are today"'. These authors put special emphasis on the fact that in everyday conversations globalisation figures as a somewhat troublesome phenomenon (as related to flexibilisation, downsizing and banking), which has a particularly painful effect on human lives at moments when 'the public (the global economy) transmutes into the private (the intimacy of the household)' (Ahier and Moore 1999: 237, as quoted in Raddon 2007: 78). The particular period in which this article was completed (Spring 2010) provides a good illustration of this point as it is marked by a banking and market crisis in Russia that is undoubtedly related to the global crisis. Whereas real estate prices are constantly rising, so are the banks' demands on those wishing to apply for home credit. News programmes show a lot of frustrated credit-seekers whose applications have been rejected by banks. There is a growing sense that as one of the 'emerging markets', Russia will have to pay for the developed markets' difficulties. And this price will be higher for those belonging to the middle- and the lower-classes.

If 'in reality' globalisation not only brings the excitement of travel and the simultaneous consumption of global cultural products but also, increasingly, a good deal of trouble, the editors and journalists of lifestyle magazines, nonetheless, strive to turn this tendency into one of the 'trends' that a lifestyle-conscious reader should take into consideration. For instance, the following excerpt from an editorial of *SALON-Interior* (one of the most expensive glossy Russian lifestyle magazines) uses 'globalisation' not as a challenge to face, but as a trendy metaphor representing an endless appropriation of ever new items as a way to prove that there's no limits in the lives of people with means.

> Globalization, the notion which, since its emergence, designates truly planetary processes, now came to embrace the sphere of private life. The word 'sphere' is not used here by chance. Our private life, while absorbing more and more orbits, is expanded in concentric circles horizontally and vertically and becomes more diverse and interesting, that is global. The nearest circle is the home. The magazine SALON-Interior is exactly about this—about matters that are most important in our life. And home shouldn't be understood as simply a sum of the walls or a sum of the walls and interior decoration. This home circle includes family, weekends, fitness, children with their education and birthdays (and their own fitness), friends' birthdays, home theater and home music salon [...] There is no limit to the circle of your life. All is in your hands. Look at the interiors, choose things, admire photos of cars and yachts [...] in order to have time for everything, that is to have time to enjoy comfort and design.
>
> (*SALON-Interior*, March 2007: 2)

'Design' is thus rendered as one of those things people with means should feel themselves entitled to; an ability to appreciate it is an indication of one's status and wealth (I shall revert to this point later). The ways Russians respond to global and local discourse about the home (and home design in particular) are mediated by the lifestyle magazines that are, in turn, part of the global media industry (Morris and Waisbord 2001). The tendency toward regional or local adoption of global media products is combined with the production of the new Russian lifestyle magazines, also globally oriented. There are more than 30 lifestyle magazines in Russia. The popularity of these magazines suggests the importance of interior design to a wide range of the public and makes them important items of cultural consumption. They are located at the intersection of culture and the economy by virtue of being both cultural products and commodities (Moeran 2006: 75). The latter is expressed in the magazines functioning as venues for promoting home decorating products. They fulfil at least three main functions: informing readers of what is possible in terms of home building, decoration, renovation and improvement; creating an editorial space that would keep potential advertisers interested in co-operating with them; and displaying and praising the work of interior designers. The magazines are published by international, national and local producers. For instance, *Lisa-Moi Uiutnyi Dom* (*Lisa-My Cozy Home*) is published by the concern Haus Hubert Burda Media; *Idei Vashego Doma* (*The Ideas of Your Home*) is published by the Russian publishing house Salon-Press; and *Letabure-Ekaterinburg* is published by the Ekaterinburg-based publishing house Univerpress. They exemplify a larger trend, which is that greater profit expectations of media companies lead to media commercialisation. As a result, the magazines appear and exist in a very competitive climate (Kerov 2007). Although just a few of them take part in global competition, all of them are included in the global circuit of goods to promote, services to offer and dreams to indulge in.

As cultural products, they are part of the cultural economy and producers of meaning. As a rule, they describe renovation using the makeover genre, dismissively accessing 'what was before' and approvingly describing 'what came after', starting from a designer's ideas, continuing with the process of negotiation with the owners and ending with the eventual, usually spectacular, results. The plural audiences that the magazines address all over Russia are consumers who are focused on the domestic and the private. However, the variety of publics that these magazines construct as home-owners and home-masters is quite broad. A well-off Tatar couple's cottage makes it on to the pages of *Lisa-Moi uiutnyi dom*. Recent university graduates buy their first home and impressively decorate it with their modest means in the pages of *Idei Vashego Doma*. The high divorce rate is reflected in the fact that a considerable number of apartments are designed for 'lone wolves' and 'independent ladies'.

What kinds of readers' identities do the magazines construct, and how do they create links between the notion of lifestyle and the clients they strive to attract? Here are some examples: 'Our client is a very hospitable person. In fact, he bought this apartment simply to be able to throw parties', says a leader of the architect and designer team that designed and implemented a spacious penthouse in a centrally located Moscow building. 'The hostess is a designer by training, a college teacher, a famous stylist who collaborates with fashion magazines; she possesses impeccable taste.' So thinks the author of an article about redecorating an art nouveau apartment. In addition to acknowledging a client's good taste, some articles are obviously written tongue-in-cheek in regard to the client's taste; it is the designers who are always there to provide an explanation for why things should be this way and to correct unfortunate flaws in taste and judgment. The magazines thus work both to legitimate the ongoing re-composition of profitable professions and to reserve a space of employability for those whose services they advertise.

The magazines addressing a very well-off audience take the diversity of its tastes into consideration by offering a wide range of home styles and interior decoration. For instance, the magazine *Salon-Interier* has a list of styles in which apartments have been done, ranging from classic to contemporary (*Salon-Interier* 2008). 'Classic' is divided into 'Gothic', 'Italian', 'Baroque', 'Empire', 'Modern', 'Art Deco' and 'Neo-classic', whereas varieties of 'Contemporary' are 'Minimalism', 'High-Tech', 'Functional', 'Ecological', 'Organic', 'Constructivism' and 'Neo-baroque'. Judging from the list of the magazine's publications on its website (from the number of clicks that each 'stylistic' gets), the stylistic leaders, so to speak, are (in descending order) 'Functional', 'Minimalist', 'Constructivist', 'Eclectic' and 'Neo-classic'. The magazines for a simpler readership show less sophistication, yet class and status issues are taken into consideration by offering a range of house renovation options that are called 'expensive', 'affordable' and 'budget' in '*Domoi. Praktika comforta.*'

Denis McQuail (McQuail 2002) differentiates between the direct and indirect selling of products and services in which the media are engaged. Whereas advertising exemplifies direct selling, indirect selling consists of various persuasion strategies. Readers are encouraged to buy a wide range of products in order to achieve a preferable lifestyle. Lifestyle magazines not only combine both kinds of selling, but their visual and written rhetoric testifies that they have elaborated successful strategies of merging the material and the symbolic. For instance, a magazine familiarises its readership with contemporary design or colour or describes shapes, having the putative goal of simply educating its readers about the world of contemporary design and art with the help of examples that comprise 'the *objects d'art*' (the everyday meaning of this expression in Russian captures the high cost of the thing in question). It is as if the magazine's message went like this: 'Look at this lovely item that costs only so much. Isn't it a nice sample of a round shape?' In other words, quite often the aesthetic education that the magazines appear to provide to their readers serves as pretext or an inventive way to promote expensive goods. This surely expresses the growing commercialisation of the media.

Lifestyle magazine readers: Leaning towards neo-liberalism?

In the rest of this chapter, I discuss some of the findings of my study on the perceptions and practices of a small group of lifestyle magazine readers in relation to the good city/good home nexus. The study was organised as follows. From mid-2006 to 2008, I conducted in-depth, one-on-one interviews with 17 people aged 23–52. In order to incorporate different social backgrounds into the study and different attitudes toward the magazines in questions, I drew roughly three-quarters of my sample from the citizens of Ekaterinburg and one-quarter from those working either as interior designers or involved in the lifestyle magazine publishing business. In the course of the interviews, I asked questions about peoples' favourite lifestyle magazines, their preferences in terms of style, the difficulties they encountered while implementing their ideas, their plans regarding their dwelling places, etc. To trigger an immediate response, I showed particular images illustrating a wide choice of designs and products that readers are expected to buy, use or display in their homes. My informants saw the majority of their renovation efforts as providing for the family, a complicated task of choosing, comparing and figuring out where and how to save. In many interviews, the understanding of home renovation as an instrumental activity during which style-related desires are inevitably put to the test by money, time, logistics and the durability of things was emphasised. Consequently, they regarded individualistic reasoning about style as something they might find themselves indulging in, but only with numerous reservations like, 'Had I had much more money…' or 'In a perfect world…'.

According to Guy and Harris, property markets should be seen as 'cultural entities, shaped as much by tradition, taste, technological and social innovation as by immediate levels of availability and demand' (Guy and Harris 1997: 126). However, the 'cultural' nature of the current Russian real estate market goes unnoticed by most informants. In fact, in many cases they speak of it as if it were the cause of their psychological trauma, as if it works as a merciless force that destroys hopes and makes one reconsider his or her ambitions. Looking at the pictures of the model homes with big windows, some remarked on the absurdity of the fact that the prices for apartments in our city and those in Spain or Italy are comparable. 'But there you have all that warmth and history and here winter lasts nine months', noted one women in her mid-fifties. On the other hand, those who recently bought apartments or homes refer to their acquisitions as miracles. 'Today, it would be completely impossible', they say with a nervous laugh. Only one informant commented ironically on the weight of conventions in the real estate business: 'They are so obsessed with the central location of the stuff they sell that they hardly pay attention to those buildings that are located just across a street comprising the border of the rectangle limiting the center of the city'. She meant that one could find a significantly cheaper place just outside of this rectangle. However, high real estate prices put especially serious limits on people's desire to move to a better place. Only four or five years ago, there was a relatively favourable period during which even people with relatively modest means could radically improve their living conditions. No longer. As one of my informants said, 'I could think as a quite realistic goal working hard in order to save enough to buy a good imported car. An apartment? Forget it'. As a result, some opt for 'cosmetic' repair, and some take a large loan that involves very frugal living for a long stretch of time in order to pay the developers who build new condominiums. Yet people say they are willing to ignore a low material standard for long periods of time while the developers are building their condominiums. As a rule, given again the high cost of 'building an apartment' (as the popular jargon has it), many end up with having 'just the walls' and express a certain sense of resentment discussing the magazines' suggestions that often involve a radical designer's intervention. 'There is plainly not much money left for doing something truly cool and fancy', one reader confesses. 'What an irony. I have dreamt of hiring an interior designer, of discussing with her what I want my place to look like, and now I just have money for plain white walls and some IKEA furniture.'

The dialectics of privatising of public space and the public elements of one's home life are described, if briefly, by Henry Lefebvre, who states that if 'the homes of the moneyed classes have undergone a superficial "socialization" with the introduction of reception areas, etc., the town, meanwhile, now effectively blown apart, has been "privatized"—no less superficially—thanks to urban "décor" and "design", and the development of fake environments' (Lefebvre 1974: 223). Critics of London's 'urban village' reproached early London gentrifiers for opting 'to be part of the city but separate from it, close to its amenities but cut off from its social problems' (Moran 2007: 101). The same attitude is widespread now when 'the public urban space has been increasingly commodified, hybridizing dollar signs of profit with cultural signs of meaning' (Barnes 2003: 486). Significantly, in Russia these tendencies are not subjected to any criticism. The city, as the traditionally understood locus of the good life, is replaced in human imagination by one's house as a place to live nicely. This is related to the broader tendency in late capitalism, namely that as communal life is the process of dissolution, the individual has to develop one's own individual identity, which is best expressed in one's habitat. As Henry Lefebvre puts it, 'When the subject – a city or a people – suffers dispersal...*housing* comes to prevail over *residence* within that city or amidst that people' (Lefebvre 1974: 222). A city might be considered good for living insofar as it can guarantee its dweller an exciting spectacle, a view of busy street life, and the diversity of its inhabitants – providing one can at any minute find retreat in the safety and predictability of one's own habitat. This is not surprising, because residential houses are clearly places that are meaningfully linked with peoples' continuing effort to fulfil their need for privacy and authenticity and to give to them sense of identity and security that are strongly connected to one's autonomy and freedom.

The connection between larger social problems and lifestyle magazines concerns a complex dialectic of the quality and size of one's dwelling place. The new cosmopolitan lifestyle involves the consumption of large amounts of living space. A Russian-American anthropologist, Sergey Oushakine, convincingly claims that it is predominantly 'quantity' that characterises the post-Soviet style of consumption. In the essays his Siberian students have written in the framework of his research, they relied heavily on what he calls the 'mindless quantity' of things while describing how they imagine the way 'new Russians' live and how they have a lot of everything. In the students' perceptions, Oushakine discerns how 'the ideology and aesthetics of success coincide with the ideology and aesthetics of excess, rather, for example, than with the ideology and aesthetics of novelty and sophistication' (Oushakine 2000: 107). In a similar vein, the architecture critic, Grigory Revzin sarcastically describes how the madness of the real estate market in Moscow expresses itself in what I would call 'the politics of ownership' of very wealthy people:

> Some Russian people are living better, and in this sense progress has taken place here. From 1992 to 1996, the average city apartment in Russian was about 200 square meters in a communal apartment from which all other

> inhabitants were forced to move out by the developers. The size of their suburban home was 400 square meters [...] on a plot of 2,000 square meters. By 2000, an apartment became a living space of 500 square meters, in a new building that was called 'elite' while the suburban house rose to 1,000 square meters, in a Victorian or some other historical style (they called them then 'little castles'). Today, a city apartment is about 1,000 square meters in housing estates that are now called 'luxe' or 'class A'. while their suburban home is now a villa, often in 'a vanguard' style. Its size is not less than 2,000 square meters, a plot of land about 20,000 square meters, with additional structures like a hunting lodge, stables, and glass- covered winter gardens.
>
> (Revzin 2007)

At the same time, Revzin's observation paradoxically shows that, although the obsession with the number of square metres one owns is strikingly present, something else is in play as well, however ironically – the level of sophistication of those engaged in this kind of practice. They no longer build notorious eclectic 'castles' with towers. It is enough to visit any cluster of upscale urban housing to realise that these people (and surely the architects they hired) do have ideas, taste and, most important, means to give them tangible expression. There is more to it. Almost everybody in this world would be glad to move to a larger home. If asked where you would prefer to live, in a well-decorated but tiny home or a bigger one, most of us would opt for the latter. We dream of having more space for ourselves, and what I think the magazines take into consideration very cleverly is that they play with these dreams and thus form our contemporary collective imagination. The idea of one's entitlement to a spacious habitat is a significant part of it.

The British sociologist Ash Amin, in his article on the good city, emphasises that 'definitions of human advancement in prosperous cities are based on high-income consumer lifestyles and bourgeois escape from ugly or dangerous aspects of urban life' (Amin 2006: 1010). Lifestyles magazines picture their readers as those who are 'rescued' from the unpleasant side of life by, first, their high income and, second, by design specialists. The way apartments are 'served' in the visual feast of listings in the magazines is amplified by the texts. One of them, for instance, says:

> If you, dear reader, think about this kitchen as being too simple, keep in mind that it is for a kitchen lady. The hostess lives in her bedroom. Look at these elegant lines and impeccable furniture, dear reader! The hostess wanted to feel endless luxury every moment of her life. We think the designer succeeded in this.

What also characterises lifestyle magazines in this regard is that they not only provide extensive knowledge to people about house maintenance and possible options for home improvement, but also offer the capability to individualise this information, to address individuals as essentially reflective consumers.

Designers, lay and professional

In the lifestyle media business, with its saturation of brands and products, brand extension is now often used to secure revenue and audience loyalty. Some home improvement magazines have successfully found a commercial niche as a source of reliable and trustworthy information that is equally appealing to advertisers and readers. Branding in this field usually entails traditional, same-genre extension. For instance, the magazine *Idei Vashego Doma* (Ideas of Your House), currently the most popular one, has a website (ivd.ru) that not only establishes the presence of the magazine on the web, making it widely available, but also provides an efficient interface with the reader. The publishing house, Salon-press, which launched the magazine in 1997, boasts that this site occupies the top position in the basic search systems, with a daily activity of 10,000 people looking through more than 100,000 pages of the magazine archive. Another reason why *Idei Vashego Doma* stands out is that its management promotes this site as a truly interactive one, allowing people to compare their design ideas with those of professionals and, through numerous forums, to seek help from both amateur and professional interior designers. This mobile environment makes people less and less patient when it comes to getting the information they need.

In the last decade, this and similar magazines used an editorial strategy in which promotion of elitism and democratisation of design went, paradoxically, hand-in-hand. The British celebrity designer Laurence Llewelyn-Bowen recently said, albeit regarding television design programmes, that in Britain this genre is indicative of a shift from an elitism in taste to a 'design democracy'.

> Two hundred years ago, having good taste was pretty straightforward and "experts" wrote books on the subject. Now everyone's got an opinion. ... We've reached a stage where we live in a design democracy: stores instantly respond to what is on TV and in magazines. Taste is no longer prescribed by the few for the majority.
>
> (Llewelyn-Bowen 2003: 26, as cited by Philips 2005: 217)

Although the Russian lifestyle TV genre is less popular than the equivalent printed and media (and their Internet) versions, the tendency that a designer commented upon, is certainly very noticeable in Russia. People's opinions ranging from the right colour of curtains (when a photo of a room and a question is posted on the forum) to whether an area in question is attractive enough to build a house on are widely discussed and exchanged. In the magazine forum, the most popular rubric is 'interior design' (72,568 messages), followed by 'materials and constructions' (65,532 messages) and 'building the suburban home' (34,810) (the forum of the *Idei Vashego Doma* online edition, 2008). Tellingly enough, the rubric devoted to local self-government, entitled 'We are the neighbors', lags far behind (1,172). On the forums, one can see modest pieces of self-promotion posted by embryonic beginners that are met, some with hostility, and others with emotional support. People also actively advise each other about those professionals whose price/quality ratio they find reasonable. In the magazine, there are articles explaining the editorial strategy in the following way:

> Can everybody become a "designer for herself"? This is not what we call for because design is a complicated business and requires special knowledge and experience. However, this shouldn't prevent one from trying. It all depends on your abilities and wishes. To those preferring to hire professionals our "school" makes it easier to find a common language with them. If you wish to personally work on your interior, you find here both theory and practical advice.
>
> (Utochkina 2000, 11: 45)

There is, indeed, an abundance of practical advice that the magazines offer. There is a catalogue of 'typical' Soviet houses (made from manufactured details and differentiated from each other as 'the series'). And there is a catalogue of 'untypical' houses, namely, those made from brick, 'panels', 'blocks', 'monolith', 'stalinki' (those made in Stalin's time) and 'khrushcevki' (made in Khrushchev's time). Speaking of interactivity, readers can send a floor plan of their apartment, list their wishes and preferences, and (if their 'case' is interesting to professionals) the magazine will publish a piece in which three or four designers present their ideas regarding the apartment in question.

However, my informants, when asked if they considered this opportunity to obtain professional advice, noted that it is too time-consuming and that the results are unpredictable. As one of them puts it:

> After a while, you can sort of predict many of their suggestions: some would be practical and some would be more radical and fancy. The trouble is that it is only when I myself begin figuring it out what it is exactly that I want my place to be, the ideas occur and, however questionable they might be from the professional point of view, I know the results will suit me for exactly the reason that I did it for myself.

Looking down

A main character in Robert Musil's novel, *Man without Qualities*, lives in the upper-storey living room of a miniature chateau. The cars, the trams, the streets and the pedestrians 'filled the network of his gaze with a whirl of hurrying forms' (Musil 1979: 7). What matters in the act of one's looking down from one's window has largely been conceived of by cultural studies scholars as relating to domains of power and visuality. A feminist historian of architecture, Beatriz Colomina, speaks of the 'domination of the gaze' as characteristic of the way modernist domestic space is organised. It is the viewer who organises the outside space, whose house frames the landscape, and whose gaze defines the surroundings (Colomina 1992: 73–130). Mary Louise Pratt described the vision of the 'seeing man': 'he whose imperial eyes passively look out and possess' (Pratt 1992: 7). Looking from above, which incorporates the acts of surveillance, transcendence, control and detachment, has been situated centrally to discussions of the symbolic use of space to prove social status and to maintain class divisions. Being able to survey surroundings from above the ground, from up there, from a pavilion built on a roof, or from one's penthouse is a position of power and a sight that allows possession. The seamless merging of the economic and the symbolical value of 'the place with a view' expresses itself in the following excerpt:

> It is known that a view from the windows has an impact not only on an apartment's value but, much more importantly, on the psychological condition of its dwellers. A distant perspective, expanse of sky, the flight of clouds and birds – it is difficult to imagine anything more calming. Besides, if one takes into consideration a significantly better ecological situation compared to the lower stories, it is clear that living "on the top" has its numerous advantages.
>
> (Shovskaia 2007: 54)

To address some more specific expressions of the connections between the city and the home, a view from a window as a part of a place's attraction is what the magazines often analyse. How to give a view a better frame, how to incorporate it in the overall style of the apartment – these are the questions they pose and answer. In a recent issue of *Idei Vashego Doma*, there is a story about a studio apartment and how both the location and the view are characterised in it:

> This red brick house is located in the new bedroom community [...], which is a housing estate of the so called economic class. The apartments are small, and the decoration and equipment are predictably modest. However, there is a lot of construction and development on this territory, and it is going to become a business and shopping center. The view from the sixth floor from the only window in the apartment is like an urban kaleidoscope and a panorama of changing [...] sky. A big window, the one from ceiling to floor is one of the few impressive advantages of this place. A sense of air and space pushes out the boundaries to the extent that one nearly forgets about the small size of the apartment (34 square meters).
>
> (Pashintseva 2007: 26)

A view thereby adds charm to a place and sometimes even becomes the owner's obsession. It is highly valued because it works in a very personal way. It is you who, since the moment you bought this place, can endlessly devour all this beauty. Thus – through your gaze – you appropriate the best dimension of urban space while keeping a hygienically safe distance from all those numerous dumps where only losers live, from unpleasant sights and smells, from unpredictable encounters you don't want any part of. This brings to one's mind 'The world as a picture', an abstract, objectified world produced by a modernistic subject. A model of visual representation 'with the viewer at the apex of a cone of vision' (Burgin 1996: 39) finds its teasing expression in the reasoning of those willing to pay a large price for a chance, while looking down from their, say, thirty-third floor, to think,

'This is my city.' Interestingly, the interviews show a more complex attitude of readers towards 'a room with a view'. It is too often that a lack of maintenance or a road expansion under one's windows turns a view into an eyesore or prevents an owner from being able to open a window.

Conclusion

There is a great deal of ambivalence at work in the relationships between magazines and their readers, as well as between designers and their clients. When people reflect on their ambivalent reactions to magazine articles, they rarely reflect on the nature of 'the right' or 'the must' that the magazines offer and why it often 'traumatises' people by virtue of being unattainable. The popular attitudes and commercial strategies of the media corporations, prevalent models of reasoning about life and value judgments, not to mention people's ideas about happiness – all become intertwined. 'The demands of how it should be' are articulated by the cultural intermediaries, the experts who act as bridges between brands and consumers and use the consumers' uncertainties and anxieties as a base on which to arrange (to position) brands they want to promote. They create the image of the ideal home, the home one must have. And they both generate and transmit social and cultural pressure to the individual. This is why, having read one especially exciting article, one can feel personally encouraged to renovate a room or a whole house. The magazines seldom discuss the details of this process nor the scope of the effort needed. And although the cost of labour and materials is often addressed, the moral cost of the whole undertaking to the family members is never discussed.

This explains why, if designers are usually enthusiastic but slightly arrogant, readers are mainly sceptical and even mistrustful. Part of their mistrust comes from a certain paradox that they discern while striving to implement the magazines' advice. As one informant puts it, 'We want to use their expertise but they are more successful in using us, in "selling" us to those who manufacture goods for the home and provide home building and decoration services'. In the end, the readers suspect that they are seen only as potential clients. People with modest means, sensing that so many options remain beyond their reach, prefer to rely on their own judgement in matters of taste and choice. Another reason for the ambivalence that many readers show towards the magazines can be explained by their anxiety about a growing social fragmentation, which, as they suspect or imagine, is expressed in one group of people's building exquisite pieces of home design whereas many others are doomed to indefinitely postpone their chance to move into even a relatively better habitat.

References

Ahier, J. and Moore, R. (1999) 'Big pictures and fine details: school work experience policy and the local labor market in the 1990s', in J. Ahier and G. Esland (eds) *Education, Training and the Future of Work I: social, political and economic contexts of policy development*, London: Routledge/Open University.

Amin, A. (2006) 'The good city', *Urban Studies* 43 (5–6): 1009–23.

Amin, A. and Graham, S. (1997) 'The ordinary city', *Transactions of the Institute of British Geographers* 4: 411–29.

Barnes, T. (2003) 'The 1990s show: how culture leaves the farm and hits the street', *Urban Geography* 6: 479–92.

Beck, U. (2002) 'The cosmopolitan society and its enemies', *Theory, Culture and Society* 1–2: 17–44.

Bird, E. (2003) *The Audience in Everyday Life: living in a media world*, London: Routledge.

Boiarskaya, A. (2007) 'Anomalii Ekaterinburga', *Afisha*, 20: 20–9. Online. Available www.afisha.ru/article/201/ (accessed 30 September 2009).

Brenner, N. and Teodore, N. (2002) 'Cities and the geographies of "actually existing neoliberalism"', in N. Brenner and N. Teodore (eds.) *Spaces of Neoliberalism: urban restructuring in North America and Western Europe*, Oxford: Blackwell.

Burgin, V. (1996) *In/Different Spaces: place and memory in visual culture*, Berkeley, CA: California University Press.

Colomina, B. (1992) 'The split wall: domestic voyeurism', in B. Colomina (ed.) *Sexuality and Space*, New Jersey: Princeton Architectural Press.

Dubin, B. (2004) *Intellektualnye Gruppy i Simvolicheskie Formy.* Moscow: Novoe Izdatel'stvo,

Eade, J. (1997) *Living the Global City: globalization as a local process*, London: Routledge.

Fiske, J. (1987) *Television Culture: popular pleasures and politics*, London: Methuen.

Florida, R. (2003) *The Rise of the Creative Class and How It's Transforming Work, Life, Community and Everyday Life*, New York: Basic Books.

Friedman, J. (2002) *The Prospect of Cities*, Minneapolis: University of Minnesota Press.

Giddens, A. (1991) *Modernity and Self-Identity: self and society in the late modern age*, Cambridge: Polity Press.

Goldberger, P. (1996) 'The Rise of the private city', in J. V. Martin (ed.) *Breaking Away: the future of cities*, New York: The Twentieth Century Foundation.

Graham, S. and Marvin, S. (2001) *Splintering Urbanism*, London: Routledge.

Guy, S. and Harris, R. (1997) 'Property in a global risk society: towards marketing research in the office sector', *Urban Studies* 1: 125–140.

Hagen, I. and Wasko, J. (2000) *Consuming Audience: production and reception in media research*, Cresskill: Hampton Press.

Hall, S. (1980) 'Encoding/decoding', in S. Hall *et al.*, (eds) *Culture, Media, Language: working papers in cultural studies 1972–1979*, London: Hutchinson.

Hartman, M. and Honneth, A. (2006) 'Paradoxes of capitalism', *Constellations*, 2006, 1: 41–58.

Jameson, F. (1998) 'Notes on globalization as a philosophical issue', in *The Cultures of Globalization*, in F. Jameson and M. Miyosi (eds), Durham, NC: Duke University Press.

Keith, M. (2005) *After the Cosmopolitan: multicultural cities and the future of racism*, London: Routledge.

Kemmis, D. (1995) *The Good City and the Good Life*, Boston: Houghton Mifflin.

Kerov, V. (2007) 'Tendentsii razvitiya zhurnalnogo rynka v Rossii', *Zhurnalist* 11: 50–2.

King, A. D. (2004) *Spaces of Global Cultures: architecture and urban identity*, London: Routledge.

Kovalenko, P. (2006) 'Stalinist high-rise living', *The Moscow Times Real Estate Quarterly*, July 1: Q3.

Kuhn, A. (2004) 'The State of film and media feminism', *Signs* 1: 1221–30.

Larner, W. (2003) 'Neoliberalism?', *Environment and Planning D Society and Space* 21: 509–12.

Lefebvre, H. (1996) *Writings on Cities*, Oxford: Blackwell.

Lefebvre, H. (1974) *The Production of Space*, trans. D. Nicholson-Smith, Oxford: Blackwell.

Lemert, C. and Elliot, A. (2003) *The New Individualism*, London: Routledge.

Llewelyn-Bowen, L. (2003) 'Taste matters', *Evening Standard Magazine* 2: 26.

Low, S. M. (2008) 'Fortification of residential neighborhoods and the new emotions of home', *Housing, Theory and Society*, 1: 47–65.

McCann, L. (2004) *Russian Transformations: challenging the global narrative*, London: Routledge Curson.

McQuail, D. (2002) 'The Media and lifestyles: editor's introduction', *European Journal of Communication* 4: 427–8.

McKenzie, E. (2005) 'Constructing the Pomerium in Las Vegas: a case study of emerging trends in American gated communities', *Housing Studies* 2: 187–203.

Moeran, B. (2006) 'More than just a fashion magazine', *Current Sociology* 5: 725–44.

Moran, J. (2007) 'Early cultures of gentrification in London, 1955-1980', *Journal of Urban History* 1: 101–21.

Morris, N. and Waisbord, S. (2001) *Media and Globalization: why the state matters*. Lahman, MD: Rowman and Littlefield.

Musil, R. (1979) *Man without Qualities*, vol. 1, trans. E. Kaiser, and E. Wilkins, London: Pikador Books.

Newman, O. (1972) *The Defensible Space: crime prevention through urban design*, New York: Macmillan.

Oushakine, S. (2000) 'The quantity of style: imaginary consumption in the new Russia', *Theory, Culture and Society* 5: 97–120.

Pashintseva, T. (2007) 'Interier s istoriei', *Idei Vashego Doma* 8: 26–31.

Philips, D. (2005) 'Transformation scenes: the television interior makeover', *International Journal of Cultural Studies* 2: 213–29.

Pratt, M. L. (1992) *Imperial Eyes: travel writing and transculturation*, London: Routledge.

Raddon, A. (2007) 'Timescapes of flexibility and insecurity: exploring the context of distant learners', *Time & Society* 1: 61–82.

Revzin, G. (2007) 'Russkie i pustota. Ob istoricheskom opyte i kvadratnykh metrakh', *Kommersant-Weekend*, 8: 4-8. Online. Available www.kommersant.ru/doc.aspx?DocsID=755648 (accessed 30 September 2009).

Ross, K. and Nightingale, V. (2003) *Media and Audiences: new perspectives*, Maidenhead: Open University Press.

Salon-Interier. Online. Available www.salon.ru/interior.plx (accessed 30 September 2009).

Sassen, S. (2001) *The Global City*, Princeton: Princeton University Press.

Sassen, S. (2002) *Global Networks, Linked Cities*, London: Routledge.

Swyngedouw, E. and Kaika, M. (2003) 'The making of "glocal" urban modernities. Exploring the cracks in the mirror', *City* 1: 5–21.

Shovskaia, T. (2007) 'V basseine nad propastiiu', *Interior Digest* 3: 60–71.

Sklair, L. (2001) *The Transnational Capitalist Class*, Oxford: Blackwell.

Smith, B. H. (1988) *Contingencies of Value: alternative perspectives for critical theory*, Cambridge, MA: Harvard University Press.

Smith, N. (2002) 'New globalism, new urbanism: gentrification as global urban industry', *Antipode* 3: 427–50.

The forum of the *Idei Vashego Doma* online edition (2008) Online. Available http://forum.ivd.ru (accessed 6 January 2008).

Trubina, E. (2006) 'Post-soviet urban cultures – symbolic productions, dynamics of power', in R. Bittner, *et al.* (eds) *Transit Spaces*, Berlin: JovisVerlag.

Turner, B. S. (2000) 'Cosmopolitan virtue, loyalty and the city', in E.F. Isin (ed.) *Democracy, Citizenship and the Global City*, London: Routledge.

Utochkina, N. (2000) 'Vvedenie v disain', *Idei Vashego Doma*, 11: 45–50. Online. Available www.ivd.ru/document.xgi?id=3104 (accessed 30 September 2009).

Warner, S. B. (1960) *The Private City: Philadelphia in three periods of its growth*, Philadelphia, PA: University of Pennsylvania Press.

Webster, J. G. and Phalen, P. F. (1997) *The Mass Audience: rediscovering the dominant model*, Mahwah, NJ: Lawrence Erlbaum Associates.

Zakharov, O. (2004) 'V poiskakh "kul'turnoi stolitsy", *Ural*, 10: 67–76. Online. Available http://magazines.russ.ru/ural/2004/10/za10-pr.html (accessed 30 September 2009).

Index